With Reservations

Musings From the Other Side

With Reservations

Musings From the Other Side

Roger Emile Stouff

Shadowfire Books, LLC
Published in the United States of America

With Reservations:
Musings From the Other Side

Copyright © 2014 by Roger Emile Stouff

SHADOWFIRE BOOKS, LLC
WWW.SHADOWFIREBOOKS.COM

For
Patches, Moses, Chance, Shadow, Daisy and Bogie.

Foreword

This little book fulfills a promise.

After my first work, *Native Waters*, was published in 2004, I promised local readers of the *St. Mary and Franklin Banner-Tribune* that another volume would follow containing those editions of my column "From the Other Side" that were not included in the first book. While over the years my writing interests narrowed to outdoors and historical Chitimacha tribal memoirs, I did not forget the kindness bestowed by those loyal "From the Other Side" readers after I returned to the Banner in 1998.

Many of those readers were not very interested in fishing or wooden boats. But they repeatedly asked for more stories about my pets, my renovations to my home, and the usual "a funny thing happened to me on the way to work this morning" pieces. I am nothing if not loyal, and those fans of the column gave me the courage to stretch my wings, begin writing in other venues, and led to the publication of *Native Waters* and all the others that followed. This little book is my way of saying thanks for sticking with me through all the cypress splinters and bamboo fly rods.

This book spans from about 1998 to the end of 2013. Many, many columns on local politics, happenings and such are not included, and some have appeared in previous books if I thought they were suited. But this little book had to happen for the faithful.

Though the title suggests a tome of indigenous nature, it is really more of an excuse. Dad was raised in Fort Worth, Texas, my mother in Charenton, Louisiana, down in the primordial swamps along the coast. That mixture is responsible for my somewhat jaded eccentricity; for example, my speech. I speak neither with a Texas drawl nor a Cajun brogue; the two somehow canceled each other out. But it was those two cultural identities, as well as the Chitimacha one dad recovered when he finally returned to his true home here on the reservation, that made me who I am. So now you know who to blame.

Roger Emile Stouff, Chitimacha, Louisiana

Day-to-Day

Jungle Fever

I was recently the star in a low-budget jungle movie.

A jungle movie is one in which the characters are in a jungle. It doesn't matter that they're doing there: Searching for lost cities of gold, fighting a war, hunting tigers, whatever. The jungle movie has that certain something which defines it as a jungle movie, namely, a jungle.

Anyway, through some cosmic twist of fate, which seems to be my lot in life, I ended up spending last week in a jungle movie. I didn't know I was there until the scene where the hero, that would be me, contracts one of those jungle-specific diseases that they always do in jungle movies, known alternately as Mango Juice Fever, Bwana Fever, and often as He Ain't Gonna Live To Find The Lost City Of Gold Fever.

It came upon me in an instant. One moment I was chatting with friends and the next I was trembling violently. My friend remarked that I was quite pale, and I remarked that I wasn't feeling too well, and he remarked that I was sweating profusely, and I remarked that I couldn't possibly be sweating because I was freezing to death, and so forth.

I ended up going home and sitting there with two blankets around me and the air conditioner turned off in summer, trembling violently. My gray tabby cat, Moses, normally oblivious to everything that concerns me, thought this a great opportunity to curl up in my lap and fall asleep. He perhaps mistook my trembling for purring.

Somehow I managed to fall asleep as well. Unlike in the jungle movies, there was no one around to build a litter out of tree branches, lashed together with vines, and carry me to my bed, so I had to get up and walk there on my own, a journey that seemed endless. Some hours later I woke up and in my dim, hazy half-sleep state I thought I had fallen into a river. Every jungle movie has a river, the Nile, Congo or Amazon. Fearing piranhas or crocodiles, I leaped up and began wrestling with my blanket, which put up a good fight, until I realized it wasn't a crocodile at all, it was really an anaconda, and I tied it up in a knot and threw it out the back door.

It was then I realized I thought I had fallen into a river because I was soaked with sweat. There are different levels of sweating. When one is nervous about a date, one may perspire. When one is working in the yard, razing a barn or the like, one may sweat. When one is afflicted with jungle fever, one sweats like hallelujah, brethren. Everything was soaked, including my clothes. I managed to clean myself up, change the bed sheets and go get the blankets out of the yard, though the dogs were decidedly unhappy that I had taken them back. Then I took my temperature.

It was 104.5. That, my friends, is jungle-quality fever. And despite the misery of the headache, body aches, sweating and chills, I felt rather proud of being the owner of a 104.5-degree fever. Then the whole cycle repeated itself, the chills for a few hours, then the sweats for a few hours, and all over again. For the next three days.

In the jungle movies, when the hero gets a fever, he often gets delirious. I think I got delirious because I mistook Moses for a man-eating Bengal tiger, and since I was sure the script called for me to save the day, I leaped on him from the sofa and we went rolling across the floor, locked in mortal combat, until he managed to escape my lunatic grasp and disappeared up the stairs.

True to every jungle movie, I was brought to the witch doctor with a bone in his nose and miniature human skulls on a string around his neck, who danced and sang and hollered and threw Johnson's Baby Powder in my face, which made me sneeze. This particular witch doctor was somewhat modernized, for he also felt a shot in the backside was in order.

As time passed I came out of the clutches of the fever and was fed fruit and spring water by beautiful native girls who all looked like Sigourney Weaver. No, wait, maybe that was while I was still delirious. Anyway, I recovered and regained my strength. The witch doctor sent me a bill for which I am to pay him two dozen pigs and a Marx Brothers video, which seems fair. I am preparing now to embark upon yet another brave, valiant and heroic adventure into the unknown.

That is, finding Moses. He still hasn't come down from the

stairs.

Barn Razing

You've all heard of a barn raising. It's what people across this country used to do when a neighbor decided they needed a new barn.

I strongly suspect it was an excuse for a party. A lot of perfectly good barns were taken down in order to build new ones, which were no better than the one they destroyed, just to have a party. The women-folk would all get together and cook ridiculous amounts of food and bake pastries; the children would scamper around and drive the livestock to a nervous breakdown, and the men-folk would wear overalls, standing around for at least a day and a half, discussing exactly how this here barn raising was a'gonna take place, consuming copious amounts of beer in the process. This is why the planning period took a day and a half, because they periodically had to take naps to clear their thinking. I believe it is recorded in the Library of Congress that one group of barn raisers forgot the required beer-drinking, nap-taking cycle and as a result built an exact replica of the Tower of London. This would have been fine, except that the cows kept jumping out of the tower windows to get away from the kids.

Now, a barn raising is different from a "barn razing,' though they sound a lot alike, and many problems have arisen during the planning stages of a "barn raising." After a couple barrels of Ol' Happyslapper Extra Stout, the men-folk sometimes forgot they hadn't actually raised the new barn at all, and in fact, forgot they hadn't even torn down the old one, and sometime after lunch on the second day, one of them would look at the old barn and say, "Yup, looks pretty good, fellas," and there'd be plenty of hand-shaking, back-slapping and everybody would go home to sleep it off.

The point to all this is that I recently participated in a barn razing. I had a barn on my property that was in desperate need of razing, and as I was also in desperate need of a party, I decided to kill two birds with one stone.

Problem is, people aren't as interested in the entire process like they used to be. I found myself on the telephone issuing invitations: "Hey (name withheld to protect the lazy) I'm going to be tearing down a barn this weekend, how about you grab a crowbar and come over and we'll—hello? Hello?"

So I was going to have to do it myself. Being the slight historic traditionalist that I am, I decided I would do this in proper style. I loaded up the fridge with beer, bought some food from the deli and some pastries from the bakery, since I was at the time single and had no women-folk around to do this for me. I don't drink beer much, but it's tradition, by thunder.

With sufficient supplies on hand, I grabbed a Diet Coke and a crowbar and headed for the back yard. The barn in question was probably eighty years old, and I feared it would fall at any moment, because the supporting corners and studs were so rotten. Now, I'm smart enough to know that you're supposed to demolish any structure from the top down, but I am also afraid of heights. So I sat down and began the planning stage, which kinda loses its appeal with Diet Coke instead of beer. At noon, I decided it was time for dinner and had a roast beef sandwich and some doughnuts, then took a nap. At three in the afternoon I returned to planning.

Sometime the next morning—I told you, planning takes time!—I headed back out with my crowbar and Diet Coke, this time armed with a come-along, a long chain and a plan.

First I removed all the clapboard siding. Then I fastened the chain to the nearest inner stud of the wall facing me, and the come-along to a sturdy maple tree, and in this way pulled each of the rotten studs loose one at a time. As each one popped free, I expected the whole structure to collapse, but I was far enough away to be out of harm's way.

By the end of the day, two walls were completely gone and half the roof, and the thing was still standing. This was the barn I feared was nearing collapse if a sparrow flew too near it, but there it stood, firm, resolute, laughing at me. I made a few phone calls and found that dynamite was not available, the National Guard would not loan me a tank, and thermonuclear weapon designs on the Internet were far too costly. Stricken, I returned to my come-along and chain, pulling at the first of the two remaining walls.

It came down. Now I had a wall and half a roof standing there. By this time, the neighbors had gathered in their yards and were sitting in lawn chairs, drinking their own beer and barbecuing while they enjoyed the show. "Ain't never seen anything like it," they commented, waving at me cheerfully. "Darned well-built barn if you ask me. Why'd he want to tear down a finely constructed barn like that?"

Discouraged, I attached the chain to the half-roof and started come-alonging. The roof came off. The wall remained. I seriously considered taking up beer drinking at this point, and entertained the possibility of having the wall listed on the state tourism registry. "See the invulnerable wall! A miracle of engineering. How did they do it? What secrets did the builders of this barn learn from ancient alien visitors which taught them to construct a barn so durable?"

So I'm standing there, looking at this wall that refuses to crumble. There is only one answer, I decided. One possibility, so daring, so bold, that I trembled just with the thought of it, but I was left with no other recourse.

Mustering my courage, I quit for the weekend.

That was the plan. Quit for the weekend. I left it alone. I guess I vaguely hoped it would think I had moved to Toledo and collapse from exhaustion all on its own while I was away. Perhaps a good hurricane would come along and finish the job for me.

None of that happened, of course, and the following weekend, there I was again, Diet Coke in hand, staring at the wall. It was an enemy. It was evil incarnate. It was a hideous beast, a demon-spawn of diabolical construction. I felt like David facing Goliath, like Gilgamesh battling Humbaba.

I looped the chain in the center of the beam at the top of the wall and began come-alonging. The board snapped. The wall stood. I tried at the corners. They came apart. The wall stood. I tried at the base, but it wouldn't budge. Without other recourse, I found a good hand saw, and started cutting. It took most of the day, but eventually I heard an unhealthy creaking, groaning and snapping and I ran like a lunatic toward the pasture. When I turned, down came the wall.

I was exultant. I was triumphant. Now *I* was the conqueror. I was Hannibal, Alexander, Patton, Genghis Khan, James Kirk, John Wayne and Chuck Norris all wrapped up in one sweaty, aching package. In celebration, I drank another Diet Coke and finished the last of the blueberry turnovers. My neighbors, who had long ago tired of the spectacle, were absent to witness my conquest. I was markedly annoyed by that.

Now, however, I had another problem. Three of them, actually. A pile of wood, a pile of corrugated tin, and a pile of junk from inside the barn. It was a big barn, and I wondered what I would do with all this mess?

That was in February. It was not until November that I returned to them. Problem was, in the months that had passed, a miniature rain forest had sprouted up among and around the carnage. I had kept the back pasture mowed, but circled around the carcass of the barn. Now nature had taken over, and supplied me with another problem.

I was vaguely concerned that, in my absence, a tribe of errant jungle-dwellers might have moved into the growth, displaced by deforestation in Brazil or Peru or some place like that. Investigation, however, proved there were no dislocated indigenous people living in the growth. I then became worried that some ridiculously rare species of bird like a Blue-left-toed Speckled Throttle Rabbler might have taken up residence in one of the mangrove trees (or perhaps they were hackberry trees, I can never tell) and the area would be declared an endangered species habitat. But I thrashed around in there with a stick for awhile and saw nothing that resembled an endangered species. I did see some pretty mean looking spiders, though.

So I started loading the trailer. It would take me, I reasoned, half a dozen loads to get all the debris hauled away. It was pleasant work. I like that kind of work, getting dirty and sweaty and exhausted, if I'm actually accomplishing something. It made me realize why a barn-raising was often preceded by a barn-razing. It was so much fun to tear down the old barn, whether it needed it or not, and drink copious amounts of their favorite liquid refreshment, heck, I'm sure the old timers did it just for grins and giggles.

Shake, Baby, Shake!

All right, now I am completely certain that the world has gone utterly, absolutely berserk.

So I'm out having dinner with some friends over the weekend, a couple, and the young lady comments to the young man, "I have a complaint about the ketchup."

Now, I'm thinking something's wrong with the ketchup itself, so I didn't pay much attention, since I wasn't having any ketchup anyway.

"The lid doesn't work the way they said," the young lady said.

That got me curious. How does a lid not work?

"It's still watery?" asked the young man, and his significant other affirmed.

Finally, I had to ask what they were talking about, and they told me. I couldn't believe it, so I went examined the bottle of ketchup myself.

Yes, it was true. A major ketchup producer allegedly developed a lid on their squeezable ketchup bottles that is supposed to prevent that watery layer at the top you get when ketchup sits for a while.

The label proclaimed something like, "No more soggy buns!" I'm not sure exactly what it said word-for-word, because I was just too appalled.

Think about this for just a minute. A ketchup bottle hits the shelves of the grocer with a new-fangled lid that is supposed to keep from getting that watery first-squirt out of the bottle! Can you see it? The consumers go wild! There are lines in the ketchup aisle, folks fighting over the last bottle with the watery-squirt-proof lid, a debacle unlike any seen since the Cabbage Patch dolls.

Am I the only one who sees the absurdity in this? To-wit:

Just shake the dad-blasted bottle before you squirt it on the stupid bun!

Is that so difficult?

Have we Americans gotten so miserably complacent and lazy that we don't have the energy to shake our ketchup bottles before we squirt them to get rid of the watery stuff at the top? Have we come to this, friends and neighbors?

Listen, I don't wanna be rude. Heck, I lived through green ketchup, un-American as it might be. I even managed to survive purple ketchup, which I still think is a plot to undermine the visual coordination of our children, hatched by the financially floundering prune industry. You want green or purple ketchup, more power to you. I'll take mine red, thank you. Call me old-fashioned. I didn't mind the squirt bottles, though they took some getting used to. After a lifetime of having to pound the side of those old glass pour-type bottles like you were fighting Jack Dempsey in the ring, it was kinda nice to just flip the cap and squirt my ketchup. After a good shaking, of course.

Imagine this for a moment. A ketchup company assembles a team of engineers—ketchup cap engineers, no doubt—in a fifieth-floor boardroom, and tells them they want a lid on their bottle that eliminates the watery stuff, so Americans don't have to worry about the single biggest threat to domestic tranquility since the Cuban missile crisis: soggy buns. The engineers, inspired into action with this great and noble task, leap into action and before long, come back with the design plans on twelve hundred blueprinted pages on just how this new ketchup bottle lid will work, and the company builds gigantic production machines to do it. They go on a marketing blitz, changing their labels to herald the advent of this incredible new lid, and America can at last sleep peacefully at night, knowing that their buns will no longer be soggy.

Never mind that it apparently didn't even work, if my friend's comment was accurate. I didn't try it for myself. I refused to succumb.

I don't think it's American's soggy buns that we should be worried about. I think it's the soggy brains of ketchup manufacturers.

Just shake the stupid bottle! Take it in your hand, move it up and down vigorously a few times and voila! You have ketchup with no watery stuff!

What next? Special aluminum cans that keep that last piece of ravioli from getting stuck in the bottom of the can like it always does, so you don't have to dig it out with a spoon?

Spigots on the bottoms of tuna fish cans so you can drain the liquid out before you open it?

Special cardboard boxes that remix your cereal because all the raisins have settled to the bottom of the box during handling?

I'm sorry. I know I'm an aberration. I know I'm a quirky eccentric. I will continue to shake my ketchup, my *red* ketchup, until the day I die. As long as I have the strength to pick up the bottle and give it a good thrashing, I'll do so. When I am too old or too stupid or too lazy to do so, I'll stop eating ketchup.

Hanging By the Pants

I was visiting with some friends—the same night as I discovered the "no-watery ketchup lid"— and they were watching what they mysteriously called "a concert" on television.

I have, it suddenly occurred to me, become my father.

When I turned into that horrible, mysterious creature known as "a teenager" my father just about disowned me. In fact, I think the only thing that stopped him from doing so was my mom, who refused to allow him to kick me out because I was her one and only. Aside from the occasional Bill Cosby-style threats ("When your father gets home, he's going to blow your face off with a bazooka!") my mom was nearly always on my side.

But when I started to veer away from things like country music —and I'm talking old country music, Jimmy Rodgers and stuff— into Bob Seger, Eric Clapton, the Eagles and the like, I suffered through innumerable comments such as, "What the bejeezus is all that noise?" and "Is somebody killing a sheep in your bedroom?"

Well, eventually we came to a consensus, when I started to appreciate blues and the like. I never did get really fond of Jimmy Rodgers' "Blue Yodel No. 75" or any of the seventy-four yodels before that, but it was okay.

So I'm sitting there and this "concert" comes on. The first act is by a group that is dressed like vagabonds. Now, when I was growing up, people who got rich and famous from making records tended to dress better. Now it seems like they dress worse, and spend more money doing it. How is it that you spend ten times more to dress like somebody that you would cross the street to avoid if you saw them walking on the sidewalk toward you? And why would you want to look that way?

Fine. My dad threw a fit when I started to grow my hair long. "Long-haired tramp," he said, but he didn't stop me. "Chitimachas didn't wear their hair long. They wore it tied up, or in a bun." I refused to wear my hair in a bun, no matter how much I revered and respected my Native American ancestors. I'm not much of a fist-fighter, and I could foresee many a good beatings in my future if I wore my hair in a bun.

So let's forget the guy dressed like he just got rescued from a desert island after ten years without a single bar of soap available, or the band after that, whose lead singer's pants were somewhere south of his equator equivalent to Cape Horn on South America. The simple fact of the matter was, the entire band and every one after that never made anything that remotely resembled music.

They all had instruments, mind you: drums, guitars, and keyboards. But I never heard a single melody. Not a chord. Not one arrangement. Not even a scale. And to make matters worse, the singing was not singing at all. I don't know what it was, but it wasn't singing.

Now, I don't mind some hair-raising, screaming rock and roll. My personal musical tastes actually run the gambit from Barry Manilow to Led Zeppelin and much in between, and I'll sing along at the top of my lungs until my throat gets sore to "Sweet Child of Mine" by Guns 'n Roses. But, durn, at least those tunes are somewhere close to a legitimate key and have a shred of rhythm!

It's like the guitar player was playing one bar of eighty-three different songs one after another; the drummer was having a bad drug trip and thought his drums were a school of piranha; the bass player kept looking for another string, and the lead singer was crying for his mommy.

I said, "Somebody fix me another drink, quick."

Now here's the funny part. There are people out in the audience, maybe a hundred thousand of them, cheering the bands on!

Yes, I looked really hard, and I'm serious. I thought perhaps that they were waving their fists at them and shouting, "Go home! You *stink!*" but they weren't. They were *cheering.* At one point, the lead singer with the Hind-End of Chile Pants got too close to the stage, and they all tried to grab him like he was Paul McCartney and it was 1964 all over again. Five guys from security had to grab the lead singer by the waistband to hold him on the stage, which relocated his pants somewhere near Antarctica. Three of the bodyguards passed out.

I hated disco. But given the choice between what I saw that night and being time-warped back to the 1970s with the requirement of being a bouncer at a disco bar, well, give me a baby-blue leisure suit and bell-bottoms and it's hello, *Saturday Night Fever*. Heck, I'll do public relations for the Village People if I have to.

I only hope I can show the remarkable tolerance my parents showed me as I exited their perceptions of good taste and suitable entertainment when my own children want to go see Hanging Jeans and the What Did You Spend the Money Your Momma Gave You For Music Lessons Band perform their No. 1 hit, "Charter Me A Sled Dog, I Gotta Find My Pants."

Just as long as they don't hit me up for the money.

Visitors

If anyone of you is squeamish about things like zits, please stop reading this column now and go read "Dear Abby."

I haven't had a pimple on my face since I was a teenager. Now, back then I was pretty acne-prone. I'm definitely not making fun of anyone with acne problems, because I had severe bouts with it and I know the misery and embarrassment it can cause. However, the reality of it was revived this week.

Sunday morning, I woke up with a slight irritation on my right cheek, just on the same latitude as my nose. I paid little attention to it, but by Monday, a decidedly pinkish pimple had emerged.

You're wondering, at this point, why anyone would devote an entire column to a pimple, but just hang in there, I'll get to that.

By Tuesday evening, the pimple had grown into a fair-sized whatchamacallit. I mean, I had this lump on my cheek next to my nose the diameter of a quarter and sticking out a good two bits. I was mortified. I had to go to a city council meeting that evening, and I was waiting for someone to say to me, "Hello, Quasimodo."

Most people were decidedly polite, however, and simply said,

"What the tarnation is that on your face, boy?"

But by Wednesday, a second visitor had appeared on my chin, and a third on my nose. The one on my chin was moderate-sized, the one on my nose, thankfully, small, because my nose has plenty enough mass as it is, thank you very much. I ran out of bandages with which to apply antibiotic cream overnight, so I bought more. These were of a different brand, and when I took them off the next morning, I had had an allergic reaction to the bandages so I now had a red rash surrounding the unknown maladies I started with.

Patches, who usually wakes me up in the morning by chewing my nose, was surprised to find a layer of antibiotic cream there in the morning, and was none too happy about it, I can tell you.

Fearful now, I went to see a nurse.

"Looks like it's getting better," she said.

"How do you know?" I asked. "You just saw me just now."

"Just keep doing what you're doing," she said. "It seems to be working."

I gave up trying to understand how she could have known this, since this was my first visit, and asked: "Are you sure it isn't skin anthrax?"

"No, I'm sure it's not," she said.

If you think about the wording of, *No, I'm sure it's not,* it would tend to leave you a little confused about what exactly she was sure of, and when you're talking about something like skin anthrax, you want to be sure you're understanding everything. This was in the days after Sept. 11 when those white envelopes with white powder were making their way through the post offices.

"Are you sure?" I repeated. "I do work for a newspaper, you know."

"Yes, I know that, but no, I'm sure it's not anthrax," she said, confusing me even further.

"I have won several statewide press association awards for my column," I went on modestly. "I declared war on two city councilmen a few months ago, and I called Osama bin Laden a girlie-boy."

"Good for you, but no, I'm sure it's not anthrax," she said.

I was getting irritated by then. "Dan Rather's office got anthrax. And Tom Brokaw's. So did the *New York Post.*"

"I heard that," she said.

"Are you saying I'm not worth anthrax?" I demanded.

"No, I'm sure you're worth anthrax," she said, and while I tried to work out what she meant by that, she left and I went home.

As things progressively got worse, someone said to me, "You ought to try some Boudreaux's Butt Paste on those," a Cajun-created ointment for diaper rash.

"What are you trying to say?" I demanded.

"No, really, it's not just for that," they said. "I didn't mean to imply that your face looked—I mean, I was just suggesting...uh, well..."

"Go jump off a cliff," I said and stalked off angrily.

After careful consideration, I have come to the conclusion that I probably had an allergic reaction to the epoxy on the boat. I don't quite understand why it didn't happen sooner, since I have been using it for several weeks now, but I may have accidentally smeared a bit of it on my face while adjusting my glasses or something and didn't notice it. Anyway, by Thursday, all three visitors had shown great signs of improvement, and I was fully recovered by the weekend.

You understand, don't you, that having an allergy to epoxy is not a good thing for a boat builder to develop. It's kinda like a mechanic being allergic to oil. Or a printer being allergic to ink. Or a nurse being allergic to coherent sentences.

One thing's for sure: You won't find any Boudreaux's Butt Paste anywhere around my face.

Reconstructions

This past weekend I was forced to embark on a reconstruction project.

Warning: This column involves the word "toilet." If you are uncomfortable reading the word "toilet" please accept my apologies, and simply mentally substitute the word "commode."

I have been aware for some time that there were some serious issues going on in the bathroom at home. The subtle indications were a) the toilet was leaning decidedly to the right...or left, depending on which way you were facing at the time, and b) I noticed Thursday it had sunk a half-inch lower than the surrounding floor, indicating I had either gained entirely too much weight or something else was amiss. These are signs of trouble as surely as when the real Gen. George Armstrong Custer said, "What's to worry about?"

So I set about work Friday when I got home from the office. I began by stripping the linoleum tile off from one corner, only to find that it rested on a layer of fiberboard. Fiberboard is this stuff that's hard as a rock when it's dry, but turns to oatmeal when it's wet. It's sawdust and glue between two layers of paper, and it's even more obnoxious than the press board that you find in most furniture nowadays. The main difference between fiberboard and press board is that press board has paper on it that's made to look like fake wood, further evidence that human beings always think they can improve on nature, usually with tragic results, as when the television collapses to the floor.

Removing fiberboard is quite a job. It was nailed to the sub-floor, which was longleaf pine. I initially had vague hopes that I could save the sub-floor, until I got about halfway through the bathroom, at which point the fiberboard and the pine both turned to garden mulch.

Apparently, the toilet had been leaking much longer than I suspected, and the water was going between the pine sub-floor and the fiberboard. This meant it all had to come out. This was quite an ordeal, but I managed to get it all up and ended the day with a sore back, stiff knees, banged up knuckles and multiple splinters.

The amazing thing is that the original cypress floor—boards 15 inches wide!—was wet as well, but perfectly sound. I put a heater in the bathroom overnight to dry it out. I thought about sanding the original floor and varnishing it, but the half-inch gaps between the boards and round holes where plumbing used to run ages ago made me decide otherwise. Now and then I could see a pair of black nostrils poke up through a hole where a pipe once existed. Just Mocha wondering what all the noise was about. Once, Patches noticed those nostrils and went over to investigate, craning her neck out to sniff at the sniffer, which then caused Mocha to sneeze and Patches spun around in terror, hit the wall as she did, and fled across the house and up the stairs.

Next day, I hauled all the cypress I had out in the woodshed into the shop and began turning it into tongue-and-groove with my router table. I took a tape measure to the bathroom and figured out exactly how much I would need to put a new cypress floor in and got to work. Naturally, I mis-figured and was about twelve square-feet short and had to setup the router to make more.

Anyway, I started with the corner by the toilet first, and rein-stalled it. Now, if you know anything about toilets, you know that they rest on a wax seal to prevent leakage. I have changed a wax seal four times before. In other words, I messed it up four times be-fore I got it right. That meant four trips to the hardware store and severe embarrassment at the register each time. This time, I bought one wax seal and prayed a lot. It went on flawlessly, and Patches and I celebrated with Diet Coke and warm milk.

So finally the new floor was in, and I gotta admit, it looked pretty darn good. I was, however, thereby bitten by the remodel-ing bug, and set about refacing the lavatory cabinet. This led to tak-ing down the mirror and reframing it in cypress, a considerable job considering the mirror is fifty-five inches by thirty-one inches and very old, therefore extremely heavy. My neighbor came and helped me carry it out of the bathroom. This further led to a new wain-scot, which is now under construction.

In the process of all this, I noticed a patch of moisture near the tub which refused to dry out, particularly after I took a shower. I see that my work is not nearly over yet. Ah, well. The joys of be-ing a homeowner. Can't call the landlord. Thus the joys of being the homeowner of a hundred-and-sixty-year-old home built by poor Indians with limited tools and countless renovations since. There isn't a right angle or anything level in the whole house, the plumbing looks like a pot of spaghetti noodles, and the back porch fell off two years ago so I had to build a new one. But you know, I wouldn't have it any other way.

Reconstructions II

Reconstruction of the bathroom at home continues.

Warning: This column probably won't contain the word "toilet" so don't worry.

As you may recall, I have installed a new wood floor, refaced the cabinet where the sink is, taken down, re-framed and reinstalled the mirror and replaced the light fixtures.

I had a little tongue-and-grooved antique cypress out in the woodshed, so I proceeded to clean this up and use it for wall covering. Now, a "woodshed" is not to be confused with a "wood pile." A woodshed is a place where you keep wood dry and stacked straight so that you can use it one day. A wood pile is a place where you throw wood for either firewood or to let slowly rot over the next twenty-five years while you keep telling yourself, "I'm gonna haul all that to the dump one of these days."

The wall covering cypress went up great. It's very "rustic." You know what rustic is. A log cabin, for example, is rustic. A ranch-style home of the older style is rustic. Cypress walling, with lots of neat nail holes, stained black from the iron decomposition around them, wormy tunnels and the occasional split are rustic. Rustic is also a word we half-baked carpenters use to describe our work. "I decided to go for a rustic look in this room," we say. Rustic, in other words, hides our otherwise inadequate carpentry skills. That badly fitted corner, that askew door frame, is rustic, not shoddy workmanship. My entire house will be rustic, of course.

There is an old window in the bathroom. Two of its panes were broken, and it had so much paint on the wood I think the trim had grown to five times it original size. So I purchased another, one of those nice little well-insulated jobs. I could not find a window the same size, so I settled on one an inch wider and taller. No problem, I figured, I probably got two inches of paint around it anyway.

Removing the old window, which I calculate has been there about eighty years, was rather like pulling up a tree stump from hard-baked clay. I removed all the framing, but there was so much paint on it I had to carefully pound on it with my hammer, trying not to break any more glass. When this failed, I pounded harder. Still unmoving, I pounded harder. When I noticed the wall was starting to come loose, I stopped pounding and got a pry bar.

The window finally gave up and, now full of hammer head marks and prying dents, was placed to the side. So I started framing for the new window. This would have been fairly easy, except for the fact that I kept dropping my stupid tools out the window onto the ground, so I had to go all the way outside to get them and come back. Now you know why I am a writer. I can build some awesome furniture, with all humility, and a pretty yar boat, but my carpentry for some reason always looks like it involved the Three Stooges and a bottle of Mad Dog 20/20.

I carefully leveled the window, trying to be a responsible carpenter. But when I stood back from it for eyeballin,' it made me dizzy. I rechecked it for level, and it was right. I figured my level was off, so I went got another (I have six of them) and got the same results. I finally realized that the window was indeed level, but everything else in the room was so far off level that it made the window look like a drunk with big eyeglasses. This may have meant I was looking into the mirror, but no, it was the window.

What to do? Leave the window level and myself disoriented? Unlevel the window and let the optical illusion balance itself? I elected to unlevel it. This worked pretty good, and by the end of the afternoon, I had finished framing and trimming it inside.

Then I completed the cypress wall around the window to the shower. That means two of four walls are done. I now need to get a new tub and shower enclosure, the installation of which I am sure will send me to a padded room somewhere.

At the end of the day, I went around to the back of the house to make sure I had picked up all the tools I had dropped out of the window and looked up at the framing I had done from the outside. Looked pretty good. Unlevel as the leaning tower of Pisa, but there you go. From five hundred feet up from a helicopter, who can tell?

During all this, Patches is sitting on the back of the commode (didn't say 'toilet!') watching me. She was extraordinarily curious about that sudden gaping open space where the window used to be, and jumped up there to look around outside, at which point a clump of insulation fell from inside the wall (the papery, fibrous stuff they blow in) and she promptly decided that the back room, behind the washing machine, was much more interesting.

At least I didn't drop her out the window.

ugh

What a nasty, mean little bug this has been. By the time I reached Thursday of the previous week, I was pretty sure I wasn't going to have much of a weekend. Friday was pretty much the same, and by Saturday, I had graduated to an unverified case of jungle fever.

I haven't had a good case of jungle fever in about four years. I guess I am long overdue. Saturday morning, a buddy of mine was coming over to do some work on my outboard engine, and by the time he left, all further plans for the weekend were pretty much null and void. That is, if I had any sense, they would have been.

But I persisted in being stubborn. I started doing some final varnishing inside the boat, touching up here and there. About midway through one stroke of the brush, my guardian spirit came to me.

Now, this is a mostly Indian thing, you understand. We all have guardian spirits, it's said, but a lot of us take it sorta like an old wives' tale, not very seriously. Indian folks usually are pretty serious about it. In the old days, we pretty much knew who, or what, our guardian spirit was. We knew this by what totemic clan we belonged to, and by the names of our ancestors.

I was therefore surprised, when my guardian spirit came to me, not to find a panther or a wolf, those being examples of the animal variety, nor the spirit of Cochise or Geronimo, but the ghostly apparition of Jim Croce.

You understand that I had been taking massive doses of DayQuil, but I am not saying this had anything to do with it. Regardless, the spirit of Jim Croce suddenly appeared inside my garage/boatshop. I doubted it was really him at first, but it had to be. There couldn't have been two people on the face of the earth who looked like Jim Croce.

"Listen to me very carefully," Jim Croce said, standing there just beyond the transom of the boat, stub of a cigar hanging from his mouth. "Put down your brush. Don't bother cleaning it. Don't bother capping the varnish can. Carefully get out of the boat, lock up the shop, and go lie down. Do this within the next three minutes, or a wave of dizziness will overcome you, at which point you will fall forward and bash your head against the cockpit hatch and suffer a concussion, the fire rescue people will come, the ambulance will take you to the hospital and you will have to wear one of those hospital gowns that are open all the way down the back."

That was good enough to me. If you can't trust Jim Croce as your guardian spirit, whom can you trust? So I did as directed and pretty much stayed on the couch for the rest of the weekend.

I did venture out once to my mom's, who insisted on being a mother and sticking a thermometer in my mouth. Since I wouldn't stop complaining about it, it didn't get an accurate reading, which was fine with me. I was pretty much convinced I had entered jungle quality fever, but I didn't want her to know it. She'd worry too much. I went home back to the couch.

When one suffers jungle quality fever, all sorts of weird things happen. The chills and sweats cycle is pretty much the worst of it. Shivering and trembling one moment, sweating profusely the next. It was so bad Sunday that Patches gave up trying to snuggle next to me on the couch and stalked off to a drier spot that couldn't be measured on the Richter scale.

I couldn't remember anyone giving me any blankets recently, so I was pretty confident I hadn't contracted small pox. It was just a good case of jungle fever. Reluctantly, I took my own temperature, without complaining: 102. I was a bit disappointed. The last time I had jungle fever, I hit 103. You gotta be proud of having 103 fever. A 102 is okay, but it's rather wimpy, more of a "deep woods" variety fever.

Monday I had firmly decided I wasn't going in to the office. But I had photos on my digital camera that were needed. I attempted to download them to my computer at home, so I could e-mail them in, but naturally, they refused to cooperate. So I had to get dressed, go to the office for an hour or so, and then went back home. The few people I ran into over the weekend and Monday were warned that I "got the bug" in advance, and they steered clear of me. I don't blame them. I thought about putting a sign on the front door of the house reading "Biohazard: Quarantined" with one of those little yellow-and-black symbols you see on hospital waste baskets, but I figured nobody was likely to come visit me anyway. Just because of that, an old friend I hadn't seen in years did come by Sunday. I hope he left uninfected.

The rest of the day was spent on the couch, watching the Discovery Channel, feeling worse and worse with each half-hour episode. It was one of those times when at first you're afraid you're doing to die, it gets worse, and then you're afraid you won't.

The fever broke around four that afternoon. I never saw Jim Croce again, which is fine by me. It's a little disconcerting to have a DayQuil hallucination wherein Jim Croce is your guardian spirit. On the other hand, it could have been Gen. George Armstrong Custer, so I guess I shouldn't complain.

Sleep was elusive Monday night, because every time I'd lie down, I'd start coughing violently. I tried sleeping sitting up, but for me, this is about as feasible as eating soup while hanging upside down. Desperation finally set in, and I resorted to that age-old, traditional and culturally founded remedy which has been proven and tested over the generations: the hot toddy.

Yup. A little honey, some lemon juice and a jigger of scotch. Maybe it was two jiggers, I don't really remember. Forget any water. Warm it up in the microwave just a bit, throw your head back and swallow it quick. It makes you jump up and down for a couple of minutes like somebody poked you in the ribs with an electric cattle prod, suddenly learning how to do a war dance right there at the kitchen counter, shake your head vigorously and shout, "Urrrgggglllleebuuughhd!" and wrack with violent tremors from pony tail to toe, but I slept for the remaining three hours of the night without coughing once. It's as if the cough reflex in me was thinking, "Well, let's not make him do that again!"

So here I am, back at the office, and back on moderate, hallucination-free doses of DayQuil. No hot toddies allowed while on duty, I'm afraid. Bother it all. The fever has not returned, however, and neither has Jim Croce. I think I'll be over this in the next day or two. My appetite, which went on vacation Saturday and had not reappeared since, is starting to come back a little Tuesday morning and I'm looking forward to lunch. That's a good sign. Maybe I'll sleep better tonight. If not, well...hot toddies are miracle workers, after all.

The Tissue Box Man

I think I have made a horrible mistake.

You see, over a year ago, a young lady here at the office got married. Hitched. Jumped the broom. Tied the knot. You get the idea. I promised that for a wedding present I'd build her something in the shop, as long as it wasn't something all-fired expensive or gosh-awful complicated.

Well, she settled on a tissue dispenser box. You know, the kind you slip over the cardboard box with an oval hole in the top, so you can pull the tissue out. I agreed, though reluctantly. My fears were soon to be realized.

I started out in the shop last weekend looking for material. I really like the contrast of two vastly different woods in one piece. For instance, some of the furniture I have in my living room is walnut and pecan. Walnut is very dark, pecan is blond. Done right, it is a nicely interesting piece. Done badly, it looks like a melted chocolate-dipped vanilla ice-cream cone.

So I rummaged around and found a couple of small pieces of Philippine mahogany, very rich brown and only slightly reddish. A little more searching in the woodshed found a nice piece of aromatic red cedar, a very purple-red-cream wood with swirling grain.

I put these together this way: The top is cedar, two sides are mahogany and two sides are cedar. I then ran a nice little routed bead along the top edge.

Then I dropped it on the concrete and nicked one of the corners badly. Not about to start all over again, I put it on the belt sander and knocked off the corner to a bevel. I did the same to the other three corners, applied several coats of varnish, and thought I was done with the deed.

Not so. Everybody's crazy about the thing. I gave it to my co-worker Tuesday, and the rave reviews began. Nobody knows that I nicked the corner when I dropped it and hid the mistake with the belt sander. Nobody even seems to care that the varnishing job is a little dusty. Now everybody wants one.

I have sold a little fine furniture here and there, and given away some, too. I don't do much furniture anymore. A curly maple armoire, an antique Douglas fir sideboard, a very clever scrap wood table are a source of pride for me.

However, I do not want to be remembered as "The Tissue Box Man."

I'm terrified of this, you realize. I mean, I don't consider myself a snob or anything, but that's just not how I want to be remembered. Imagine the scene, fifty (hopefully!) years from now:

"Hey, did you hear Roger Stouff passed away?"

"Really! Wasn't he The Tissue Box Man?"

"Yeah. Quite an artist. Known for his beveled corners on his tissue boxes. Revolutionary!"

"I know. I hear there are some of his tissue boxes in the Louvre."

"Me, too. Christie's is auctioning one right now, the bidding opens at a hundred and fifty grand."

"Wow. Hmm, didn't he also do some writing or something?"

This is not how I want to be remembered, folks! I want to hear:

"Roger Stouff! Oh, the master boat builder? The guy who raised the art of curly maple armoire and scrap table building to a whole new level? What a sad loss! The world will never be the same. Didn't he win the Pulitzer? Or was it the Nobel?"

Now that's more like it. I suppose it's only important that one be remembered at all, but if it's to be as The Tissue Box Man, I'd just as soon be forgotten.

I have been debating for some time jumping into trying to sell some of my woodwork. But I am told I am too high-falooting. I want to build sideboards and armoires and secretaries. People, I'm told, won't buy that around here. They will buy paper towel holders with little crawfish figures, and tissue boxes. I feel like Rembrandt handed coloring book and a box of Crayons (the glitter kind, for Pete's sake!) and told, "Here! This is what people want!" Nope. Ain't gonna happen. I may be a cheesehead, but I refuse to be cheesy. Not in this lifetime, pal. What, Stradivarius should have given up violins and made toilet paper roll holders? Michelangelo should have given up sculpting and rolled kid's plastic putty on the comics page? DaVinci should have been playing with wooden blocks?

But then I hear that for a nice wood tissue box the stores get about twenty bucks. Let's see, at twenty dollars for a really nice tissue box, I could pump those puppies out at about ten a week, that's two hundred bucks, eight hundred a month...minus materials, say, six hundred a month, times twelve, that's over seven thousand a year–

Nope. Stop it. I will not lie under a tombstone which says:

HERE LIES THE TISSUE BOX MAN.
MAY HIS ENDS ALWAYS POP UP THROUGH THE
HOLE.

Ain't gonna happen.

Now, where did I put the rest of that mahogany and cedar...? For an armoire, I mean. Really.

The Shrinking Jeans Epidemic

It's become all too clear to me that I have developed a months-long case of the lazies.

This is totally unlike me. But since I finished the boat around the first of May, I haven't done pecan in the shop.

I mean zero, zip, zilch, nothing. I think those final months of getting the boat ready for launch were such a rush of adrenaline-pumped activity, I haven't had the gumption to get out there and do anything new.

I had recently acquired a 1963 Thompson mahogany boat thanks to the generosity of a very fine gentleman here in town. I had said I wasn't going to start that project, the restoration of it, until after I had done quite a bit more work on the house. That's not been hard, because I've been in neither the mood nor had the energy to do either.

I have great plans for my next phase of remodeling. Never mind that the bathroom still isn't finished, and the kitchen cabinets are not done, either. But I just don't seem to get around to doing anything. I come home from the office each weekday, and on Monday, Tuesday, Thursday and Friday, I just kind of laze around all evening until bedtime, playing on the computer or watching the tube or eating. Wednesday and Saturdays I go to to dinner with friends, and Sundays I lie on the sofa all days planning what I'm going to do to the house when I get started.

I began to think that I was getting taller. I knew that I was also getting taller because, when I bend over to tie my shoelaces early in the morning, it is getting increasingly difficult to breathe while doing so. This, my analytical mind informed me, is obviously because I am getting taller, and thus my shoe laces are harder to reach because they are farther away from my hands.

Next, I realized that if I was getting taller, I must be doing so proportionately, because my jeans are getting tight. That made sense. If you're getting taller, you're not just elongating, you're also gaining breadth.

But a quick check of my driver's license and the use of a tape measure revealed that I was not, in fact, getting any taller, much to my disappointment. I figured that my jeans had shrunk, and caused them to be too tight, and their tightness, therefore, made it harder for me to breathe, therefore more difficulty in tying my shoes. So I went to get new jeans, and when I tried on the same size I had bought before, I found the most amazing thing had happened: All the jeans of that size in the entire store had shrunk too! What do you think are the chances of that?

I complained to the manager that all his jeans in my size had shrunk. He assured me that this was impossible, but I said, "No, it's true. None of them fit me anymore, and I've already verified that I am not getting taller." I showed him my driver's license as proof.

The stubborn man refused to believe that his store's stock of jeans had shrunk, so I left angrily and went home to brood.

So a couple days ago, I went to visit my godchild, and his mom said, "Roger Stouff, are you gaining weight?"

I was stunned and insulted. Me? Gaining weight? Of course not! Didn't she see that my jeans had shrunk? That would make me look like I am gaining weight, I guess, so I forgave her humiliating remark, but I went home again to brood.

I am sure there is no correlation between my inactivity in the shop and the fact that my jeans are shrinking. I am also sure there is no connection between my jeans shrinking and my belt moving up one hole toward the end. Obviously, my belts are shrinking too.

Now, just so you don't think I'm nuts, let me explain this to you scientifically. The weather we've been having lately is the obvious cause of this. All that rain has caused humidity to be very high. Because of this, things swell. But at the same time, the intense heat of the summer days we've been having causes them to dry out, and this rapid succession of swelling and drying causes things to shrink from cellular damage due to desiccation. This is why your wash rag in the tub, if you use it and let it dry then use it and let it dry a few times turns into a thinner, shrunken mat.

The weather has been so screwy lately, in fact, that not only have my jeans shrunk, but also the jeans in all the stores around the area.

Rather than go up a size in jeans, therefore, I decided to wait until fall when the seasons start to change and my jeans will once again acclimate to the climate and I'll be able to wear them comfortably again.

And since it will be fall before that happens, and since I don't do remodeling in the house wearing dress slacks, I'll have to wait until fall to get to work on the kitchen, you understand. Nobody does carpentry work in their Sunday-go-to-meeting pants. Wearing uncomfortable, weather-shrunken jeans doing carpentry work can be distracting, which is a safety hazard when working with power tools. Safety is my middle name, so I won't take any chances, no siree Bob.

That means I've got a couple months of waiting for the weather to get right so I can get into my jeans and start working on the house again.

Oh, well. I guess I'll have to see what's on the tube and make sure I have a good supply of chocolate—I mean, celery, yeah, that's it, celery sticks on hand in the fridge.

Demolishing the Kitchen

These things just happen. I never know when they're going to happen. They pounce on me like predators.

I would like to think that, after reading my column on having a bad case of the lazies, all the good thoughts you kind folks sent to me were received and motivating. Since I haven't moved much off the sofa since Noah came ashore, I was a bit surprised Saturday morning to find myself demolishing my kitchen.

It's true. I was finishing up my last cup of coffee and watching Norm Abrams finish up a toy wagon with letter blocks in it, and the next thing I knew, I had a hammer and a crowbar and was in full-swing demolition mode. Now, what I had intended to do was go for a boat ride early in the morning, before the jet-ski demons and bass boats began turning the lake into a churning mass of human pestilence. Sorry. I get cranky about that. Anyway, I had charged up the battery and filled the fuel tanks the night before, ready to take off.

But instead, the next thing I knew, I had removed the paneling from the entire wall between the kitchen and living room, on the kitchen side. I had been thinking for some time of building a kitchen bar there, and though I hadn't firmly decided to do it yet, my natural instincts took over and there was no stopping it.

The problem was, the wall is in the center of the house, and supports the floor of the upstairs room. I knew that I couldn't just tear out a wall like that and not invite disaster, but I reasoned that if I took out one stud at a time and replaced them with the cypress beams I intended to use as posts for the bar, with an appropriate large header above the bar itself, I would be out of trouble.

Of course, this was not the case. As soon as I took the first stud out, I saw the ceiling—i.e., the floor on the second story—sag about an inch.

I panicked as few people know how to panic anymore. Panicking is an art, and a fading one. Many people panic nowadays. Panicking is easy, in today's society. We panic when our stocks plunge. We panic when our Internet connection goes down. We panic when we can't find the television remote. We panic worst of all when someone knocks on the door when we're in our underwear running around the house looking for the television remote.

But I panic the old-fashioned way. I yelled a single word, very loudly, a word which I am not at liberty to repeat here. Then I rushed out to the back yard and grabbed a ten-foot long four-by-four, made a mad dash back to the kitchen and propped it under the sagging ceiling, pounding it into place with my trusty mallet.

In other words, I panicked in the proper manner, by doing something about it. Other people might panic by running around in circles in the middle of the kitchen, trying to contact their surgeon, or their second cousin's wife's uncle, who knows someone he went to school with years ago who now is a building contractor, for advice, or on the telephone contacting the vo-tech school to take a state-certified, accredited class to teach them what to do when you take out a wall stud and your ceiling is threatening to fall into your kitchen sink.

With said reinforcement applied, I had the good sense to then put up three more braces before I proceeded to take out more studs.

It was, however, at this point that I noticed that when I had gone to get the four-by-four from outside, I had left the side door open.

I am not perfect. I may have panicked in a way which immediately solved the problem of the sagging ceiling, but when I suddenly thought that Patches might have escaped while I wasn't looking, well, I panicked again but without nearly so much presence of mind.

First I shut the door, then went running all over the house, calling her. "Patches," I said, and realized that my panic might have made me sound irritated, in which case she surely wouldn't come to me, so I soothed my voice and called again, "Paaaaatcheeeeesss, come here, my sweet, where's that kitty? Come here, Patches. Paaaatcheessss, oh, where's the good kitty?"

Having not found her in a few minutes, and a bit tired of sounding like one of the Brewster sisters, I got my flashlight and investigated every one of her known hiding places as quickly as I could. No Patches. I was then left with the undeniable conclusion that she had gone outside.

Patches is not an outside cat. She's never been outside, because there are too many stray dogs around. So I ran outside, calling for her as I peeked under the porch, under the house, under the boat, in the boat, behind the azaleas, under the back porch, beside the hackberry tree, here, there and everywhere. I was just about to lose my mind, thinking she had been picked up by a falcon or something.

"Have you seen my cat?" I asked my neighbor.

"Do you have a cat?" he replied. My neighbors don't visit me inside the house very often, you can tell.

So I rushed back inside to call the FBI, demand they have every available agent in the district down here pronto, and that includes Fox Mulder and Dana Scully, and as soon as I got in, there she was, napping on the sofa.

Now, I am positive she was not there before. The way I figure it, when I went outside to search, she decided that perhaps all the noise and excitement of my reconstruction project was over for the moment, and emerged from whatever unknown hiding spot she was within to take a nap while there was time. She looked up at me sleepily as I stood there, frowning at her with my hands on my hips, as if thinking, "What?"

After I calmed my nerves with a Diet Coke, I got back to work on the kitchen. Before the weekend was done, I managed to get the wall disassembled where the bar is going to go, framed up with cypress two-by-sixes, and the header installed so I could relieve the ceiling of the support timbers. And amazingly, it all worked out great!

I have a lot to do before the kitchen is done, but at least I'm making progress at last. I guess a house that's been around for a hundred and sixty years is pretty patient, and I'm glad of that.

I just need to make sure that when I close the wall back up, I don't close up Patches in there. I'll probably go stark raving mad looking for her in Jeanerette or somewhere, and they'll come get me with a padded truck.

Quitting

I am pleased to report that I am no longer a Diet Coke fiend.

Well, maybe that's not quite true. I am not as big a Diet Coke fiend. You see, it occurred to me that I had been drinking more Diet Coke than was be good for me. I was somewhere in the neighborhood of six to eight cans a day!

Now, there are multiple reasons why I decided that this made about as much sense as getting in a fist-fight with a circular saw.

The first was the allegations that aspartame can cause, among other things, memory loss. I have a notoriously bad memory, much to the consternation of my friends, employers and my mom.

It's not uncommon for me to get up from my desk with purposeful intent, get halfway to wherever said intent was to be fulfilled, and completely forget what the heck it was I was intending. Sometimes, I'd walk from the boatshed into the shop to get a tool, then stand there for fifteen minutes trying to figure out what tool I was going fetch. Sometimes I had to walk all the way back to the boat to see what I was doing and jog my memory to recall what tool I needed to do it. My mom gets the worst brunt of it. I tell her I'll do something for her and promptly forget about it.

So I decided that the Diet Coke had to be severely cut back. My routine is this: After my coffee in the morning, I started on the soft drinks. I drank them all day. On weekends, working in the yard or on the house or boat, I drank Diet Coke to stay cool.

But the plan became that I would drink one after my coffee in the morning, one after lunch, and perhaps one in the evening. That was at least a reduction by half.

The first morning was on the weekend. I chose this morning because that way, if I had some sort of withdrawal fit, nobody would see it but Patches, who is pretty much used to me throwing occasional, mysterious fits anyway. I decided that I needed to keep hydrated while working in the oppressive heat, so I considered my options:

Beer: No good, I use power tools. Safety first!

Tea: Making tea is about as fun as getting in a fight with a circular saw, and I'd have to sweeten it anyway. Sweetening with sugar was out of the question, and that left aspartame, so I was right back where I started from.

Scotch: Same as beer.

Juice: Too expensive. Most of them give me heartburn, too.

Wine: Same as beer and scotch.

Those Ginseng and Whatever Power Drinks For Energy They Sell Now: I won't drink anything I can't pronounce.

So I had my first Diet Coke after the coffee, then set about drinking water while cutting the grass.

I had forgotten how good a glass of ice water is. I was impressed. Mowing along in the morning, with my big red plastic glass of ice water, I thought, "This ain't so bad at all."

About an hour later, I found out it was that bad, after all.

After the caffeine went through my system, it seems, things were not nearly so hunky-dory. I started getting a strange tingling in the back of my throat, and my tongue turned to a wad of cotton that had been soaked in kerosene then dried out again. Then waves of anxiety started pulsing through my limbs like ants crawling over me. I was, I realized, in serious trouble.

When someone has an addiction, I now realize, it's easy to justify another fix. I did so by reasoning that if I suddenly started having a conniption, I could seriously injure myself with the lawn mower. This gave me ample excuse to run into the house and pop a top. I tell you, the sudden *Snap! Swwiizzle!* was enough to start my mouth watering. I gulped down Diet Coke and felt my whole body relax. The anxiety faded, the tingling in the back of my throat went away.

Cheerfully back to mowing with my trusty soft drink by my side, about halfway through the can I realized I had fallen into the trap again. I cursed myself for a fool, and promised to do better.

I managed to make it until after lunch, and then until the evening. I drank enough ice water to float Noah's ark. The next day, I started the process all over again, and did better.

I haven't noticed any improvement in memory yet. I have, however, noticed more frequent trips to the bathroom. This means, I reasoned, that I was absorbing more of what was in the Diet Coke than I am in the water. Upon reading the Diet Coke label, I learned these were, namely, aspartame, caramel color, phosphoric acid, potassium benzoate, natural flavors, citric acid and caffeine. I was drinking ninety-six ounces of a kid's chemistry set every day.

What the devil are "natural flavors" anyway? As far as I know, that could be beetle dung. Beetle dung is a natural flavor. Why don't they say what "natural flavors" they mean? Beef broth? Pasta? Snap beans? Rocks?

Anyway, I'm down to two Diet Cokes a day, rarely three. I can be satisfied with two a day, I think. That's not all that bad.

The next step, however, is kicking these dadgum cigarettes. That will be a much greater challenge. I have quit before, for six months, and was dumb enough to start back again. I remember that when I quit last time, living with me was less fun than getting in a fight with a circular saw.

Would anybody care to baby-sit Patches for a few weeks?

Backyard Banking

For the past week or so, I've been called upon to prepare the daily stock listings here at the office whilst someone was on vacation. In so doing, it always amazes me watching those numbers go up, go down, relax a little, plummet, skyrocket, or just never do anything except sit there stubbornly refusing to budge. In one way, it bothers me that I don't have any money invested in stocks, bonds or mutual funds. That's what responsible people are supposed to do, isn't it? It makes me feel like I should be watching those numbers dance around with more interest. However, on the other hand, I am rather glad I don't have any of those things. I think I'd be a nervous wreck by the end of a week, and go back to six to eight Diet Cokes a day. Or six to eight scotches.

Heck, I only grudgingly have a checking account. If I didn't have to mail (pre-Internet) bills, I doubt I would even have that. Call me eccentric but I prefer the old cash thing. I always complain about the fact that nowadays banks charge you in most cases to put your money there, which they in turn use to loan to other people or invest. This is the strangest thing I've ever heard of. If a bank has $100 million in customer money, they really don't, because they've loaned some of it to Joe Blow, and invested some of it over somewhere else, and if all of us decide one day we want our money, they couldn't give it to us, and it'd be 1929 all over again. They call this banking. The interesting thing is that if you and I do it, it's different. We have a certain amount of money with a certain amount of bills, and we often borrow from one to pay another until that one gets to where they're banging down the door or ringing the dadblasted phone off the hook, so we borrow from the third to pay that one, and the cycle continues. This is called "robbing Peter to pay Paul" but if you're a bank it's called "banking." Similarly, if all your bills decided to demand payment on the same day, you'd go into a Depression, just like if everyone went to the bank to get their money at the same time. It's just different kinds of depression, I guess.

Me, I like the old ways best. Bury it all in Mason jars around the back yard. Warning: I am heavily armed, so don't get no funny ideas. The spot where my moolah is buried is also lined with C4 explosives, booby-trapped with land mines and I also have a trained attack cat. The dog, however, will happily dig up the loot for you in exchange for a scratch behind the ear, but you didn't hear me say that.

My grandfather used to tell the story about how, when he was a young boy, if they grew low on money in the house, his great aunt would lock all the kids in the house and walk down to the bayou. She'd return in an hour or so with a few silver coins and dirty hands. Similarly, in ancient times, Indians built little "pimple mounds" along their hunting paths to store tools, supplies and other whatnots. Kinda like a pre-historic ATM machine. Therefore, I have to believe that backyard banking is a decidedly Indian tradition, and well, you know what a traditionalist I am.

Watching the stocks for a week or so, I can see why some people get upset and jump off the hoods of their BMWs to their deaths. It would drive me mad. I am also amazed by the idea that, if you open a CD for, say, ninety days, and you decide you want your money back early, you pay a penalty for getting it. What's up with that? There's no penalties when you go out in the back yard with a shovel, under the night sky and take out what you need for Christmas gifts. Penalties for getting your money. Gimme a break.

I hear that some banks are also charging to make deposits. What a load of malarkey! Charging you to let them keep your money, so they can go loan it to Joe Blow down the street? What if you don't even like Joe Blow because he dumped your sister or something? What if you know Joe Blow is just going to spend it all on loose women and booze? For this you gotta pay to make a deposit? Joe Blow can hock his television and Nintendo if he needs the money, for all I care.

Now, when I need a loan, I'm sure you'll all realize what an up-standing and witty fellow I am, and graciously oblige in letting the bank make me a loan. But I promise, it won't be from one that charges deposit fees!

Here's another thing: Some big city banks are charging you to actually speak to a real person. What? Is this someone's idea of a joke? Those automated things are nice, and online banking is even nicer, but sometimes it's great to be able to speak to someone with a pulse. For this you get charged?

I want to make it clear that I am not making fun of bankers. I have some good friends who are bankers. I just don't understand the philosophy behind the entire process, or how it came to be. But come to that, I'm sure they have similar consternation about the newspaper business, or wooden boat building, or cat ownership. To each their own, I guess.

Gotta run. I need to stop and get some more Mason jars on the way home. And some ammo. And some dog treats, just to keep her on my side. I'll pay for it all with a check, of course.

Old Folks Weren't So Dumb

You see, what's happened is, modern "convenience" has become entirely inconvenient.

When we get all bothered about a hurricane churning up a kettle of witch's brew in the Gulf, everybody starts making preparations. More often than not, these preparations are not only costly, but also time- and labor-intensive.

Here again, the old curmudgeon in me comes out. We of modern times think we're smarter than the old folks were. Time and time again, we are proven wrong.

So what do we do? We run out and buy plywood to board up the windows when a storm comes. We buy plywood until there isn't any plywood left. We go through great and complicated pains to cut and fit each of these pieces of plywood, screw them into the window frames, or if we don't want to make holes, concoct some conglomeration to keep them in place consisting of rope, chains, chewing gum, Scotch tape, a block-and-tackle and several mules.

In the old days, the old folks did something extraordinary when a storm came. Brace yourself now, this is going to be shocking and, to some, hard to accept without freaking out:

They closed the shutters.

Yup. That's it. They closed the shutters. It required no trips to the lumber store, no screws, no inventive measures, no mules. It went something like this:

"Pa, I think there's a big blow a'comin'."

"Sure thing, Ma, my corns have been hurtin' somethin' horrible!"

"Better close up the windows."

"Okay, Ma."

Five minutes later: "All done, Ma."

"Thanks, Pa. Took you a little long, didn't it?"

"Naw, just what it always takes."

"No, I think it took longer. You wasn't gawking at that floozy over the fence taking her unmentionables off the clothesline again, were ya?"

"Now, Ma!"

But somewhere down the line, house designers and architects and builders decided that shutters were either a) no longer necessary since there is a lumber store around the corner, b) not very pretty, c) too much trouble to build on a house that costs $175,000 but really is only worth $95,000, or d) the builder/architect/designer had been drinking furniture polish.

If you look at houses since that time, you'll see a spattering with shutters. However, if you go try to close these shutters, you'll yank the vinyl siding off the house, because they aren't really shutters at all, they're vinyl decorations. Thus the logic went: We don't need shutters anymore, but we might put something that looks like shutters on the house if it makes you feel better, until you go to close them when a storm comes, and find out they don't even have hinges. This some people don't find out until the morning before a storm arrives because they thought for all years they've been living in that house that the shutters were real and not, in fact, phonies.

So instead we all run out to get lumber. Now, no matter what you do, no matter how carefully you number the pieces to correspond with the windows they went on—some people even draw little pictures of the house on the plywood with a big X marking which window that particular piece covered—when you go to put them back on for the next storm, they don't fit. It's one of the rules of nature: Plywood cut to cover your windows for a storm in 1994 will not fit the same window in 1997. Scientists have been working on this problem for decades, and so far have only come up with the explanation: "The windows shrank."

When I was growing up my dad kept a stack of galvanized, corrugated tin in the back yard. This served two purposes: He nailed this tin over the windows for a storm, and if the storm took any tin off the roof, he'd have a good supply to make repairs. No plywood ever made it on the windows of our house. Any plywood that came onto the premises was apt to become a boat, or a piece of furniture or a box to hold tools. Plywood on windows was sacrilege.

And speaking of Ma and Pa, modern meteorology still has nothing on the old ways. You can throw all the super computers in the world you want at predicting a storm, but a good set of corns and a touch of arthritis is still the best storm prediction device in the world. I've known corns in Charenton which could predict a tropical wave in the Atlantic out past Bermuda. I've come across cases of bursitis that could tell you if the fish were biting, too. What I haven't found is an arthritic elbow that was any help at all on the stock market.

You can say all you want about modern informational technologies: We track storms now with the television, the radio, the Internet, whatever. But when the power goes, you're sitting in the dark in the shelter feeling like you've just been cut from the umbilical. Battery powered radios are great, but you always forget the batteries, don't you? Okay, maybe you don't but I always do. That's when I start wondering how the Professor rigged up that bicycle thing with a bunch of wires and stuff and made Gilligan peddle it so they could listen to the radio. Of course, the reason they're on that island is because somebody didn't know there was a storm coming, so there you go. If the Professor could build a bicycle thing that would run a radio, why couldn't he fix a two-foot hole in a wooden boat? And what kind of skipper was the Skipper, really, if he didn't know a storm was coming? And how did Mr. and Mrs. Howell pack everything they owned on that little boat, and why? Why did Ginger bring evening gowns? Did the Skipper and Gilligan never have spare clothes, and how did the colors stay so bright all those years of washing in the surf? And —

Never mind. I often wonder, though, what the really old folks thought of hurricanes. I mean, back when the Indians were the only ones on this continent, before Columbus came along and discovered it for us, to our great surprise. Here we were, just minding our own business, cooking up some garfish and wild blueberries for supper, watching the young 'uns playing on the shell mounds and wondering if the little woman was paying far too much attention to that young brave in the next hut over who was taking his loincloths off the clothesline, when all of a sudden *BAM!* The next thing you know, there's two hundred mile per hour winds, trees bending into pretzels, a storm surge the size of a courthouse, and this storm picks your whole family up and drops you somewhere in Kansas. This, you recall, would be where Dorothy was transported to Oz some four centuries later. You had to worry about it a lot, because it's common knowledge that the tribes of indigenous people in Kansas don't think much of folks dropping in for supper in the middle of a big storm. They get especially irritated if it turns out the brave in the hut down the way hadn't quite gotten his loincloths off the clothesline as yet, and all the pretty young ladies are giggling and turning red. Er, redder.

Driving On 90

Dave Barry claims that Miami has the worst drivers in the world because he was once passed up at six hundred mph by a man watching music videos on a screen where the car's sun visor should be.

Dave has never driven on U.S. 90.

He really should try it sometime. Driving on Highway 90 is something like going through the various circles of hell to the center, that being New Orleans.

If you start on Highway 90 in Lafayette, things are pretty bad. This just gets you geared up for the road ahead. Outside of

Lafayette, once you get past Pinhook, somebody in the state decided to install traffic signals every ten feet. Since the average car is twelve feet long, that means that somebody is always stuck in the middle of the intersection under a traffic signal, while a pickup truck full of cypress porch swings is trying to get through from the other way and the driver is honking his head off at you, as if someone is in desperate, emergency need of a cypress porch swing as a life or death matter. There are also truck stop casinos every five feet, so there are at least two between each signal light, with people who are trying to get back on the highway in a bad mood from losing their money, or people eager to get off the highway to go lose their money.

Once you clear Broussard, things get a little better, and you might start to think driving on Highway 90 is actually no big deal. Until you get to New Iberia. The Center Street exit is the place you want to avoid here. If you've gotten onto Highway 90 from the Center Street exit before, you'll know that the on-ramp and the eastbound lane itself are a deplorable lunar landscape, which somebody tried to fix by pouring too much asphalt into the craters. I don't know why highway repair crews don't understand that if you put five gallons of asphalt into a four-gallon hole, you get rid of a crater and end up with a gopher hill. If you get several dozen of these bumps in any given twenty feet of highway, you are in effect airborne more often than you are in contact with the road surface.

So moving down Highway 90 at the Center Street exit and entrance, you need to veer to the left to get out of the way of people who are entering the four-lane at seventy-five mph, airborne, and driving compact cars so low the bumps of asphalt are actually higher than their floor boards, so they just kind of skid over them in a shower of sparks and leave their mufflers and drive shafts behind. If any of these vehicles entering the highway is a pickup truck carrying a load of lumber from Lowe's, or worse, a Volkswagen Beetle with a bathtub tied to the roof, your best bet is just to drive off into the median and hope your injuries are minor.

After you pass New Iberia, things get just calm enough to make you believe the worst is over. The weirdest thing is the signal light at Sorrel Road, which most people ignore, but then you get past that and it's on past Franklin, smooth sailing, across the western end of the parish, to Calumet. Thankfully, that area just before Ricohoc is much better now, and you don't feel like you're riding a roller coaster in AstroWorld anymore.

As you get to Patterson, you have to suddenly hit the brakes and nosedive because the folks over there decided they wanted a fifty-five mile per hour speed limit on a future Interstate highway. If you manage to get through this area without going to jail for the rest of your life, you make it to the bridge over the Atchafalaya River and, after figuring out that the Federal Avenue exit is not, in fact, the way to New Orleans, nor is the East Boulevard exit or the business district exit, you proceed on through the swamps on U.S. 90 until you get to New Orleans. The greatest danger here is avoiding tourists who are driving too close to the embankment trying to look for alligators. Alligators, in fact, have better sense than to be anywhere near Highway 90.

Not long ago, I had reason to go to New Orleans and arrived there at about four in the afternoon on a Friday. The first thing was the Luling Bridge. I don't like bridges. The Baldwin Bridge makes me edgy. The Luling Bridge turns me psychotic. Driving across the Luling Bridge and looking at all those huge cables, you realize that they are in fact only anchoring the bridge to itself.

Now, do try this at home. Tie up your dog to himself and see if he doesn't run off. Tie up a loaf of bread to itself and see if it stays on the ceiling when you put it there. Tie up a chair to itself and kick it, see if it moves. How can you make a bridge that is cabled off to itself? How does it stand up? These are not the things that need to occur to you when you're driving over it. I refuse to drive over the Huey P. Long Bridge at all. It is not a bridge. It is a footpath on steel girders.

But having passed over the Luling Bridge and into New Orleans proper, I found myself among a thousand other cars which were heading into the city. On the opposite side, there were thousands more cars leaving the city. Whenever someone wanted to get onto my side from an access road, they just closed their eyes, put the accelerator pedal to the floor, and aimed toward the flowing mass of cars on the highway, hoping they'd hit a space in between and not end up under a tanker trailer.

If someone wants to change lanes in New Orleans, and there's only enough space between you and the car in front of you, they have a little button on their dashboard which says "Ignore Laws of Physics." Only residents of New Orleans are allowed to have these buttons in their cars. Visitors have to wing it. When they press this button, their car miraculously fits into a space it could not before. If the space is too small even for this button to work, there's another button which is labeled "Suspend All Driver's Belief in Physics" and they try to get into it anyway. These buttons are not limited to New Orleans, because in fact many drivers on Highway 90 seem to have installed them.

I swear, the same car passed me by eight times. I saw this little red car pass by, get off at an exit, then a few minutes later, pass by me again and get off at another exit. I strongly suspect the driver— who was hunched over with both hands on the wheel, looking decidedly suspended of belief in the concept of time as well as physics —was stopping for pizza, groceries, videotapes and flowers for his wife then zooming back onto the highway until the next exit where he needed something came up. On the other hand, there might just have been a lot of little red cars with little guys clutching the steering wheel on the highway in New Orleans.

If you get into the old town, you will learn that the streets go nowhere. You miss your turn, for example, so you think, "I'll just go up a block and circle back." But if you do this, you end up in Abita Springs, where they make great beer and have garnered a small fortune off customers who missed a turn in New Orleans and decided it wasn't worth going back to try again. There are people who have ended up spending their entire lives in Abita Springs drinking beer after missing their turn in the Big Easy, and their families never heard from them again.

You also learn that you cannot make left turns anywhere in New Orleans. Everyone in New Orleans turns right, never left. That's because they learned a long time ago that if you turn left in New Orleans, you drive into the lake. Lake Pontchartrain is actually littered with sunken vehicles from before Orleanians discovered this. When they come to visit Franklin, they spend a lot of time going in needless circles, thinking they might drive off into Bayou Teche if they turn right.

But I managed to get out with my life, and all the paint on the truck intact. So come on, Dave. You think Miami's bad? Let me take you for a ride from Lafayette to New Orleans on U.S. 90. You even get to drive!

Shopping at the Big Boxes

It's a good thing I know a little bit—just a little, you understand —about what I want when I go to buy something at the home improvement centers.

Now, not to take anything away from local merchants, but sometimes if you're out of town already, or it's after-hours, you end up at the Big Blue Box or the Big Orange Box. You know what I mean by those two descriptions.

It seems, however, that when you ask for help at the BBB or BOB, you very often get a person who hasn't the faintest idea how they even got to work that morning, much less where the blades for a twelve-inch Delta planer might be found. That's not to say that all employees are this way, so don't go starting a tar-and-feather party, okay?

Someone I know went to either the BBB or the BOB to buy wood stain. You know, it comes in a can and you make wood look like any other kind of wood you want. She had some new furniture made for a bedroom, and wanted to stain the wooden knobs the same color as the original furniture, so she took the knobs with her.

She asked an attendant if a certain stain would look the same as the picture on the can if applied to oak. The attendant said he was sure it would, but that there was a much bigger problem.

"See, the wood on the picture, the grain is running up and down," the attendant said.

"And...?"

"Well, look at your knob. The grain is running left and right!"

I kid you not. In another case, a friend of mine went to get some insulation board. He needed three-quarter-inch stuff, and asked an attendant where it might be found.

The attendant looked at the stacks of material and said, "There it is, up there."

My friend looked. "No, that's half-inch. I need three-quarter."

"Oh." The attendant looked some more. "Is that it right there?"

"No, that's one-inch."

"Oh."

"It's the little '3' with a '4' and a line in the middle," my friend offered helpfully.

"Oh."

Now I myself have had similar experiences at these giant home improvement centers. Once I went looking for glue.

"Oh, that's over with the other glues," said the attendant.

"Which would be where?"

"Aisle six. Or is it four? I don't remember. Come on, we'll find it."

After following him down aisles four through six, we still hadn't found the glues and my feet were starting to hurt.

"They must have moved it," the attendant said.

"To Toledo?" I asked. He thought this enormously funny, and after the laughter died, he asked someone else, who pointed out that glue was actually on aisle nine. They didn't have the kind of glue I wanted.

Here's the other thing about those places. You have to get one of those big carts to get big stuff. If you want plywood or lumber, you have to get this ten-foot long cart with iron tubing on the sides and in the middle. You find what you are looking for, and have to sort though the errant sheets of half-inch plywood that have been wrongly placed with the three-quarter, and the two-by-six lumber obstructing your way to the two-by-fours. You then negotiate the cart, loaded with eight sheets of plywood and a dozen two-by-fours, back to the register. In the process, you knock over the display of water faucets, wipe out the rack of copper tubing and roll over the toes of an eighty-four-year-old woman who had been searching the store for light bulbs since May.

Once you get to the checkout, they use those scanners on the end of a coiled cord to scan your merchandise. Nobody told you that there were labels with the bar codes on each piece you have, and in the process of loading them, you have half the labels on one end of the cart and the other half on the other end. More often than not, the sales clerk won't count to see how many sheets of plywood you have, scan one and multiply it by that number. Instead, they assume you are a thief and have slipped one piece of good stuff in with the mundane sheets. So you have to let them scan all the labels on one end then turn the cart around—wiping out the register display as you do—and get the other end scanned. At this point, you're wondering if it wouldn't have been easier just to go cut down your own trees for the lumber.

Another thing: You need to go to the restroom. You are at the front end of Aisle 1. The restroom is all the way to the back. You have this big cart full of plywood and lumber and you have to negotiate it all the way to the back of the building, leave it there, do what you have to do, and when you come out, you find that some attendant has taken your cart and put all the lumber and plywood back on the shelves. Not surprisingly, he's put the three-quarter plywood on the half-inch pile and the two-by-fours with the fence boards.

Oh, and don't go looking for something simple like a piece of molding. Forget it. Even if your house was built last year, you'll never find that piece of molding. You'll find molding that's too wide, or too thick, or not the same shape. You'll find molding exactly like you want, but it's that strange "medium density fiberboard" stuff, and yours is cherry-stained wood. You'll find, if you are brave enough to search to the back of the display in hopes that the one piece you are looking for somehow fell behind the rest, the skeleton of some other customer who made the same mistake years before.

Thus the pitfalls of being a "do-it-yourself" type. A trip to the home improvement store ranks right up there with flogging. If you find exactly what you need and manage to get it out to your truck without knocking down the building on your head, you then must unload it and head for home.

Nine times out of ten, it rains on the way home. When you get there, your two-by-fours look like pretzels and your plywood like poppies.

Rather than go back to the store and take another flogging, you make do and use these convoluted materials anyway, changing your home interior design concept from "post-modern conservatism" to "middle-late Sanford and Son," and shoot yourself for not going to the local merchants.

Throw Your Own Fit

On the way out of Lafayette one day, Susan and I stopped at a supermarket. When we went to check out, next to the rows of cashier aisles was one empty corridor with a bunch of computer screens and no cashier. I was told by that this is a "check yourself out" aisle.

While I considered making a noisy scene, howling loudly about the utter insult upon my sense of decency, I thought better of it, but secretly threw a hissy fit inside. I remember one supermarket I visited which had a "bag your own" policy, for allegedly reduced pricing.

You know, I'm easily as cheap as the next poor slob, but there's something about bagging your own groceries that really hacks me off. I'm not sure what it is: A combination of feeling insulted, embarrassed, tacky and fear that you'll over-stuff one of those flimsy plastic bags and spill your frozen lasagna boxes all over the floor, not to mention breaking the beer bottles. I have to wonder if it's a "clean up your own mess" policy as well.

But I guess what irritated me the most about bagging your own groceries was the fact that some poor bag boy was out of business. To make matters worse, he was put out of business by a nationwide corporation that didn't give a rip that the young lad, or perhaps a retired gentleman, would be relegated to obscurity and poverty forever because of their stupid bag-your-own gimmick.

Being a bag boy is an American institution. Bag boys and paper boys are historic icons of our culture. Now, when corporate, nationwide supermarkets come into a community promising to hire local people, they also ignore the fact that they'll be putting bag boys out of business and making the shopper feel like a lower class life form to boot. I thought our foraging days as a species were over?

But that wasn't enough. It wasn't bad enough to put the bag boys out of business, now they're trying to put the cashiers out of business, too. Check out your own groceries! What a technological breakthrough! The latest and greatest convenience! What's convenient about it? I like standing in the wings, watching my groceries get checked out by a real live, breathing person, with whom you can make idle conversation about the weather, the tabloids, the price of eggs nowadays. Though I didn't actually try it, making small talk with the computer screen at the check-yourself groceries aisle, I am quite sure it would have been rather boring.

I've got an idea for nationwide stores, of whatever kind, who come into local communities to do business: Act like you give a rat's behind for the people there. Don't try to dazzle us with your "price saving" gimmicks like bag-your-own groceries and self-checkout, not to mention those silly savings cards.

Here's a novel idea: Employ local people, pay them admirable wages, reward their years of service, and become a part of the community by sponsoring civic groups, supporting nonprofits and being a good neighbor.

Otherwise, don't come in at all, so in the end, I don't have to shop your gimmick-ridden metal buildings of ill-repute when I can't get something in particular locally because you've shut down all the local outlets that might have had it for me.

Yes, I'm on a tirade. A torch-carrying crusade toward martyrdom, I'm afraid. It's a pathetic situation the way customers are treated these days.

Take for example the bank. The bank decided that if I sign my payroll check and fill out a deposit slip for "less cash received" I have to submit it in person. Nobody else can do it for me. They have also decided that if I have $5.98 in the account and I'm depositing my paycheck and I want $50 in cash I can't have it. Never mind that a payroll check from the Banner-Tribune is surely bounce-proof. I bet they'd cash one from a metal-building superstore.

Add to the misery, you can't have your money until the next business day, even if you get there before closing. I had a knock-down drag-out fight with a teller one Friday because I deposited a check the day before I was going Christmas shopping, and was informed my funds would not be available until Monday.

My exact words were, "I'm going Christmas shopping tomorrow, and there better be money in there when I want it or I'm coming through that little tube to get it, ya folla?"

It's my stinking money, after all. Don't make rules about my money, don't tell me when I can have my money. Don't forget, there'd be no banks without our money. I'll bury it all in Mason jars in the back yard if they get snippy with me just one more time...

I remember a friend of mine telling me about how, years ago, when his son turned eighteen and had a new job with the oil industry, he told the boy to go to the local car dealership and pick out a used car up to a certain price. Then, he told the boy, go to the bank and ask for Mr. So-and-so and tell him to loan you the money for the car and a year's worth of insurance. The father said to tell the banker he'd be there Monday morning to sign the paperwork.

The banker complied without question, and the father was in there bright and early Monday morning to settle the deal.

Those, my friends, were the days. Days before check-your-own and bag-your-own groceries. Back when customers were treasured.

What a colossal rip-off.

Blissful Socks

Last weekend I experienced one of the greatest joys in my life.
I bought new socks.

Yes, that's what I said. No, I am not deprived, nor bored to tears. Okay, sometimes I'm bored to tears, but not very often.

See, buying socks is a special thing, at least for me. I tend to wear socks down to about a half-dozen loosely conjoined threads before I get new ones. I know it's time to go get new socks when I get thread burns between my toes.

I wear one style of socks: Black. Basic black matches anything I happen to be wearing. No patterns. They are also all of the identical weave. This is what makes buying new socks something of a challenge. I must buy exactly the same weave and style of socks, because I absolutely, positively refuse to put my socks together out of the clean laundry basket. Hate it. Dumbest waste of time I can think of, even dumber than pressing underwear or raking leaves. Forget it. If I have all socks the same weave and style, I just throw them in the dresser drawer and no matter which two I grab, they match. There may be some slight color differential between the old ones and the new ones, but long as they're close, who's looking?

It's kinda fun going through the rows of socks hanging from the store hooks, looking for the right pattern, weave and size. Finding them is a "eureka experience."

I also bought a new pair of shoes, but I accidentally bought them too small. Just half a size, mind you, but they were a bit uncomfortable. I am cursed with a wide foot, and as wide-foot shoes are growing increasingly difficult to find, I just go up half a size or so.

"Fill two Ziploc bags with water," a buddy of mine said. "Stuff one in each shoe and put them in the freezer. The ice will expand and stretch the shoe."

At first I thought this was some sort of joke, because my bud is a notorious prankster. Also, I was reluctant to try this method of shoe-stretching because I was afraid that in some half-awake state I might mistake them for Hot Pockets.

It didn't work. Still too tight. I had a little trouble getting the plastic freezer bags out of them, but managed to do so and keep the shoes in good enough condition to go exchange them for the proper size, which is what I should have done in the first place rather than trying something daring.

Shopping for clothes in general is an exercise in frustration that I despise greatly anyway. Socks are pretty easy, but when it's time to start buying new jeans and shirts, I usually end up nearing a nervous breakdown.

You know, we have regulatory agencies for just about everything in this country except the clothing industry. Now, I'm not one for over-regulation, but I think there should be a federal oversight agency in charge of making sure that every brand of shirt, pants or whatever sticks to defined size guidelines. No more do you have to worry that a medium shirt in this brand might not be the same as a medium shirt in that brand. If you buy a medium shirt, you know it's going to fit you, because it's been inspected by the USDA or at least Homeland Security.

I hate buying underwear. Call me modest, but there's something I just can't get over about buying underwear. I carefully wait until there's no one in the whole mens department before racing down the aisle and throwing a pack or two of underwear into the basket, hoping I grabbed the right size and any color besides hot pink, then suddenly disappear and materialize again in the fishing tackle section as if nothing ever happened. Then I have to check out. I always feel my face is red when some lady cashier runs my underwear over the little price scanner thing. Instead of keeping my mouth shut, I try to be cute and say something witty, usually like, "Well, you know, they make those in Bangladesh sweat shops. People in Bangladesh don't even wear underwear, so why should we trust them?" Soon as I pay, I rush away before I say anything else stupid.

Jeans are my worst nightmare. Ideally, I wear a twenty-nine-inch inseam. Don't ask me what the waistline is, because I ain't telling. It's difficult to find twenty-nine-inch inseams around here, because stores tend to believe everyone is taller. They make few allowances for us short people. In the same way, the racks are usually chock full of shirts from large to XXXL, as if nobody wears anything smaller. By no means petite (and less so every month!) I get really tired of looking through all those L's and X's for a lousy medium shirt. They oughta hang a sign on the door, "IF YOU ARE AVERAGE OR SMALLER, GO AWAY!"

I used to buy Levi's jeans for twenty dollars, which in today's world is a low-priced pair of jeans, but in my world is a couple of trips to the waterin' hole. I finally decided that I didn't give a jolly rip what the brown label on the waistline reads, long as I am comfortable and at least basically presentable. Same with shirts. I do not need people to make an impression about me based on Duckhead, Ralph Lauren or Tommy What's-His-Name. I'm comfortable, I'm not violating any indecency laws, what's the problem?

Truth be known, clothes don't make the man, as the old adage goes. Actually, a fine fly rod does, but that's a subject for another day.

Hanging On

Another recent acquisition of mine was a new set of sheets, pillow cases and comforter.

Yes, my old set was getting rather decrepit. They were seven years old. Have you noticed that I tend to hold onto things obsessively? It's true. I still have pairs of eyeglasses that date back to the 1980s. I can't see the broadside of a barn through them, but I keep them in their little padded cases anyway, just in case I need parts.

I suppose I am either the typical or atypical male. Things like bedsheets and the like just don't mean much to me. In fact, I prefer when they get that well-worn, soft, comfortable feel. Faded color? Who cares? Frayed hems? What, I'm high society now? I tend to spend a lot more time making sure my fishing tackle and boats are in tip-top form than anything else.

But I finally gave in and got a nice set in one of those oversized plastic zipper bags, which I seriously thought would make a good tackle bag. Anyway, after a good washing and running through with fabric softer, the sheets and pillow cases came out okay, though still a little crisper than what I'm used to.

The comforter, on the other hand, will stand up in a corner on its own. It is also so incredibly slick, somehow, that it refuses to stay put.

I mean, this baby will slide. It actually levitates. It seems to generate some sort of electrostatic charge between itself and those crisp new sheets. If I even turn over during the night, it flies completely off the bed like a magic carpet and into the dining room. If I breathe too hard on it, it turns completely around. One night Patches jumped into the bed with me, the comforter took flight, and the more frantically she tried to escape this lunatic floral-patterned demon, the more electrostatic energy was created, and the comforter ended up in the yard and Patches hid for three days.

This is why I hate buying new things, but in three or four years I'll have it nicely broken in.

I'm told my sofa is in need of replacement. I just got that sofa, second-hand, a few years ago, and it is by far the best napping sofa on the face of the planet. I have finally compressed the cushions flat in just right the places and puffy in just the right other ones. When I lay down on my sofa, it fits the contours of my body perfectly. What else could someone want from a sofa? The idea of acquiring a new sofa, which will require years of napless break-in, appalls me in a way I can't fully describe.

It was suggested to me that, to firm up the cushions, I should put a piece of plywood under them. I was aghast with horror. If I want to sleep on plywood, I'll go nap on my workbench. Why on earth would I want to do that? While I am not like the princess and the pea about such things, it would be a shame to ruin a perfectly broken in napping sofa by putting plywood under the cushions.

My armchair was my grandmother's. It's brown, threadbare and ugly as sin. But it sits in the exact same spot she had it, and I cover it with an afghan—suitably worn and lackluster in itself—to dress it up a little. It's comfortable, it was Granny's and I hate to think that one day I'll sit down in it and it will collapse into a hundred pieces, forcing me to retire it. It gives me great pleasure to sit there, where she sat, in the same spot. One of the reasons it's in the same spot is that there is exactly one and only one way to arrange the furniture in my living room, owing to the fact that there are no electrical outlets on the inside of the exterior wall where the front door is. Not a single one. So I have to be near an outlet for my reading lamp and laptop, and the television and stereo simply must be in the same place they have been for as long as there's been such devices in this old house.

I have a kitchen drawer full of remote controls. Ten or more of them. Some of them go to electronics I don't even own anymore, but I keep them anyway, because who knows when an old remote control might come in handy?

Two other kitchen drawers are the mandatory "junk drawers." This is where I throw stuff that I can't find any other place for, or am too lazy at the time to go put it in its proper place. There's a wonderland of stuff in those drawers: coins, wire, old greeting cards people sent me, bullets, a guitar tuner, dead batteries, photographs, screws, nuts and bolts, small nails, picture frame hangers, nail clippers, you name it. I could probably find an outboard motor in there, except that I keep those in the walk-in closet behind the bathroom. This gives some people pause when being nosy, and they peek into my bathroom closet and see two small-horsepower outboard motors on the floor.

Not wanting to admit that they snooped in my private domain, but unable to coalesce logic into what they just saw in their despicable spying, they say, "I dropped the Charmin and it rolled through the slightly ajar door of the closet and I had to go get it, and I was wondering, why do you have two boat motors in your bathroom closet?"

I explain patiently that both of them were my father's, and they have great sentimental value; they are good old engines that I may use someday; I do not want to store them in the shed outside for fear they might get stolen, and lastly, you have worn out your welcome, please go home and mind your own business.

One of the things slowing my renovations of the house is that, when I finally get up the nerve to clean out and renovate a room, I have to move everything to another room. I am rapidly running out of space downstairs, and have begun storing my hoard upstairs. I am fearful that if I continue this way, the second floor will collapse under the weight of all my accumulated goods.

"You ought to have a rummage sale," someone told me. A rummage sale! To call this "rummage" is to call King Tut's golden mask a trinket. How dare they! These are my old science-fiction books that I will likely never read again, my dozen remote controls that don't operate anything, my boxes and boxes of CDs I don't listen to. Rummage! This is not rummage, this is a stack of old editions of newspapers I worked for that are no longer in business, this is a crate of computer cables and other wiring, an old dial phone which may save my life if the tone system ever crashes, a broken paddle I intend to epoxy back together one day, and a stack of luggage that I have never used and probably never will. Rummage. Bah.

I tend to hold onto things, I know. I am far less interested in acquiring the latest and greatest than keeping stuff that has been faithful to me, even though it's outlived its usefulness.

I told Susan I intend to restore Dad's old 1963-vintage Mercury

9.8 horsepower outboard, complete with new decals and paint, and display it in the living room next to the bar. She took a dim view of this idea.

Perhaps I could put it under the cushions on the sofa. Maybe so. But I have my concerns about where the prop might fall.

Things That Bug Me

Here's a small collection of some of the many, many things that bug me in this world.

I was told that if you dial the number in the local telephone book for the local post office, you get some lady on the East Coast. What's up with that? I am sitting about two hundred yards from the post office on Willow Street, but I can't call them from my office? I tried it, and after twenty minutes of punching menu options, talked to some nice lady near the Atlantic Ocean, I was finally able to talk to the person I wanted to talk to: the post office employee in Franklin.

Speaking of phones, it's nearly impossible these days to know how to dial a phone number out of your immediate calling area. I want to dial someone, so I dial the (for example only!) 555-1222 number.

"We're sorry, you must first dial a one or a zero plus the area code," the automated recording tells me. So I dial one and the area code.

"We're sorry, one and the area code are not necessary when dialing this number," the recording then says.

I dial the number without a one, just the area code and number.

"We're sorry, no area code is needed when dialing this number," the recording says. "If you feel you have reached this recording in error, dial zero to speak to an operator."

Fed up to the gills by then, I dial zero.

"Good morning," says a friendly voice. "United States Postal Service, may I help you?"

There is a conspiracy at work here, I am convinced of it.

Drive-thru fast food lanes bug me. With all the technology at their disposal, such as mega-ovens, soda machines, huge lighted plastic signs and the like, you'd think they could install intercom systems that work clearly. I hate to drive up to the thing and hear:

"Ajouh afadfoin agagada, ooo affdaf ohnpadfa?"

"I'll take a bacon double cheeseburger and a large chocolate shake, please," I say helplessly.

"Arft sparnfargle sooloo zipalltooitz?"

"No, no fries," I guess. "Don't super-size it, either."

"Zepft hazbalgathrun bereer indoustoo," they say and I drive around to the second window, where the lady with the fast-food restaurant uniform opens the window, smiles and says, "Peergloot-ten vaadlimnistal oongalla." I hand her a five, receive my food and change, and high-tail it out of there in terror because I actually understood that last part.

Long as I have your attention—a rapidly deteriorating condition, I'm sure—it really bugs me when you see a television promo for some movie with "Joe Blow, star of *The Lord of the Rings*," and you have no idea who Joe Blow is. So you check the film credits for Lord of the Rings and find that Joe Blow was an Orc in the battle toward the middle of the second movie who got killed by Gimli in a half-second of footage.

Here's another thing that bugs me: stuff that's packaged in thick clear plastic then welded shut. You know, you buy, oh, say a socket set. It's in clear plastic hanging on the hook in the store. You get it home and start trying to open it. I tell you, they could make tanks with this stuff. You first try to rip it apart at the seam, but then you realize it isn't really a seam at all because you see the slightly melted edge where someone used a high-intensity laser to seal the package. So you go after it with the a pair of scissors, but you might as well be trying to cut hardened steel. Out comes a big knife, which does little more that scratch the stuff. You hold it with your foot and bash it with a sledge hammer repeatedly, run over it with the lawn mower, throw it into the path of a freight train then finally give up and take it to someone who has an acetylene torch.

Really high on the list are television commercials for bodybuilding equipment. Look, I'm as happy looking at a pretty girl as the next guy, and I'm sure the gals like the buff guys, but it's the attitude these commercials take. If you don't own the brand-new Super Body Firmer 2000XL, complete with instructional video and a year's supply of a powdered protein supplement, then you, sir or madam, are no more than a slovenly couch potato who should be too embarrassed to show your sagging, rotund, pitiful behind in public. Go hide in a closet, they seem to tell us, you're not fit for public consumption. I usually go to the kitchen for a handful of Oreo cookies during these advertisements.

Zipper bag-packed products, like ham or cheese, bugs me. Why bother? They never work. As carefully as you try to rip off the strip above the zipper, it will tear. And have you ever tried to remove or put back in a block of cheddar cheese without scrapping it over the zipper, thus rendering it so clogged with cheese as to be completely unzippable?

What happened to screw-tops on gallon milk jugs? Has the dairy industry gotten so pathetically lazy that they can't put screw-tops on milk jugs anymore? Instead, they most often put those pop-on tops. After your pull off the little ring of plastic that secures them to the milk jug, they are never secure again. God forbid that you should happen to bump the milk on the rack above it as you're removing a nearly full jug from the fridge, because the top will pop off and the sudden jarring will throw milk everywhere. That really bugs me.

Why are ripe bell peppers more expensive than green bell peppers? Does it really cost that much more to leave them on the bush a little longer? A definite bug.

New soft drink machines bug me. Old soft drink machines had a little light on the side of each selection with the words "Sold Out" next to it. New machines do not. So after you deposit your money, and press the button for Diet Coke, it tells you it's sold out. Invariably, the coin return is broken on these machines—or are they really broken? Maybe they make them that way on purpose. So instead of Diet Coke, you have to make another choice, and all they have left in the whole machine after you've punched every single selection button is Fresca. It's a good thing the automobile industry doesn't sell cars on such terms.

These are just a few of the things that really bug me. Perhaps there'll be more later. But then, maybe that bugs you. Let me know, and I'll try not to do a follow up. I'd hate to bug anybody.

More Things That Bug Me

Here's a few more things that bug me.

While grocery shopping (a thing that bugs the bejeezus out of me in itself) I noticed that there are new ketchup containers which sit upside down, with the lid at the bottom. This way, it seems, you don't have to shake up your ketchup to get it to come out.

Such laziness leaves me speechless. Why, in the name of all that is Freudian, would anyone feel the need to buy an upside down ketchup bottle? Have we, as a nation, become so pathetically lazy that we can't shake our ketchup down to the lid when we want it? Are we so miserably stupid that we can't figure out the physics involved?

Grumbling about the decadence of a society gone to the dogs, I bought two bottles.

Now, another thing that really bugs me about grocery shopping is the little signs they put on the shelves under some product or another advertising, "$2.50 ea., 2 for $5!" Do the math. Yet people who don't need two cans of condensed milk buy them anyway because of the tremendous bargain they have been offered.

Here's one of my favorites: You pull up to a stop at an intersection. Another car pulls up to at the exact same time. The next few moments play out this way:

You motion for the other driver to go on.

The other driver motions for you to go on.

You insist, being gracious, that the other driver go on.

He is determined to be more gracious than you are, and motions for you to go on.

You both go at the same time.

You both lurch to a stop.

The other driver motions for you to go on.

You motion for the other driver to go on.

Neither one of you is about to go on, because you're sure you'll kiss bumpers, so you sit there glowering at each other until one of you runs out of gas, then the other goes on.

One of my favorite inventions, for a Luddite anyway, is pay-at-the-pump gas stations. One of my biggest irritations is that half the time the machine is out of paper, so I have to go inside to get a receipt anyway. What's the point?

Know what else really bugs me? The way they package DVDs. Ever tried to open a DVD? Sure, the shrink wrap comes off with little to no effort, but then they tape the seams of the box shut with strips of clear tape printed with the name of the movie on it. These never come off in one piece, so you have to take off one millimeter shreds at a time, at the end of which you're so exhausted you never get to watch your movie.

Television commercials for new medications bug me. Half the time, you don't have a clue what the medicine is for, based on the imagery of a cute couple walking along a beach, or a retired citizen playing golf, or a puppy trying desperately to break free of his leash, but you have been informed you must see your doctor for a prescription, so you figure it's not for you since you don't have anything that serious bothering you. Out of curiosity, you look up one on the Internet, and wish you hadn't.

Those shirts which are printed with "No Fear" on them. Leap into a pen of half-starved Bengal tigers, pal, then come back and tell me that.

Second to that are those little Calvin stickers on truck windows showing the little guy doing something which I won't describe here, usually on the logo of a brand of truck different than the one the sticker is on. Of course, the guy with that brand of truck has the same sticker but the logo has been changed to the first brand. Truth be known, I'd appreciate it if they'd keep their personal hygiene habits to themselves.

It really bugs me that television advertisements are played louder than the movie I'm watching. Just after the hero makes the startling announcement that he's going in alone, there's a crescendo of music which is pleasing to the ear and plot situation, a brief fade to black and, "GET NO PAYMENT FOR 12 MONTHS ON YOUR NEW TOYOTA COROLLA!!!" which blows you against the rear wall of the living room, ears bleeding and a half-eaten slice of pizza in your eyes.

People who think a piece of red plastic will make a broken tail light all better bug me.

Louisiana's license plates bug me. I do not want a license plate where the first three letters read "BRO" or "FAT" or "BIB." It's not a conversation starter, it's an irritation. My license plate should not read, "COP," because I'm not one, nor should it read, "BAR" if that's not where I'm going, and for Pete's sake, if I get one that reads, "NDN," I'm suing the state office of motor vehicles.

All the flap about the Ten Commandments in public buildings and the mention of "under God" in the Pledge bugs me. You don't like it, don't look at it, don't say it, or better yet, get out of the country. Perhaps, though, the words "or at least a select few" should be added after, "with liberty and justice for all."

Microsoft's choice of wording, "This program has performed an illegal operation and will be shut down," bugs me. Illegal how? Was it robbing a bank? Purse-snatching from a little old lady? Exercising unfair competitive business practices?

Telephone automated switchboards bug me. What if I don't know the extension of the person I want to talk to? I have to use fifty-four keystrokes to find the right number, then they're out, and they ask if I a) want to hang up, b) want to leave a voice mail, c) want to return to the automated switchboard, or d) want to speak to an operator. There is, by the way, no operator on duty, and their voice mail is full.

In the same vein, it bugs me when you call a company and the recording says if you want to speak to a customer service representative in English, press 1, or *Para hablar con un agente de servicios al cliente, oprima el número 2.* Call me what you will, but if you want to reside and do business in this country, proudly retain your native language but learn English, too. My people had to.

Instructions on shampoo bottles bug me.

Seeing people cutting their grass when you can't even tell where they just passed with the lawnmower bugs me.

People who make lists of things that bug them *really* bug me.

Extinction and the Bajoon

Complaining about the weather, a Louisiana pass time, is entirely flexible depending on the current conditions.

Sure, just a few weeks ago I was complaining about the constant rain. Now the rain isn't so constant, and I'm complaining about this miserable heat. I'm a Louisianian, it's tradition.

Of course, the moment I sit down to write regarding the heat and all, a cool front comes through and makes things downright tolerable.

But let me tell you, friends and neighbors, it has been downright hot in the afternoons around these parts. Because of this, I have had a bad case of the "don't feel like doing pecan" syndrome from about noon to just before dusk It's too painfully hot out there.

I'm sure over the last few summers it couldn't have been this hot, and I couldn't have been that much younger. I mean, it was just two summers ago I built a mahogany runabout. I worked on the house. Now, just because I am two months or so shy of my fortieth birthday, I can't take the heat anymore? Bah.

But if I go outside about two o'clock on the weekend to, oh, say pick up the garbage container from the road, before I'm halfway back to the house the sweat is pouring in to my eyes, my hair is matted to my scalp and I'm seeing mirages of palm trees, water ponds and Jeanie-clad Arabian girls. A trip to the road to pick up the garbage container is like a journey across the Sahara. I keep wanting to drop to my knees and dig a hole in the sand with a stick in search of water.

I don't know about global warming and all that, but it's hotter than it was. I don't remember it being this hot when I was a kid, when I could explore the bayou all day, ride horses, shoot my BB gun, swing on the swing set in the back yard, whatever. Now it's all I can do to get the key in the door and rush into the house before I collapse into a desiccated pile of leathery skin and brittle bones.

The air conditioner runs almost all the time. I don't remember the air conditioner running that much in previous summers. I know my electric bill is a better indicator of global warming than any ice sheet in Antarctica. Talk about sea level change? I could change the level of the river basin just by sweating into Bayou Teche.

And when there's that ever-present threat of rain in the forecast, whether it comes or not, it drives the humidity up, which only serves to make it hotter. I look at the weather forecast and see it's going to be ninety-five degrees, but with the humidity, you get a heat index of one hundred and three! Who thought up the idea of heat indexes, anyway? I mean, isn't it bad enough to say, "It's hot as the dickens today," without some smarty-pants know-it-all adding, "Yeah, and the heat index is one hundred and *FIVE!*" It's the summer version of wind chill in the winter. Did I really need to know about wind chill? Does it make me feel any better to know that the wind is making me feel colder, just like the humidity makes me feel hotter? How does this advance the culture of humankind? More importantly, isn't there enough suffering in the world without making up heat indexes on top of everything else?

"Man proposes and the Good Lord disposes," my dad always said, and though I still haven't a clue what in the world that meant, I suspect it had something to do with heat indexes. Next the know-it-alls will concoct some geometric, algebraic, trigonometry-based calculation to determine that the angle of the sun through the earth's atmosphere, compiled with the amount of vegetative growth within forty feet of an individual, and coupled with the severity of solar flares, has actually risen the simple temperature of ninety-five degrees on the thermometer to one hundred and forty-six degrees. At that temperature, brain fluids begin to boil.

It sure is hot, though, that's the bottom line. I went out to wash the truck this weekend, and vultures were circling overhead by the time I got to the windshield. This morning on the way to work I think I passed the bleached-white skeleton of a door-to-door salvation salesman, an irony in and of itself. Me, I'm just heading to the bajoon for a cold one.

I have a half dozen quarts of chili in the freezer. Who wants chili when its ninety-five degrees in the shade (never mind the stupid heat index, I don't want to know about it.) I have the fixins' for a big seafood gumbo in the freezer too, but who wants a hot, steaming bowl of seafood gumbo when it's so hot the crawfish are burrowing to Anchorage, the shrimp are somewhere in the Marianas trench and the blue crabs are just begging to be put in an ice chest?

They say that Neanderthal man could not biologically cope with the change in climate at the end of the ice age, and went extinct either due to heat stroke or interbreeding with modern *Homo sapiens*. This may mark the event horizon of another extinction wave: My kind, nearly-forty fat boys who spend eight or more hours a day in air-conditioned offices and meeting rooms, are heading down the road to extinction via climate change. We'll be fossilized, or perhaps mummified, and thousands of years from now they'll dig up our bones and study them in labs, trying to figure out why we expired. If we are in fact mummified, perhaps there will be enough of our internal organs left for tissue samples which will reveal that our sweat glands went China Syndrome and our livers have suffered that inevitable by-product of climate change, too many trips to the bajoon for a cold one.

Sure is hot, ain't it?

Yet More Things That Bug Me

Yet more things that bug me.

"One size fits all." That, my friends, is a very large crock. You mean to tell me, the same glove that fits me is going to fit Andre the Giant? If that was the case, no gloves would have appeared in OBJ.'s trial. One size fits all. Gimme a break.

Those Geico commercials bug me. I don't mind the ones with the little lizard guy, he's kinda cute. It's the ones that start off like a real commercial or a real news alert. Take the episode where there's this handyman, quite clearly a mockery of Bob Villa, working with a couple who just bought a beautiful New England colonial home. He tells them the floor joists are rotted out, the plumbing's shot, the electrical system is kaput and termites have eaten away the entire second floor. But there's good news! He just saved a bundle on his car insurance!

At this point, the couple should ask to borrow his nail gun.

Morning radio shows bug me. There's nowhere to get good music in the morning on the radio anymore. Instead, we are served the allegedly comedic routines of three supposed deejays who make fun of everyone, make lewd comments to their female callers and have about as much talent as a slab of pork hindquarter.

People that think American commercial beer is real beer bug me. You want real beer? Try Guinness Extra Stout. It has the consistency of used motor oil, and tastes pretty similar. One sip will usually be enough to swear you off of beer for the rest of your life.

It bugs me if I come home and Patches does not greet me at the door. A very rare thing, but it does happen. Usually by the time I get to the front door, she's scratching at it eagerly. Sometimes I come home, and she's dozing on the stair, and I feel neglected. I stand there at the bottom of the stair, hands on hips, and say, "What, you don't love me no more?" She opens a single eye and peers unconcerned at me over her paw. Disgusted, I settle in for a nap on the sofa, glowering at her up there on the stair, so content and solemn. About the time I am drifting off to sleep, she sneaks down the stair, across the living room floor and leaps on my face.

Car wash tokens bug me. You go to wash the car, need change. You put a five in the changer, and get twenty tokens, of which you only need six to wash the car. Now you are stuck with fourteen tokens which only work in that car wash. So you figure next time, you'll go through the automatic wash system, treat yourself, pamper yourself a little, right? Guess what? The automatic car wash at the same place does not take tokens.

Soft drink machines with slots for debit or credit cards bug me. But at least they don't dispense tokens. Most of the times they don't even dispense a soft drink, no matter how much you kick them. If you feed them a dollar bill with a half-millimeter crinkle at the lower left corner, they won't take it. Give them a crisp new dollar bill straight from the Federal Reserve printing office and it takes it, but gives you no soft drink and the money return button never works.

Stores which remove all their lawn care, garden supplies and outdoor products in October in Louisiana bug me very badly. What, they think nobody cuts grass in Louisiana by Halloween? If you need a lawn mower belt or a new garden sprayer on Nov. 1, you have to wait until March.

The Weather Channel's hurricane coverage bugs me. While a hurricane may be centered some two hundred miles from where they mistakenly positioned their reporter, the poor slob continues to stand there in a yellow poncho with hood, a slight breeze ruffling his hair under at most overcast skies, saying, "Make no mistake! This is still a very dangerous storm, and we could be feeling its devastating effects even here! Business owners are boarding up their windows, and the exodus of evacuating residents is clogging the highways!"

But behind him, folks are frolicking on the beach, playing volleyball and fishing.

People who don't give greetings when they call you bug me. You know what I mean. The phone rings, you answer it by saying, "Hello?" like a normal person does, and:

"I just found out that Joe and Jane are getting a divorce," they say. No "Hey, what's up?" or "Hope I'm not bothering you," or even a simple identifier of who the heck is calling, such as, "Hi, this is so-and-so." Instead, they just launch into a discussion. That really bugs me.

Movies which take the title of a classic work but bear absolutely no resemblance to that work bug me. DVD releases of movies bug me. You see a great movie in the theater and you want to add it to your collection, so the minute it comes out you buy it for $22.95. A few months later, they release the Director's Cut. A few months after that, the Special Extended Edition. And even a few months after that the Director's Cut Extended Edition with Restored Deleted Scenes. By this time you've spent nearly $100 and are writing nasty letters to the distributor.

Speaking of, musical artists who re-release their material remixed bug me. Not too long ago, I was looking for my collection of James Taylor's Greatest Hits because I wanted Suze to hear "Something in the Way She Moves," one of the most wonderful songs JT ever did. I never did find the CD, so I went to buy a new one. I found a repackaged version of the same collection, with "BONUS TRACKS NEVER BEFORE RELEASED!" and thought, "What a bargain!"

So I rush home, slap it in the CD player, all a-quiver with anticipation, and I get...a remix. About two beats faster with different arrangement. That really bugs me.

People who talk with their mouths full bug me. I don't want to see a mush of chewed up macaroni and cheese when you're talking to me. Besides, all I hear is, "Grouafaoh fadadfjoyu fadfafe." Swallow, then talk to me. My mama would have slapped me upside the head.

And finally, list after list of things that bug people, run into the ground until they get pretty lame, because the author doesn't have a clue what else he might write about this week...that really puts me over the edge.

Birthday and Columbus Day

The great thing about birthdays is all the attention you get.

Having turned forty—that's right, the big Four-Oh—on Sunday, I really was overwhelmed, humbled and grateful for the kindness I was extended. It started really on Thursday. Three of my co-workers and friends, namely Geri, Lana and Debbie, sent me a gift certificate to Cabelas. If you're not aware, Cabelas is an online mega-sporting goods store. I quickly ordered a dozen and a half strike indicators and a dozen black wooly buggers before they changed their minds. Strike indicators are what fly fishermen refer to as a bobber. It's very much smaller, though, of course. Wooly buggers are...well, they're...indescribable, but the bass love 'em.

Vanessa, managing editor, got me the tee-shirt that has a photo of a few Indian warriors on it, and the words say, "Homeland Security: Fighting Terrorism Since 1492." My kinda shirt!

Now, Friday night the staff threw me a little party at Polito's Cafe in Franklin, complete with the prerequisite chocolate cake, my favorite. I wore my Homeland Security T-shirt, which was a hit with all the patrons of the cafe.

A group was gathered in the back to watch the presidential debate. I wandered in at some point and after making a few snide comments about George W. Bush, learned quickly that I was in a room full of Republicans who have no sense of humor whatsoever when it comes to politics. For the record, I'm registered "no party" but geez! Lighten up a little, folks! Feeling outnumbered, and wearing my Homeland Security tee, I figured I was safer back in the main dining room when the Republicans started giving me that "The only good Indian is a dead Indian" look.

Saturday, my gal and I celebrated both our birthdays (hers is in September) at Mr. Lester's Steakhouse at the casino. I had steak and lobster and a piece of New York cheesecake with blackberries, two glasses of a darn fine Merlot, sauteed mushrooms, green beans and I gave the bread basket serious grief, I can tell you. I don't go to Mr. Lester's without getting my due. We left with doggy bags, too, the contents of which I don't have to tell you the dog never got a whiff of.

Sunday was a grateful day of rest. We watched movies all day, literally. Monday I had to go back to work. Monday is bad enough, having to go back to work and all, but this Monday was also Columbus Day.

People don't quite understand why I'm so hard on ol' Chris. I mean, it was more than five hundred years ago, right? Sure enough. If I had my druthers, he would have been justifiably forgotten, or at best, his mug would be on the wall of the post office. It just irritates me that Columbus has his own "day" on the calendar. The only other person in American history who has his own day is Martin Luther King Jr., who certainly deserves it. But Columbus? Gimme a break. The Marx Brothers would be more deserving.

Let me review the pertinent historical facts regarding Christopher Columbus' voyage, as interpreted from an indigenous viewpoint. A long time ago, Christopher, who was Portuguese, began trying to convince Ferdinand and Isabella that the world was round, not flat, and that he could sail to Asia. The Spanish crown got so bored with hearing his tirades that they gave him three ships to go away, hoping he'd fall off the edge of the world and they'd be done with him for good. It was worth three bedraggled ships to them, you see, for a little peace and quiet without all that babbling.

Unfortunately, the only thing Christopher was ever right about was the world being round. He simply believed it was, in scale, of golf ball circumference whereas the earth is more like a basketball. So he sailed west, and sailed, and sailed, and the men were getting pretty cranky, since they still hadn't bought into this whole round-earth thing. By the time they had enough and were tying ropes with knots which Christopher realized had nothing to do with seamanship, all the while eyeing the yardarm and Chris' stiff neck, he ran aground in Hispaniola, saving him from certain lynching.

There they met the Taino people, who Columbus praised as being so generous, kind and friendly that, he wrote to Ferd and Izzy, that they'd make wonderful slaves. After throwing Columbus a big feast, he and his men thanked the Taino by kidnapping a few to bring back to Spain, along with all the gold the Taino people could give up by force. Before all this, the Santa Maria gave up the ghost and sank, so Columbus left a lot of his men behind while he went back to the palace to show off those kind, generous, friendly people, who later died.

Now, Ferdie and Izzy were so delighted to have him back they made Columbus Viceroy of the Kind, Friendly People With All the Gold, and sent him off again with a whole buncha men and more ships. Upon arrival, Columbus found that the Taino had gotten sick and tired of the Spaniards pushing them around and abusing their women and disposed of the sailors he had left behind.

Columbus in turn proved how friendly, kind and generous the Europeans were by systematically killing or maiming every Taino he could get hold of. The rest he put into slavery to dig gold.

He justified this by reading to the Taino—who could not understand English, of course—the Requirement, a Spanish document approved by the king and queen, demanding the Indians become Christians or else, "I will take your women and children and make them slaves. The deaths and injuries that you will receive from here on will be your own fault and not that of his majesty nor of the gentlemen that accompany me." Some historians have noted that Columbus and later Conquistadors read the Requirement to trees and empty huts when no natives were encountered, mumbled it into their beards as they attacked a sleeping village, read it from the decks of ships, or after natives had been captured.

So any Taino who resisted were hunted down with war dogs. Or used for sword and archery target practice. Columbus casually noted in his journals that his men took quite a liking to the young Indian women. Girls ages nine or 10 were among their favorites. These were men who purported to be civilized Christians, and the Taino were heathen savages, you will recall.

Rather than be worked to death or maimed by the Spaniards under Columbus' command, thousands of Taino committed suicide, often taking their own children's lives to spare them from the cruelty of the "discoverers" of America. Spanish historian Peter Martyr would write in 1516 that "a ship without compass, chart, or guide, but only following the trail of dead Indians who had been thrown from the ships could find its way from the Bahamas to Hispaniola."

In 1492, the Taino population was somewhere between one and two million. By 1518, there were about sixteen thousand left. As of 1570, there were only a handful surviving.

Christopher Columbus, "discoverer" of America and perpetrator of the first genocide in the "New" World, died penniless and in obscurity, still believing he had reached Asia.

And for this, Columbus gets on the national holiday schedule.

Homeland Security. Yup.

Pilgrims and Shoe Leather

Recalling that the first Thanksgiving was given by the Pilgrims to thank God and the Indians for helping them survive the cold northeastern winter, we must remind ourselves that our heroic settlers—who wore buckles on their hats and shoes as well as their belts—were on the verge of starvation in the "New World." This is defined by Webster's as "ill-prepared" and by Merriam-Webster as "leaping before you look."

One of the Indians nearby apparently saw what was going on, and went back to his chief.

"Listen," the young brave must have said. "We gotta help those guys. They're about to eat their shoes."

"*With* the buckles?" the chief asked, horrified.

"I don't know," said the brave. "But their hats have got to be next!"

So the Indians helped out, and the Pilgrims survived the winter. There were a couple other Thanksgiving events later, and George Washington declared it a National Day of Thanksgiving in 1789. Later, President Thomas Jefferson said, to paraphrase, "That was a really dumb thing to do."

However, in 1863, President Lincoln made Thanksgiving a national holiday in its present form, disregarding Jefferson's remark as the result of too much pumpkin pie. It's been here ever since.

The first event lasted three days, and everyone had a dang good time. The Indians impressed the Puritans by their prowess with the bow, and the Pilgrims impressed the Indians by blowing things to bits with their muskets. The Indians probably thought this pretty silly, since the noise scared off every other wild game for miles around, and figured that's why the settlers were starving.

It wasn't too long after the first Thanksgiving that the Pilgrims got really jealous of the Indians and started shooting them on sight and stealing their food. It wasn't too long after that when the other colonists all across America did the same. It was quite a bit after that, though, that John Wayne made movies in which he called everybody he didn't like "Pilgrim," because John Wayne liked Indians. The fact that he shot more of them than any other cowboy star in the movies remains a mystery.

Of all the foods brought to that first feast, there were many meats, but turkey became the national, traditional Thanksgiving main course. Benjamin Franklin considered the turkey a prime candidate for the United States national bird—I kid you not—but luckily, the founding fathers realized that you couldn't have a national bird that was also the main course at Thanksgiving dinner, so they chose the bald eagle instead. It's a good thing, too. If the national bird had been the turkey, we'd all have to eat pigeon at Thanksgiving.

Turkey is perhaps one of my least favorite foods, though I don't despise it. It's tolerable, at best. The best turkey can't compare to even the worst chicken, if you ask me. You would think turkeys grew up in sub-Saharan conditions, as dry as they are. Oh, don't give me all that, "You gotta know how to cook it," stuff. Turkey is dry no matter what you do to it. Douse it with a fire hose, it doesn't help.

Pumpkin pie is pretty good, but give me pecan pie over pumpkin pie any day. And cranberry sauce? I'd just as soon suck vinegar out of a bottle through a straw.

Now, cornbread dressing is the bomb. That's a Thanksgiving feast all in itself. I could live off good cornbread dressing for weeks.

I also like good rice dressing, though this is getting increasingly hard to find, because folks nowadays only make rice dressing with beef or, horror of horrors, pork. If somebody would make me a good rice dressing from liver, like the old folks did, I'd be a happy man again. An oyster dressing rates at the top of the list.

But I remain thankful at Thanksgiving, to the Creator and to the Indians. I am thankful to the Creator for a loving family, my health and good friends among many other things.

I am thankful to the Indians for saving the Pilgrims from eating their shoes, buckles or not. This would have been a very big faux pas to allow such a thing, and the Indian's reputation as the "noble savage" might well have been even worse, something like the "stick-your-head-in-the-sand savage." We made the right call on that one. History will recall that little act of kindness, though they'll never quite get the whole Christopher Columbus thing straight.

I am thankful that we don't all wear buckles on our hats and shoes anymore, but I wish that the Pilgrims had come to Louisiana instead of Massachusetts. If they had, Thanksgiving dinner today would have been fried catfish, boiled crawfish with corn and taters, raw oysters and muscadines!

Settling In

The good thing about December, though, is that the wanderlust begins to fade when the temperatures drop. It's hard to be a bonafide, dyed-in-the-wool wanderer when you hate to go outside in cold weather. Wandering around the house gets pretty boring.

It's funny how the spring seems to be so hectic and rushed, since I know that I have only so many days to get out and do the things I want to do. On the other hand, the winter seems to stretch out in front of me endlessly, like a long dark tunnel with only a pinprick of light at the end, miles away. That's how I look at winter: a long dark tunnel.

Should I ever be physically and fiscally fit enough to be a real-life wanderer, I'll do it from like April to October. I could do a lot of wandering in that time. If I did it by water, in a husky little gaff-rigged catboat, I could be to Maine by June, just when the weather's warming up. There I could catch lobsters and steam them on the beach, or fish stripers and go visit Norm Abrams for a little while. When it gets too close to winter in the northeast again, I could cut across and catch the Intracoastal Canal in Maryland and follow it home by September, giving me a month or so to spare if I decide to stop off at the Grand Banks or something. Assuming I don't get run over by a big ship or something in one of the industrial corridors.

Wandering is a hard job. Oh, sure, you could just stuff some clothes and a pocket knife in a back pack and thumb your way, but what's the fun in that? My luck, I'd thumb a ride with a psychotic, or worse yet, a Petula Clark fan with a whole collection of eight-tracks.

But that's spring and summer talk. It's December, the heater's running in the house and folks are bundling up. I really respect the ladies who work in offices where they're required to wear skirts. I could never be a lady in an office where I'm required to wear skirts in the winter. First of all, I'd freeze to death before I got to work, and second, I don't have the legs for it.

One of the worst things is winter clothes. I hate long sleeves and snug collars. Drives me nuts. Makes me feel like I'm suffocating, claustrophobic. First thing I do when I get home is jack up the heater and put on a short-sleeved tee-shirt with a big sigh of relief.

Patches doesn't like cold either, being a short-haired tortoise-shell calico (that's far too many adjectives for such a tiny cat.) In fact, I think she hates it worse than I do. If I am lying on the sofa watching television, or sitting in my chair reading, whatever, she snuggles up next to me in a tight little curl and stays there for as long as I do.

But when I go to get up for some reason, I have to give her fair warning.

"I'm going get a Diet Coke," I announce, rubbing her ear to butter her up.

She looks at me from one open eye, daring me.

"I'll be right back," I say. Testing the waters, I just kinda shift positions a little.

"Grrrrrrrr," Patches expresses her displeasure.

"Look, I'm getting bed sores I've been here so long."

She closes her eye and pretends to doze, a bundle of warmth and contentment. I decide it's dumb to be intimidated by a napping cat, and so slight of one at that, so I go get up anyway.

"*GRRRRRRRRWWWWWWWW!!!*" Patches warns me in no uncertain terms.

This is when I literally fly out of the chair before she can get me. I go do whatever it is I had intended, and when I get back, Patches has claimed the warm spot where I was.

"Okay, let me back in," I say.

She looks at me with complete disdain and yawns.

"I warmed that spot up, it's mine," I whine. I sit down next to my spot, shoving her over with my behind. She puts her ears back, and I decide that shoving her with my backside was probably not the wisest idea, having provided her with a generous amount of surface area to attack.

So gritting my teeth, I pick her up, sit or lay down, and put her back where she was, in her own warm spot, as quickly as possible. Usually she just jumps down and stalks off to the back room, perturbed.

"You coulda done that to begin with!" I tell her retreating form. It always gives me satisfaction to get in the last word.

It's always a good time to catch up on my reading, in the winter. At least, I try to. Lots of times, I guess because I'm getting older, I fall asleep when I'm reading. This is extraordinarily annoying. When I wake up, I completely forget where I was in the narrative, and Patches is sleeping on my book.

"That's my book," I say. "You don't even know how to read."

She opens one eye and stares at me with a distinct message of, "Are you sure?" Realizing that I'm not sure that she can't read at all, and that it wouldn't surprise me if she could, I just go back to sleep.

So I reckon I'll be reading a lot over the winter, probably re-reading a lot of things. When I was a lad, soon as it got cold I would start *The Lord of the Rings* and it would occupy me through the winter if I paced everything right. There's nothing better to read in the winter than Tolkien. But now, with all the movies out on DVD, I figure I'll just spend a weekend with them like a true 21st century lazy bones, and save myself from picking cat hair out of the book spines.

Bizarro Dreams

Suffering from a bit of pre-insomnia lately, I've been watching a lot of late-night television.

I call it pre-insomnia, because it only happens when I'm trying to get to sleep. I always eventually get there, but the road to LaLa Land is pretty rocky lately. So I get up and watch television, hoping it will bore me to sleep.

However, I made the mistake of tuning into TV Land one night. I love TV Land. I mean where else can you get Gilligan, Dick Van Dyke and Archie Bunker all at the same time?

Ah, the golden age of television. I miss it. Back before *CSI* and *Survivor*, when the most important controversy in the industry was whether or not Lucy and Ricky should have separate beds on the set. Back before Al Bundy (who is just a lobotomized Archie Bunker) when Andy would sit Opie down and tell him the facts about right and wrong, or stop Barney from shooting himself in the foot while trying to load his one bullet into his pistol.

Just the other night I saw an episode of *You Bet Your Life*, the game show hosted by none other than Groucho Marx. Though the episode on that night was funny, it wasn't my favorite. In that one, a woman contestant is telling Groucho that she has something like eleven kids, and the reason for this, she tells an amazed Groucho, is that she really likes her husband.

"Well, I like a good cigar, but I take it out of my mouth every now and then," Groucho said, and the network executives of 1950s television went berserk. Funniest moment in game show history, if you ask me. The network execs of those days would have keeled over toes-up if they saw but a single episode of *Desperate Housewives*.

I miss classic cop shows, which were far, far better than what we have today. Remember the true greats, like *Mannix, Barnaby Jones* and *Canon*? The introduction of each one featured this booming voice over your television's one-and-a-half inch speaker thundering,

"A QUINN MARTIN PRODUCTION!" While I admit it was hard to adjust to former Jed Clampett star Buddy Ebsen playing Barnaby, it was even more difficult to imagine William Conrad running down a street in pursuit of the bad guys with a snub-nosed .38 in his hand looking like a kid's cap pistol.

But they were great, those old shows. I'll tell you who was a lethal weapon, and it wasn't Mel Gibson. It was Angie Dickinson as *Police Woman*. Angie was a lethal weapon if there ever was one. Blonde bombshell cop chases down the bad guys, can cook, carries a gun. What man could ask for more? Angie Dickinson was lethal, believe me.

However, she would certainly have met her match with Lindsay Wagner as *The Bionic Woman* who could outrun any bullet and arm wrestle like nobody's business.

I liked *Adam-12*. And *Dragnet*. When I'm suffering from pre-insomnia and watching TV Land to try to get to sleep, Jack Webb can put me in a coma faster than anything else. With he possible exception of infomercials. Just the facts, ma'am.

Old television police shows were educational, too. I learned to speak Hawaiian from *Hawaii Five-O* thanks to Jack Lord: "Book 'em, Dano," however, is as far as my command of the language goes.

There's the comedies, too. *Gilligan's Island* is among the best for pure slapstick. I never missed an episode of *The Jeffersons, Happy Days, Good Times* or *Barney Miller*. Those were real comedies.

And the Saturday morning cartoons! Gosh, they don't make Saturday morning cartoons that are worth pecan anymore. I grew up on the greats like *Scooby, Hong Kong Phooey* with the indomitable voice of Scatman Crothers, *Super Friends*, the or *Land of the Lost*. Now there was a great live-action Saturday morning series. Will, Holly and dad Rick Marshall get sent into this alternate reality full of ill-tempered dinosaurs, as well as cute cuddly ones, and these lizard-looking creatures called Sleestaks that mostly just hiss at you until you run away. Kinda like *Canon*, come to think of it.

We always watched *The Sunday Night Mystery Movie* at our house. Each week, a different crime mystery featuring McMillan and his wife, Colombo, Banacek, McCloud or Hec Ramsey. I loved that show. We also watched *The Wonderful World of Disney* and *Mutual Of Omaha's Wild Kingdom* with Marlin Perkins and Jim Fowler. Marlin, recognized as one of the foremost naturalists in the world, safe in his television studio wearing a nicely-pressed suit, would tell us with the excitement just seething from his voice, "And when we come back after the break, Jim is going to wrestle that twenty-foot crocodile into the back of our Jeep after which we're going to relocate it to the Nile River to be with its family again." Sure enough, after the commercial break, Jim would wrestle the crocodile into the back of a Jeep and deliver it to its new home. We'd cut back to Marlin, who'd say, "Boy, that looked like rough work, Jim!"

Now and then I catch an episode of *Lost In Space*. This, you may not know, was the television series that CBS turned down *Star Trek* in favor of. Still, it's a lot of fun watching young lad Will Robinson get attacked by an alien monster with the zipper on his costume running down the back, clear as day. All the while poor Will is being snarled by the dozen tentacles of the zippered-back monster and carried off to its den, the robot is waving it's accordion arms and yelling, "Danger, Will Robinson! Danger, Will Robinson," and we're wondering why the robot doesn't shoot electricity out of his claw-like appendages to subdue the creature, like he did in the last episode.

For a temporary insomniac, late night classic television is a real hoot. Finally I fall asleep, and dream through the night that I am on a dinner date with Angie Dickinson, and the waiter is a Sleestak who hisses at us when we order crocodile burgers. Angie invites me in for a nightcap, but as soon as she reaches out with her key to unlock the door, she turns into H.R. Puffnstuff. Luckily, this is when my alarm goes off and I wake up before anything crazy happens.

Sleeplessness

This insomnia business really is for the birds.

It's not as drastic as some folks have described in their personal experiences. I do get some sleep, it's just that it takes me forever and a day to get there when I tuck myself in.

Insomnia makes people crazy. I never really understood the whole concept because I never suffered from it until a few years ago. Even then, it's a very rare thing for me. Probably it comes from having too much on my mind, too many tangles I'm trying to unknot, but the ol' noggin needs rest!

Usually a shot of NyQuil does me in, but this method has resulted in limited success this time around. NyQuil would in the past knock me down for the count, and DayQuil makes me hyper as a seven-year-old. This is probably because I normally avoid taking medication at all costs. I hate taking medicine; the idea of putting that stuff in my system gives me the willies. I gotta be pretty sick or in pain to take medication. The recent controversy surrounding Vioxx and the like did nothing but confirm that my paranoia is justified.

But I take a shot of NyQuil an hour before I should be going to bed, and when I finally turn off all the lights, check all the door locks and head for the sack, I toss and turn for hours. This is equally unpleasant for Patches. Whereas she normally will wait for me to settle in then find a comfortable spot to nuzzle up next to me, my constant tossing and turning disturbs her comfort level. Every time I move, she must readjust her position, and eventually she gets sick and tired of all the commotion and, with a growl, stalks off to the far corner at the foot of the bed.

"Don't gripe," I say to her. "At least you can sleep."

And sleep she does, while I'm unable. I tried drinking a good beer before bed instead of NyQuil. I tried a glass of wine. A glass of warm milk. No good.

I lie there, and the gray matter is rolling at light speed, jumping from one subject to the next without even completing the one before: *Gotta pay this bill, what's the due date, where did I put that fly leader, need to get the toilet fixed so it'll quit running all the time, feed the dog in the morning, where did I put that crescent wrench when I was working on the boat, who the heck stole my soft drink from the ice box at work, where is Malta, when does the time change, how do calculators work, did Amelia Earhart live out her life on some uncharted island, why are horses' noses so long, just what kind of animal is a shrew, how the heck did marsupials ever evolve, do I have enough var-*

nish left to finish that bamboo fly rod I'm rebuilding, where the devil has Carole King gotten off to???

It's tough being responsible for solving the mysteries of the universe, take my word for it.

When I was a teen, I could sleep until noon. Now I require about six hours sleep, no more, no less. If I go to bed at ten, I get up at four. If I go to bed at midnight, I wake up at six. So if I get to sleep at last at two and the clock goes off at six, I slap at it like it's an annoying bug that's buzzing around my face. One morning the phone rang at a quarter to six, and I slapped at the alarm clock for two or three minutes before I realized what was going on. The next morning the alarm went off, and I got up and answered the phone.

At least I'm not getting cranky from too little sleep. Well, no more cranky than usual, anyway. Over the course of my life, nearly every decision I've pursued has made my cranky, or to put it more aptly, cantankerous. When I was fifteen and decided I wanted to be a newspaperman, nearly every member of that breed I knew was cranky, so I figured that's how newspapermen were. Later, I became cranky because that's what a good fisherman is supposed to be. And later still, I became cranky because it was just a hard habit to break. Cantankerous, I mean. Ornery. Stubborn as a mule and set in my ways. Add insomnia to the mix for long enough, and you end up with a Genuine Grade A USDA-inspected reprobate.

People offer me solutions to insomnia that frighten me.

"Put two olives in a glass of milk, warm it in the microwave, then drink just the milk," they say. "Throw the olives out the back door and say, 'Ollie, Ollie Oxen Free!' six times while standing on one foot. Works every time for me!"

Or, "Read *War and Peace* under candlelight with Mozart on the CD player. Make sure you're barefoot."

Even, "Put a baby bottle nipple on a fifth of scotch and nurse on it until you pass out."

I'll find my own cure, thank you, and one that does not involve voodoo, alcohol or Tolstoy.

I have a friend who suffers with bouts of severe insomnia. To see him in the daylight during one of his spells is frightening. His eyes are bloodshot and puffy, he looks pale and thin. You have a sudden urge to either throw him down and hit him with a defibrillator or run for your life because you think he's a zombie from a George Romero movie. I have not gotten that bad yet, I hope.

These little spells have happened before, and they always pass, so I'm just biding my time. Too much TV Land will make you worse, I've found, because you lay there in bed longing for the good ol' days, and wishing that Dr. Marcus Welby was still practicing, because he'd surely know how to cure insomnia. My luck, I'd probably get Jack Klugman, aka *Quincy, MD*, who was a coroner.

Mardi Gras Mambo

In an attempt to be more cheerful—despite the fact that the cold is gnawing the tips of my nose and ears off, my teeth are fractured from chattering and I am in about as good a mood as a flaming badger—I submit the following solely to take up space.

Next week is Mardi Gras. I am only dimly aware of the approach of that most beloved of south Louisiana holidays, since I'm not much into Mardi Gras. No offense, of course. Some people don't like fly fishing, though I can't fathom such disinterest.

Anyway, next week is Mardi Gras, ye olde Fat Tuesday. This weekend will be the famous Chitimacha Parade wherein the Indians, in retribution for that ill-conceived sale of Manhattan Island about four hundred years ago, now throw the beads back at the Europeans. I've used that joke every Mardi Gras for seven years, and you can count on hearing it again every Mardi Gras until they run me outta this joint.

Folks in south Louisiana either get off a whole day or a half-day from work Tuesday, but we in the newsroom have to go cover the Franklin Mardi Gras Parade. Otherwise, I'd be at home hunkered down under a blanket sipping hot cocoa. It's not that Franklin's Mardi Gras parade isn't super, it's just not my thing. I can't recall my parents ever taking me to a Mardi Gas parade when I was a kid, though I always suspected that Mardi Gras parades were partially what my father meant when he confided to me early on, "It's crazy out there, boy," meaning off the Rez. For some period of his life, my father seemed to believe a passport should be required to leave the reservation.

Please don't throw me any beads. I appreciate it, really, it's a really kind gesture, generous and thoughtful, but I am carrying around an eight pound camera during the parade, and any further weight around my neck will cause me to topple face-first into Main Street. Those who have done this tell me there's a whole community of people down there, folks who have toppled due to being overloaded with beads around their necks, all at ankle-height and discussing the various merits of concrete, culverts and curbing.

Pass down any street where the Mardi Gras Parade passes and you'll see people have snatched up all the beads, cups and doubloons and most of the candy.

You're already thinking I'm just a party-pooper and an old fuddy. Not true. Remember, I have to work for the parade, so I am not able to really let my hair down and enjoy myself. My idea of Mardi Gras parades is standing around the krewe stands waiting for the royalty's toast, and hoping an errant airborne hard candy doesn't crack my camera lens, keep going and impale in my eye. Listen, I enjoy a good *fais-do-do* as much as the next person. If I could have a lawn chair and an ice chest full of Abita Ambers to enjoy the parade, I'd be as sociable a Mardi Gras reveler as you're ever likely to find. That is, if the weather isn't especially nice, otherwise I'd probably be fishing. But hey, at least I'd fish with some fly or lure in purple, green and gold.

Of course, I could just be grumpy because of the lousy weather, so don't take any of this seriously. In fact, I know I'm grumpy. I've been cabin bound for too long. Come Tuesday, if temperatures are above sixty degrees, you might even find me dancing a jig on Main Street, neck full of beads, wearing one of those specialty beer-drinking hats. I don't mean hats that drink beer, of course, I mean the ones that hold two cans of beer on either side of your head, with straws from each that come down to your mouth. This keeps your hands free to catch beads. The problem is, if one of the beer cans gets hit by a hard candy the ensuing foaming eruption could very well be devastating. On the other hand, I hate canned beer, and since glass bottles aren't allowed on Main Street during all the festivities, I'll settle for Diet Coke in a plastic bottle.

But I made it through another Mardi Gras, and don't have to face such joy and revelry for another year now.

Tuesday morning, we came into work here at the Banner and got out a quick paper. It would have been much quicker, actually, had we not been fielding telephone calls from kind folks who were hoping we'd slip up and reveal who the royalty was for the krewes. Back in the old days, we used to hide that information in the safe, locked up tight. We were laying out pages by hand back then, ye olde cut and paste, and on Mardi Gras morning nobody but bonafide newsroom personnel were allowed in the paste up room. You didn't get to know who the King and Queen were until the fire department threw the papers during the parade.

Regardless, we got done and outta here and I arrived home at ten wondering what I'd do with myself until parade time at one o'clock. You recall that we news people have to work for the parades while all you happy Mardi Gras revelers enjoy the festivities. Don't you feel sorry for us? So I stood there in the kitchen for a while, sipping a Diet Coke, and thought I could do some writing, or I could clean house, or I could take the dog for a walk, I could even take a nap.

Instead, I grabbed a bamboo fly rod and my tackle bag and high-tailed it to a pond.

Oh, don't get me wrong. I knew my chances of catching a fish were virtually nil. The water has not had a chance to warm up, and the front of rain that moved through surely had given my scaly little finned friends a severe case of lockjaw. But off I went on my merry way. The fog was still thick at that time of the morning. I assembled my three-piece Granger Victory, a nine-foot bamboo fly rod more than 60 years old and attached a medium-sized fly to the line tippet. I spent a relaxing two hours at the pond, there in the fog, casting for fish. One small and very cold bream took the fly, and was brought happily to hand to be released again.

It had been weeks, perhaps a couple months, since I had been out on the water what with this screwy weather and all. This old Granger, a product of the Goodwin Granger Co. of Denver, Colorado, was made before World War II and is known as one of the finest production bamboo fly rods ever made. It sings hymns like a celestial choir when I cast it with a six-weight line, becomes a stunning soloist with a seven-weight. That may mean little to nothing to most of you kind folks, or even to the fishermen out there who have never cast a fine fly rod, but for me, it was two hours of happy peace.

Then it was off to the parade. The fog had lifted to reveal gray, threatening skies. When the parade finally got downtown, those of you kind folks who read my last column regarding Mardi Gras were gracious enough to throw me tons and tons of beads, apparently in the hopes of seeing me actually topple face-first onto the street. Not that I don't appreciate the thought, of course, but forgive me for handing off the beads I caught to the nearest little tyke. Besides causing me to topple face-first onto the street, they tend to get tangled around my camera and I end up nearly choking myself to death trying to get a picture of the royalty toasting the krewe.

Soon as I was done, I headed out of town before the festivities were over. I was amazed at the number of beads still lying on the streets, and the crushed candy had soaked up the high humidity in the air to become a suitable resurfacing of Main Street for a little while at least. I did, however, find I had to press the accelerator of the truck harder than normal to get up to the speed limit. I suspect that was because the tires were bogging down in smashed candy. Next truck I buy will be four-wheel drive just because of Mardi Gras.

!@#%&

I find I cuss more this time of year than any other.

Now that's not to say I am a foul-mouthed varmint who is in dire need of having a bar of soap for dinner. What I mean is, seasonally speaking, I am a lot more prone to launch into tirades of what my grandfather called his fourth native language, the four being in order, French, Chitimacha, English and Profanity.

I don't cuss much during the spring, summer and early fall. This is because I'm usually a pretty happy guy. I do tend to cuss more when I'm fishing, even though that's when I'm happiest. The oxymoron there is that I get severely hacked off when lure-eating trees consume my fishing flies, or the trolling motor shaft snaps off when I hit a log, interfering with my bliss. Normally, though, I am as genteel a person as you are likely to find, a true southern gentleman.

Except this time of year. When my feet hit the cold oak floor of the living room, I let loose a stream of adjectives and adverbs designed solely to superheat the air with sheer vehemence. When the water takes forever to warm up for my shower and I forget and jump in anyway, a spew of expletives gushes forth like an erupting volcano. When it's raining all weekend, every time I pass a window I launch into a violent fit of unsavory language.

Please don't misunderstand. I am not a troglodyte. I don't spit in polite company, never fail to say "ma'am" and "sir" when required, and have been referred to once or twice as, "That nice young man." My cussing comes naturally, almost by inheritance.

Proper cussing, in a gentlemanly fashion, has strict limitations. There is a certain set of acceptable cuss words, and a set of unacceptable cuss words. Use of only the acceptable words marks you as a distinguished manner of person, one who has learned patience, restraint and composure. Using the forbidden set of words marks you as uncultured, uncouth and possessing a hairline that begins just a fraction of an inch above your rather prominent brow ridge.

Take some of the menfolk in my family for example. With complete dignity, restraint and composure, any one of them could cuss the wallpaper clean off the wall, not even leaving a sticky residue behind. When angered by one of us youngsters, they could scald the skin with words so that red welts rose on our arms and faces. All in cuss words Group One, remember. None of the menfolks ever stooped to use of Group Two words, and as far as I knew, to do so meant being disowned by the family. It's not so much the words as how you use them. I can say, "Frog!" with relatively no sense of threat involved. But with the proper inflection, venom in the voice and show of glistening teeth, "Frog!" can cause your shoelaces to knot right there on the spot and your teeth to fracture. It's all in the delivery.

At this time of year, you never know when it's going to happen. Usually it is facilitated by The Weather Channel. Soothed and tranquil by a bout of temperatures in the seventies and sunny skies on Monday, I tune to find a one hundred percent chance of rain on Saturday with temperatures falling to the forties. And it's like someone threw a switch. Dr. Jekyll, the brilliant scientist and gentleman suddenly begins to choke, convulse and gag, and he grows hair all over his body, his face grows distorted and rather Neanderthal, he slouches over and several of his teeth fall out. He stares down at the television screen where The Weather Channel is predicting the weekend conditions and suddenly roars a long soliloquy of naughty words that would have gotten him expelled from elementary school, if Neanderthals had such things as elementary schools.

But I try my best to be compassionate and careful. Never mind that, genetically, I am in possession of the DNA to cuss a magnolia tree into going deciduous. It's late winter that causes my tantrums and lack of manners. I can't be blamed. I am not responsible. It's somebody else's fault. I am, as Curley said, a victim of circumstance.

Now, the women in the family cussed exceedingly rarely. Almost never. Almost. If one of the ladies in the family used even the mildest of Group One words at you, you knew immediately to snap-to, pay attention, boy, and pray that any further instructions did not involve soap, and if they do, they do not involve your mouth.

I am remorsefully aware that George Washington once noted, "The foolish and wicked practice of profane cursing and swearing is a vice so mean and low that every person of sense and character detests and despises it."

There is retribution, however, in the fact that Mark Twain, a far greater hero in my book than Ol' George and much more deserving of being President, said, "The idea that no gentleman ever swears is all wrong. He can swear and still be a gentleman if he does it in a nice and benevolent and affectionate way." Who ya gonna abide, the man who created Huckleberry Finn, or a man with wooden teeth?

The art of gentlemanly cussing is an ancient one. It is one thing to speak in certain syntax while out with the boys hunting quail far in the field. It is quite another to speak in the *Reader's Digest Abridged* version when at the royal ball. It is a difficult skill to master, and often only becomes second nature after being thrown out of enough royal balls on your coattails. As far back as when humans began tinkering around with language, this skill was elusive.

"Grunt-grunt, burf-burf," says Mr. Neanderthal Man.

"Grunt?" queries Miss Dainty and Polite Neanderthal lady.

"Grunt-grunt, burf-burf," he replies. This is in actuality the origin of the Germanic, Latin and Slavic languages, and several hundreds of thousands of years later would translate to, "Bring the mastodon carcass to the dump yourself, wench."

To which she replies, "Grumph-grumph ugh-ugh," which in a few millennia will become, "That's it, you sleep on the rock by the cave door tonight, buster."

"Pflat-phlat, gurgle-hack," he says, pleadingly, which means, "But snoog'ums, I was only kidding!"

If you believe that writing an entire column about cussing without actually ever cussing is easy, you are quite mistaken.

If you also suspect that I have lost my *phlat-grumph-ugh* mind, you're probably quite correct.

Particulars

Though I don't consider myself very picky or choosy or high-strung...well, okay, maybe I am kinda high-strung...there are certain things I am very particular about.

Most of these involve food and drink. For instance, do not ever serve me a microbrewery beer or scotch in anything other than glass. No plastic, and for cryin' out loud, putting good scotch in a Styrofoam cup is considered a capital crime in some countries. I can almost tolerate beer in a plastic cup, but I don't really enjoy it.

Coffee belongs in a special cup of porous ceramic. I'm not married to this philosophy, but I prefer it. I will drink coffee out of just about anything if it's good coffee, but I have two mugs at home that are rough and porous but glazed ceramic. Slick, tight ceramic is not acceptable. And never, never, never ever wash a coffee cup with soap! This will get you five-to-ten in the slammer. A good rinsing with hot water is all that a good coffee cup should ever get, rather like a black iron pot. Warning: It's advisable to use dark coffee cups when treating them this way. That's why "black" iron pots are "black" and not yellow. Keeps the revulsion level down.

Coffee needs to have taste, not simply be hot brown water. If you can see the bottom of a cup of unsugared, uncreamed coffee, give it to the potted plants. Your cup should hold more coffee than the ratio to sugar and cream, too. Chicory is good for cleaning floors, like Pine-Sol, but that's about it.

I'm not bad about food except in a couple of areas. I love mixing peas or corn with crawfish stew, but don't *ever* get anything into my mashed potatoes. Mashed potatoes can be completely ruined if something crunches in them. Mashed potatoes should *never* crunch. An errant kernel of corn or onion from a hamburger steak will ruin mashed potatoes just as surely as if you doused it with ball bearings. Yuck.

I despise white beans with a passion deserving of Spanish inquisitors, but I adore red beans, especially with ketchup. Yes, I said ketchup, also great on scrambled eggs. Adds a little zing to red beans. Does nothing for white beans which, as far as I am concerned, have absolutely no redeeming qualities whatsoever.

Cafe Bayou at the casino has the most delectable chocolate shakes I have ever encountered. They serve them in glasses, but give you the leftovers that won't fit in the glass in a stainless steel beaker. Once the waitress is safely out of sight, I pour the shake from the glass into the beaker, because it tastes a bazillion times better in stainless steel. There used to be a doughnut place in Lafayette that kept milk in stainless steel canisters, and I once or twice strongly considered asking if I could just put my mouth over the tap. I love dairy products served in stainless steel.

Salad forks are the dumbest things ever invented for dining. What's the point? So the tines are a little shorter. For what practical purpose? So you won't gorge yourself on salad before the main course comes? Salad forks are ridiculous, and I ignore them in even the finest of restaurants, opting for the real man's fork instead.

Pizza is among my favorite of foods, and though I love almost all toppings, most of the time I prefer mine with pepperoni only.

Anything more than pepperoni is simply gratuitous. Black olives cross the threshold into toxic waste. Pizza, by the way, is American food, not Italian. Tomatoes came from the Americas and were brought back to Europe by the explorers. Prior to tomatoes, spaghetti and pizza were pretty boring stuff. Lasagna was bad enough to weep over.

Give me my fries crispy, please. If I want mashed potatoes, I'll order mashed potatoes, which of course should not crunch. Fries should crunch. If you bring me fries that droop when I pick them up off the plate, we're going to have words, I promise. Fries should never droop. My mama's fries never drooped, and were cut fresh from real potatoes.

If I request a hamburger, please don't pile the onions and pickles at the exact center of the bun. This adds four inches to the height from that narrowly stacked tower of dills and onions with a beef patty teetering precariously between them. Spread them out evenly. I like a bit of onion and pickle in every bite. I'd prefer Hellman's too, but that's negotiable.

If there is a perfect food in the world, it has to be eggs. I could live on eggs, though I am sure the span would be short. Eggs are the perfect food. You can do anything with them. Eggs you buy in the supermarket today are mislabeled. They are not really eggs, they are facsimiles of eggs laid by facsimile chickens. Real chickens —chickens that scratch around for bugs and seeds in the yard—lay real eggs, with firm, deep yellow yolks and not much whites. Supermarket eggs are like instant coffee: about as far apart from the real thing as a Chihuahua is from a wolf. Cartons of supermarket eggs should be clearly labeled "Facsimile Eggs—No Scratching In The Yard Included." Duck eggs are even better. For a duck egg fried in a black iron skillet in olive oil I would slay a dragon.

Rice should be, for me at least, a collection of individual parts, not a cohesive mass of sticky goo. I like the kernels of my rice separate, not conjoined into an unidentifiable mass that you can't distinguish from mashed potatoes. Some people say my rice is too firm, but at least the kernels keep a polite and respectable distance from each other. When you go for a spoonful of rice, the whole pot should not come with it, and you should be able to retrieve the spoon.

Come to think of it, I guess I am kinda picky and choosy as well as high-strung. Gimme a break. And you can probably add stubborn to the list, especially when it comes to crunchy mashed potatoes. Gross.

By Any Other Name

There are some really great off-the-beaten-path roads around here, and I enjoy driving them. You can have your four-lanes and your incessant need to make good time, do seventy-five miles per hour and haggle with big trucks and the new signal lights every mile and a half from here to Lafayette. Give me the scenic routes any day.

One weekend Susan and I were driving along one of the many wonderful roads around these parts, just enjoying the day, and reading the handwritten signs along the way.

CORNS FOR SALE, read one, which really cracked us up. "Do they sell them by the kernel, ear, or bushel?" I wondered aloud.

"No, silly," she said, "It's not those kinds of corns, it's the kind of corns like on your feet."

Well, that cleared things up, but it's kinda disgusting that someone would sell such a thing, ya folla?

A little further down the road we saw BUNNY RABBITS FOR SALE.

"*Bunny* rabbits for sale," I noted with emphasis.

"What's the difference between a 'rabbit' and a 'bunny rabbit'?" Susan asked.

I explained that it's like puppy dog, or kitty cat. It's kinda an affectionate thing. Obviously, the bunny rabbits would be sold for pets, while the plain rabbits are sold for cooking purposes. You never hear conversations like this, or at least, I pray you don't:

"Hey, Calinda, you coming to the house for supper, *cher?*" *(For the foreigners to Cajun country, that is not Cher, as in the singer, it is 'cher' pronounced 'sha' and equates to 'dear' or 'sweetie' or the like.)*

"*Mais* yeah, Tee-Bub, what y'all got cookin'?"

"Bunny rabbit spaghetti!"

No, the idea of "bunny rabbit spaghetti" does not appeal to me at all. You do not hear people talk about, "Shut up that mangy puppy dog from barking all night!" or "Keep that scraggly kitty cat from walking on my car!"

Of course not. Bunny rabbits, puppy dogs and kitty cats are terms of endearment, measured in heart-swelling feelings of affection, not serving sizes.

Incidentally, our managing editor here, Vanessa, noted in passing Monday morning, "Man, I smothered a rabbit this weekend."

To which I replied, "Oh, the poor little thing! How did you keep the pillow over its little face?" but I did not inquire as to whether it was, in fact, a rabbit or a bunny rabbit but knowing how kind-hearted she is about animals, I am confident it was not of the bunny variety.

I also have a tradition that when driving to Lafayette, somewhere around Broussard, there is a sign that reads "Cracklins" except the "l" is faded, so as soon as I see it I yell, "Crack-ins! Let's go get us some Crack-ins while we're here!" I don't know if it's really funny every time, or if Susie's just being polite, or if we don't go to Lafayette often enough and we both forget I used that pathetic excuse for a joke before, but at least she always laughs about it.

Interestingly enough, if you look at many of the products claiming to be Louisiana vintage, they're not. I'm particular about that. Okay, there's a few things I'm particular about. Well, to be honest, there's a whole lot of things I'm particular about, but here's just one of them: If you are not from Louisiana, just please don't try to say, spell and least of all manufacture products from Louisiana. It's like some company trying to sell Chinese mud-bugs down in Louisiana as "Peeled Crayfish Tails."

Let's get this straight: It's not *crayfish* it's *crawfish* and nobody peels anything *but* the tails. You suck the fat out of the heads (don't frown until you've tried it!) and nobody is going to buy a produce called "sucked crayfish heads" no matter if they're from China, Louisiana or Peru.

I am also always amused by the bags of frozen Gumbo Shrimp from Maine, the Crab Claw Meat from the Carolinas and the shrimp cocktail from New York. I sure wish we lived near some decent seafood-producing waters, you know?

But I digress. We were talking about scenic roads off the beaten path and odd things we find along them. I am not sure if it's still there now, but there used to be a little company on the road to Abbeville called Quail Tools. A friend of mine once wondered, "What kind of tools does one use to work on a quail?" but we later, in fact, learned that this was faulty thinking. It is the kind of tools quails *use* when working, of course. Precisely what quails work on, I'm not sure.

"Satsoomas." That's always one that gets me right in the funny bone, too.

I mentioned not long ago that I completely despise that a circle with a line through it is now used to designate if something is not allowed. I fussed that, in the old days, and rightly so, if something was not allowed, you used X over it, and I don't know what happened to the whole X thing, why it was replaced by that silly circle with a line through it.

I have found out. The highway department, you see, started using X as short for "crossing." Actually, as short for "cross" because you see signs now like "Railroad Xing." What the devil does that mean? Who left the highway department in charges of word usage and redefining? "Crossing" becomes "Xing" because, well, after all, an X is two crossed lines, right? Then you see signs like "Deer Xing" and you really just don't want to know.

There's grounds for a civil suit there, I'm sure of it.

Yawn

I believe the only way I shall sleep properly again is to go back to Montana or get sick again.

I slept like a baby every night in Montana, though I suspect it has nothing to do with the state or its locale, it was of fishing like a work mule from dawn to dusk, climbing ridges and working fast-moving water for trout. I don't have that kind of option here, unless the good ol' newspaper would like to make me their Outdoors Field Editor. Hear that ominous silence...?

The only other time I have slept well was last week when I contracted a horrific stomach bug. The first and possibly second nights I slept great, but that's because I was exhausted from illness, so it really doesn't count.

I have done all I can think of to get over this, but nothing is helping. For instance, I am pretty famous for napping. I have written column after column about the fine art of napping, but in light of my nighttime sleeplessness, I gave up napping earlier this summer to see if that would help. No cigar. I tried over the counter sleep aids, which I think made me yawn one night, and that was it. It's getting to the point where...well, you know how you feel when you're just so worn out you have this dazed, foggy feeling in your head? That's how I feel most of the time. It's for the birds, I can tell you.

Warm milk, cold beer, bologna sandwiches with sardines, a raw egg mixed with tomato juice, I've tried all the homespun cures (okay, some of the previous I did make up, but you get the idea) and nothing has helped.

But here's the odd thing: I can lie on the sofa with the television on but just barely audible and I doze in and out, only awakened by a flash of light from the screen or a spike of volume that is a little louder. This is as near to good sleep as I get, and it's still not there. At last I turn the television off and go to bed, and I am wide awake. I tried just turning the television off and staying right there on the couch, but I still lay wide awake.

"You're working yourself up to it," they tell me. "You're so worried about not sleeping, you don't." That may well be, but what to do about it? I'm supposed to just think, "Well, tonight I'm going to toss and turn for four or five hours before getting just enough sleep to exist relatively sanely but be miserable through the rest of the day...but hey, who cares?

This frustrates Patches nearly as much as it does me. Patches likes to sleep cuddled up next to me, but when I'm tossing and turning and frustrated into throwing covers off when I get too hot, or putting them over me when I get too cold, well, it's hard for Patches to cuddle properly.

She will wait for me to be still for some predetermined amount of time known only to her after I lie down, then sidle up next to me, circle three or four times as cats have a habit of doing, and settle down to rest...just in time for me to get frustrated with my situation and turn over or toss covers. Then we repeat the whole process, over and over again, until eventually she gets aggravated and goes to sleep on the sofa in the living room.

Now, one of my other symptoms of insomnia is after a while I get so frustrated with trying to sleep in one place, I go try another. So I get up from the bed and go to the sofa, where Patches is rolled up into a slumbering calico ball. For an insomnia-suffering person to see this coiled, purring bundle of contented, blissful sleep...well, it makes me mad and sometimes kinda crazy.

Usually I'll just pick her up, lie down, and let her sidle back near me and we try the whole routine on the sofa. But sometimes, just the picture of her contented slumber is too much for me to handle, so there in the half-light, I tiptoe up to her, curl my fingers into claws and leap on the sofa, tickling her stomach like a mad hatter, all the while yelling, *"COOTCHIE WOOTCHIE COOTCHIE KITTY COO!!!"* at the top of my lungs. This is at two in the morning, you understand, so the cat bites and claws in frantic escape, scurrying across the floor sideways, and lights are popping on all over the neighborhood from the noise. Smug and satisfied that if I can't sleep nobody else will, I bandage my hands then lie down on the sofa and mentally count calico sheep in my head. Eventually Patches will sulk back, jump on the sofa and express her displeasure with my rudeness by walking all over my head a few times, chewing my finger, then finally settling down to rest at about the time I'm ready to abandon the sofa and go back to the bed.

Well, that's about how it goes, anyway. See, it's three in the morning right now as I'm writing this. My eyelids are drooping, my brain fuzzy (Naw, ya think?) and I swear I could curl up on the sofa right this instant and sleep for days. Won't happen though.

I guess I just need to fish myself into exhaustion, like in Montana. I suppose the high altitude helped, as my brain wasn't getting enough oxygen, but then, when does it ever? No comments, please.

Super-size It

One morning I walk into the advertising office here at work, waiting for a document to come off the printer, and I remark,

"Boy, I'm gaining too dadgum much weight."

It's true, I've gained a few pounds since I quit smoking. I mean, I don't think I'm ready for a piano case burial or anything, but I do notice my clothes are tighter and there are these rolls on me where they weren't before.

You also have to understand that in my office, besides me and the publisher, the full-time staff is all women. The sports guy and press guy are men, but they're part-time. I therefore observe and note how girls react to each other.

For instance, if one of the girls in the office complains to me, "I'm getting so tired of being fat," I am obliged as a well-raised Southern gentleman to say, "Oh, you're not the least bit fat, quit being silly, it's all in your head." Now, when they talk to each other, they say, "Girl, I know, I went from a size-whatever to a size-whatever (women's sizes make absolutely no sense to me) and I feel like a big moo cow!"

"Oh, Lawd, I know, I look like one too!" the other says and they get to giggling like a coupla schoolgirls.

Since I don't feel like "one of the girls" around here, I expected a return of courtesy such as I myself give out. But instead I get:

"Join the club," the advertising rep sitting near the printer says to me.

So there it is. Men, you understand, are expected in the company of females to be polite. We are expected to say things like, "You are a bean pole, you are a will o' wisp, you'll blow away at any moment!" But the courtesy is not reciprocal. She might as well have said:

"Yeah, ya slob, you are looking a little like a lumpy potato sack these days, ain't ya?"

It just ain't right. There is the cultural fascination with weight, especially how it relates between men and women. Look at the aforementioned sizes. Women's jeans are for example sold in sizes: Six, eight, 10, 12, whatever. Men's jeans are sold in inches: 30, 32, 34, 36, whatever.

See the cultural bias here? The whole clothing industry, because it ain't just jeans, is so afraid of offending women they turn 32 inches into size 14 (that's a near approximation, please don't deluge me with Letters to the Editor shouting that a size 14 is actually 31½ inches, demanding retractions and boiling tar and plucking chickens, okay?) The other reason is that women know that men don't understand that size 14 is (approximately!) 32 inches, and since women like to keep men perpetually confused, it all works out for the best.

A guy goes to get a pair of jeans, 36-inch with a 34-inch inseam, he's right where he needs to be. Girls go get a size 10 petite. What the devil is "petite" as compared to "average" and "long"? Once again, it's all designed to keep men confused and women from saying, "You big long-legged heifer!"

Now let's get back to my waiting-at-the-printer discussion. I am expected, when a female says something disparaging about her weight, to disagree strongly, compliment highly and exit a perfect Southern gentleman. In proper society, then, a woman will do the same for a man in normal circumstances. However, I am in hybrid circumstances, in that I work with these gals and am in some ways "one of the girls" and in other ways still some kinda disease-ridden outsider.

So if you carry that to its logical conclusion, when one of the girls says to me, "I feel like an oil drum," and I say, "You look more like an offshore platform," I'm just being one of the girls, right?

Ah, no. They just don't see it that way, and that's when it happens. You guys, you all know what I mean. Their faces split open and a molten-lava skull comes out, fire shoots from their hair and lightning from their fingertips and their heads spin around six hundred and sixty-six times and they start yelling, *"DIE MAN-SCUM, DIE!"* while shooting bolts of electricity into your head and frying your brain.

Don't make jokes about it, either. Some in the same group of gals that I work with, go to lunch with every day and who are my buddies, my pals, I mention to them that my belly is getting so big I feel pregnant and I get a forty-five-minute lecture about how I have no idea how it feels to be pregnant, no man can know how it feels to be pregnant, long diatribes about beached whales and orcas feeding on sea lions, so on and so forth.

I mentioned this to a friend of mine—someone I don't work with and who really is a friend, unlike these hybrid friendships I have at work—and this is what she said to me:

"Petite means short, except we don't like to be called short, petite seems so much prettier! And if I had to look at the size of my waist in inches every time I put on a pair of jeans, I'd just wear a mu-mu instead! And get this, different stores have different sizes. Some stores have wizened up and they'll actually put a six label on a pair of eights or 10s. Hell, I'd rather sport a smaller number no mater how bad they looked! I'd leave the tag on it for all to see. I'm a six in some stores, eight in others. Can't believe I actually told you that!" That last line—and the entire imagery of fried brains—is why you shouldn't even bother to ask me who told me this.

I guess the safest thing to do is just to never bring up the subject of weight with girls when you're a guy, even if it's about yourself, and wait until I'm around my guy friends, where the conversation usually goes like this:

"Man, I'm getting too big."

"Heck, me too."

"Not me, I still wear the same size jeans I did in high school."

"Yeah, but in high school you buttoned them *over* your stomach, not *under* it."

(Big laughs and back-slapping all around, another round of beer.)

"Well, if you worked hard like me, in a real job, instead of that pansy newspaper stuff, you wouldn't have that problem."

"Yeah? So what's your excuse?"

"I got thyroid problems."

"You got *beer*oid problems, that's what you got."

"Me? You the one who can balance three mugs on that gut of yours."

"Ha! Better'n a pizza pan, ya gorilla."

"You got a built-in serving tray, ya bum."

"You guys shaddup, we all got six pack stomachs."

"More like a twelve-pack!"

"Or a case!"

(More big laughs and back-slapping all around, another round of beer.)

And so on and so forth and so it goes. I guess the best thing to have done was not even write this column, because I'm sure I'm going to get in trouble over it from my so-called friends, but then, I can outrun most of them anyway.

Five Months

Well, I'm coming up on five months now since I quit smoking. I am proud of myself. I admit there was always a doubt in my mind that I could do it, but after the first few weeks it got to where I don't even think about it anymore except in rare times of extreme stress. One of those was getting on an airplane to Montana then getting on another one to get home (including the layovers and changeovers in between) but I didn't fail.

Not smoking is something I haven't experienced in twenty-two years. Next month I'll be forty-one—I say, I say listen to me when I talk to you, boy—forty-one years old. I started smoking around age eighteen, being respectful enough at least to my parents to wait until I was legal.

It wasn't but a few weeks ago when I noticed Susan smelled really nice. I commented on this and she laughed. "Skin lotion. Same lotion I've been wearing forever," she said. "I quit wearing perfume years ago because you just never noticed."

I felt extraordinarily guilty about that, like I've been neglectful or something due to my previous addiction.

Not smoking has taken some stranger turns, though. I have also been for twenty-two years or so, a scotch drinker, when I drink, that is. For the record, that's regularly but not excessively, if you get my meaning. It's sort of a family tradition: The men in my family didn't drink often, maybe once or twice a month at a fish fry or barbecue or crawfish boil, but when it was time to drink, they didn't believe in doing any job shabbily.

Anyway, I seem to have lost my taste for scotch since I quit smoking. I don't enjoy it as much as I used to, strangely enough. Instead, I have grown increasingly fond of beer.

The inherent problem here—and the point to this column, which I am sure has you wondering why I am spending so much space espousing the evils of indulgence—is that a scotch and water amounts to about sixty calories. A good beer is about two hundred. The problem therefore lies in the waistline: Scotch adds far less to my midsection than beer.

Now, don't start preaching to me about, "Well, you need to stop drinking, too!" I ain't buying it, I ain't going there. I don't drink much, I do so safely and responsibly, and I refuse to give up all my vices.

Most of my problem, though, is my choice of beer. I refuse to drink American commercial beers. Anything with the word "light" in it does not qualify as beer, it qualifies as (in my humble opinion!) imaginary beer.

There are many evils corporate giants have inflicted on this proud nation, such as canned vegetables, frozen dinners, lemon juice that has no lemon in it (read the label, it's true) and squeezable mayonnaise bottles...but how they ever convinced us to give up real beer for light beer is perhaps the most cunning example of mass hypnosis and the most compelling evidence for subconscious suggestion via chemicals put into our water supply by the CIA than I have ever seen to this day. The second best example is store-bought tomatoes. Yuck.

Since I quit smoking, I have not changed my socializing habits, I still hang out with my friends who do smoke. It rarely bothers me, though sometimes I do get to feeling like I am being suffocated. I just politely let my pals know that I am feeling uncomfortable with their smoke, as delicately and non-preachingly as I can. Usually this is accomplished by flailing my hands in front of my face vigorously, mouth agape, uttering gasping and choking sounds and holding my breath until I turn blue.

And they say I'm being melodramatic. Go figure.

I haven't caught my breath back in only five months, but I do find it easier to breathe in general. Yes, I've gained weight, much to my dismay, and I am trying to do something about it. I have been "cutting back." Herein lies yet another debate I have with my cohorts and with society in general.

When someone says "cutting back" in relation to food, people automatically think "diet." They actually don't hear the words "cutting back" because some layer of cerebral tissue filters the entire phrase "cutting back" from conscious assimilation and substitutes it with "diet."

"Diet" then, at the cerebral level, is automatically filtered again and miraculously transformed into "starve" though people seldom say this out loud.

I do not believe in diets nor do I believe in starving. I believe in "cutting back" which may require hypnosis or surgery for you to even read on this page.

For instance: My friends laugh themselves heartily to the point of near suffocation at me when, instead of a lunch plate of baked macaroni and cheese, brisket, mashed potatoes and fried bread, I order a chef salad with extra Thousand Island dressing, understanding that while my lunch may not be zero-cal, but is about a quarter as much as theirs.

"That's not dieting!" they protest.

"I'm not dieting, I'm cutting back," I say.

That cerebral filter kicks in and they furrow their brows at me in confusion and ask, "Why are you repeating yourself?" Then go off on a tirade about the salad.

"It's got cheese!" they rail. "And eggs! Do you know how bad eggs are for you! Your cholesterol will go through the roof and combined with already overweight status will give you a coronary! And then you're eating extra Thousand Island dressing! That's a diet?"

"That's cutting back," I say.

"Why are you repeating me, now?" they ask, because they never heard the words "cutting back" they heard "diet." The brain can do miraculous things in denial.

Anyway, I'll soon make five months smoke-free and I'm mighty proud of it, despite these changes I'm undergoing. I'll slowly get my weight back to something I'm happy with, of course. But then the masses will preach to me that I have not done a proper job of "dieting".

"You could lose another fifteen if you tried," they'll say.

"I could," I'll reply, "But then I'd have to starve myself."

The other interesting thing about the human brain is that people who convert the words "cutting back" to "diet" and then associate and assimilate the word "diet" to the unpleasant word "starve," which they try not to ever mention, when they hear the word "starve" they suddenly go all glassy-eyed, slack-jawed and rush to the nearest drive-in for a super-sized sundae.

Adventures in Salad

In an effort to control the ever-increasing girth of my waistline I have become quite a salad fan.

Now, it's not that I didn't enjoy salads before, but for me a salad was mainly something you enjoy as an appetizer before that big ribeye and baked potato with loads of butter, a meal finished off with a slab of chocolate cake.

However, recent newsworthy events of revolutionary activities along my equator have necessitated an in-depth study of salads. Now, I am not a believer in radical diets. I do not think that I can safely lose a dozen pounds in a week. I am of the opinion that I inflated this spare tire of mine gradually, I need to deflate it just as gradually. I am not perfect. I fail miserably at times. We all go to lunch, the Banner crew, and I am quite eager to sink my teeth into a large chef's salad. But the lunch special of the day is something like lasagna and when the waitress asks, "What can I get you, sir?" my mouth opens and my lips make the words *chef's salad* but a voice that sounds auspiciously like mine reverberates "Lasagna, please!" It's a frightening experience, really.

I saw that a fast-food joint was featuring these "fruit and walnut" salads and thought that was pretty clever so I got one. I was disappointed to learn that these salads have no lettuce, carrots, purple cabbage or anything else, it's just what it says, "fruit and walnut." The dressing was also yogurt. Yogurt—let's be very clear on this, friends and neighbors—is many things...it is *not* a salad dressing. But since this wasn't a salad, I guess that's appropriate.

So I went to the grocery store and decided I would do it right even if they couldn't. Here's what I bought: Romaine and iceberg lettuce with carrots and purple cabbage; apples, walnuts, pear halves and pineapple chunks in juice, not syrup; raisins, grapes, strawberries, and ranch dressing. I put all this together in a stainless steel salad bowl with a bit of cubed baked chicken and cheddar cheese (sharp, always sharp!) You'll note that there are no tomatoes in my salad. Unless I grow them myself, I'd as soon not bother with store-bought tomatoes. I'd as soon eat a baseball.

But as far as my salad, man, I gotta tell you...that was some good, yeah, *cher!*

But here's some observations I made about salads. It really isn't the salad that helps you to lose weight, so far as the caloric or fat or carbohydrate value therein. It's the effort. I mean, unless you're eating a basic salad with just lettuce, you have work at that puppy to keep it right, because gravity is always working against you. If you do not constantly stir at it while eating it, the salad ends up like this, in precisely this order from top to bottom: Lettuce, fruit chunks (largest first) chicken cubes, cheddar cubes, slivers of carrot and purple cabbage, grapes, raisins, lastly the walnuts. Precisely that order, because the lightest stuff stays at the top based on bulk, the smallest stuff falls to the bottom based on tiny-sizedness, and the other stuff kinda suspends in the middle. I learned in geology class in college that this is also how sedimentary layers accumulate in soil and rock strata. Geologists, therefore, probably are salad fans.

Like I said, I don't believe in radical diets. I don't think diets are good when they begin, "First, buy two dozen crates of grapefruit." I did not, as mentioned, go on a chocolate, cream cheese, cordial cherry and Double Rocky Road ice cream binge for thirty days to acquire these extra pounds, I do not expect to go on a tofu and sesame seed diet for a month to lose them. Gradual's the word here, up the ladder and down.

I was pretty much doomed to gain a little extra cargo this year, really. I mean, I quit smoking and joined the nefarious "over forty" crowd all in the same year. My greatest fear is that, if it's true that the camera really adds ten pounds to you, I'll look like I'm capsizing the boat when my television appearance on *Fly Fishing America* airs in the spring.

Usually I'm not interested in numbers when it comes to weight. I'm interested in how my clothes fit, how hard it is to tie my shoes (very hard at the moment!) and things like that. I am not really worried, usually, about bathroom scales, but just for grins and giggles a couple weeks ago I stepped onto one. Morbid curiosity, I guess. Like rubber-necking at a wreck with fatalities.

I'm not telling you what the little numbers said, no matter how much chocolate cheese cake you bribe me with. Let's just say that I cussed that poor little bathroom scale like a dog, ya folla? It was such a loud and ceaseless tirade of emphatic disagreement the cat hid under the sofa and didn't come out until nightfall. My fig tree shed all its leaves during my hissy fit, and that was before the first cold snap. Paint peeled from my walls, crown molding snapped loose—well, you get the idea. I was not a happy puppy.

"Terrific," I said to Suze after the explosion was over. "I quit smoking, saved myself from lung implosion and now will expire from cardiac over-expectation. I'm doomed."

But that's when I decided to get on with a gradual decline back toward some semblance of what I call "neither too much nor too little" so far as physique goes. I am, of course, doing this smack dab in the middle of the two most indulgent holidays on our calendar. I never was good at timing.

I always believed Patches, my calico kitty, was descended from a lineage of mountain lions. Some scientists believe you can tell where domesticated cats originated from by their behavior: If they like high places, they were probably mountain lion-stock that liked cliffs and ledges. If they like low places, they were probably tundra or savanna saber-toothed tigers, etc.

Patches is certainly of high-altitude stock, because she has found that my tummy is the perfect place to perch aloft and take a nap.

Brain Food

They say that fish is not only good for you, it's also "brain food." *They* being people who go to college to study such things (and I decided to be a writer...go figure.)

It's all about those Omega-Delta-Buick fattening acids and anti-oxidations, I think. Supposed to make you smarter, somehow, because those are the chemicals the ol' noggin works best on, sorta like a steam engine gets hottest when shoveled with coal instead of grass clippings.

It really doesn't make sense to me. Fish, you see, are not that smart. In fact, one of the great topics of angling literature has been why fishermen such as myself gear up with hundreds, in some cases thousands of dollars worth of equipment to go and try to fool a creature with a brain the size of a grain of rice into *eating*, for cryin' out loud. C'mon now, that's pretty much all they do, eat and swim and occasionally make a little romance when the moon is right. The notion that fish are smart simply because they like to be in schools was something developed by a marine biologist who was sidelining as a standup comic.

So maybe that's the key as to why fish are brain food: They aren't that smart themselves, and all those El-Camino-acids and fancy-pants oxidations just kinda collect in their system, so when we eat a big helping of fried fish we get it all for ourselves. Hey, works for me.

I know that whales are considered extraordinarily smart, but then, whales are not fish, they are mammals, just like ourselves and, believe it or not, so is a porcupine, which is scary. Whales may be so smart by eating baitfish and tiny shrimp, further evidence to support the whole "brain food" hypothesis.

Now to make matters worse, for those of us who are watching our girth as well as trying to raise our intelligence quotient into the triple digits, sugar and carbohydrates appear to be brain food. These are, of course, the very things we girth-minded zealots try to avoid. So are we in fact taking a mind that can do calculus and exchanging it for a six-pack tummy? Does this explain the whole phenomenon behind supermodels?

Research recently has shown a chemical called choline is an excellent brain food. "Choline" is not to be confused with "chlorine" which will whiten your brain and kill you. "Choline" is found in the following foods in order of which contains the most: Beef liver, eggs, beef steak, peanut butter, oranges and potatoes.

Well, all right! Now we're talking a menu, friends and neighbors. Let's start with a breakfast of fried eggs, medium-hard, with hash browns and orange juice. For lunch we'll have a serving of catfish fillets with fries. If we need a snack sometime in between lunch and supper we'll have a peanut butter sandwich. Or a Reese's cup. For the evening meal, a porterhouse with a baked potato fits the bill quite nicely, or beef liver, smothered with onions, with mashed potatoes for the gravy.

The fact that beef liver is considered a highly regarded brain food only serves to reinforce what I've always believed anyway: People who like liver are smarter than those who curl their noses up at it and complain loudly about the smell. (Whoa! Look out Mr. Postman, the Letters to the Editor are coming!)

If we use the premise that since fish are dumb but therefore make great brain food, then we can extrapolate perhaps that turkey is an excellent brain food, but a careful observation of the facts does not bear this out. For one thing, a turkey is so dumb it will drown itself staring up at the rain in puzzled awe. For another thing, people who gorge themselves on turkey for Thanksgiving rush out the next day and get in fights at Walmart over the new X-Box. Turkey is definitely not on the brain food list.

Of course, the fish-as-brain-food hypothesis starts to fall apart as well if you examine it too closely. If fish are so dumb, why do you hear fishermen saying, "The fish were feeding all over the place and I couldn't get them to bite!" Fish maybe aren't so dumb...or maybe the fisherman was a catch-and-release only angler? There's just too many variables to draw a firm conclusion.

In fact, scientists tell us the smartest animals are, in ascending order, squirrel, squid, raven, dog, pig, parrot, elephant, monkey, dolphin, primates (that means us.) You'll notice there are no fish, cows or chickens laying eggs on the list. The lesson in the above list is clear, though: We should not eat pig, since incredibly they're smarter than Labrador retrievers (though it's no surprise they'd be smarter than poodles), dumber than parrots, and would get stepped on by elephants in a chess game. For the record, the dumbest animals, scientists believe, are the armadillo and possum. Well, that explains the whole roadkill thing...

This is why PETA's argument also falls apart. This group of animal rights activists who, apparently, eat absolutely no beef liver, fish, beef steak or other such brain food, has published a comic book called "Your Daddy Kills Animals!" It shows Dear Old Daddy in a fishing hat and with tackle all around him. He's holding a big knife and gutting a fish with maniacal glee. The lower headline reads, "Ask your daddy why he's hooked on killing!"

Nope. No brain food consumption here. PETA might be better served if they all went out for a lunch of peanut butter sandwiches twice a day. Do peanuts feel pain? Hmmm...

Battling Big Brother

Nope. Ain't gonna happen. Forget it. Uh-uh.

Last week, you see, due to a series of unimportant circumstances, I got my paycheck from the boss and decided to cash it rather than making a deposit. It was easier to get to the bank the check was drawn on rather than my bank, so I hopped over there right before lunch.

I've done this many times before. I have a sore spot in my heart for banks and financial institutions in general. This sore spot rapidly became a gaping wound Friday when I signed my check, put it and my driver's license in the drive-thru canister and *Poof!* It went to the teller.

After the usual holiday pleasantries the teller asked if I had an account there, and I said no, but the check was drawn on their bank. She then said something to me I couldn't quite make out and the canister came back to me. Inside was my check and a small container about the size of a half-dollar. I looked across the rows of drive-thru stalls at her questioningly, and she said, "I need you to put your thumb print on the front of the check."

The look on my face must have been comical because it was one of complete puzzlement. The rage would come later. "Pardon?"

"Your thumb print," she said. "I need your thumb print on the front of the check."

"What the devil for?" I asked.

"It's company policy," she said.

I noted that it must be really new policy because I had been there a few weeks earlier and no one had asked for my thumb print. This did little to solve the problem, however, because the teller was just waiting there, looking expectant. I asked for my driver's license back and departed, I'm sure leaving the employee to wonder if I was an escaped con or a spy. It wasn't her fault, it's the company policy, she just works there, but that don't mean I gotta take it.

I pulled up at my bank and the usual holiday pleasantries came over the speaker, to which I replied, "I have been a customer of yours for fourteen years, are you going to ask me for a thumb print to cash this check?" They did not, and everything was fine and I then went on my way, but in a nasty mood.

Now, pay attention closely here, because I'm only going to say this once: It's bad enough that they track my buying habits through my cards; it's a foul, foul circumstance that I have to give my driver's license to cash a check in my own hometown, but hear this and hear it clearly:

They ain't getting my thumb print, finger print, palm print, retina scan or hair sample and I ain't gonna tinkle in a cup for you, either, ya folla?

The *nerve* of some people.

Listen up, I'm not a criminal, I am not doing drugs and until you have reasonable suspicions that I am, my various prints, body parts and fluids are my property. Just like, by the way, that check that was written out to me. I do not give thumb prints to get my money from the bank.

"But it's for your own protection," someone tried to explain to me.

From who? Let's go over it again: It's my money, the check was written to me. Why do they need a thumb print to protect me from myself? While it may be true that I could use a good dose of common sense and frugality with my finances, I still don't think it's worth a thumb print in the CIA database. I don't want Michael Chertoff thumbing through my DNA or, for God's sake, George W. Bush reading my emails and finding out where all my best fishing holes are.

"But, what if someone else got your check and cashed it?" was the reply.

Sorry, that dog won't hunt. They didn't get ID'd? Not my problem, that's the bank's. I always give my ID, even though it disgruntles the heck out of me. Some clown walks in with my check and cashes it without an ID, well, that's just tough luck on the bank's part. If he presents an ID with my exact name and mugshot on it, well, the poor slob is gonna have a rough time of it in life anyway, just like me.

Now, to make matters worse, I come down with a cold Christmas Day, but manage to get through until Monday when I go to get some medicine. I could barely breathe and my face felt like an overinflated balloon. Instead of my usual misery-relief medicine on the shelf, they got a card that I have to take to the cashier. I could smell a fight coming, but did it anyway.

First, she had to get my driver's license. I thought about arguing, but decided that it was kinda like cashing a check, so I gave it to her. Then she pounded on the touch-screen that I couldn't see for about five minutes and asked for my phone number.

"What the devil for?" I demanded.

"It's company policy," she said.

"What, I'm going to get a 'get well' call from the CEO?"

Blank stare.

"You have my driver's license. You have my address. If I turn out to be a drug pusher who's getting kids hooked on Sudafed, are you gonna give the cops my phone number so they call me first to make sure I'm home so they can come arrest me?"

Blank stare.

I gave her a fake phone number, so I'm sure I'll get the FBI's attention and they'll put wiretaps on my real phone and monitor my email, but who gives a rip? I paid with cash instead of my card just to be ornery. Trace *that*.

I am not going to be treated like a criminal, sorry, corporate America and U.S. Government. I ain't done nothing wrong. I won't be printed, sorted or cataloged. I won't be analyzed, cross-referenced or digitized. You ain't putting a transducer implant in my earlobe to locate me. I'm not a number, a data set or a profile. My DNA double-helix sequence is private, thank you very much. I got a name, it was my daddy's name, and his daddy's before him, and none of them were criminals as far back as I've cared to dig up the ol' family tree, though I did locate some references to moonshine, but that was an awful long time ago.

Thumb prints to cash a check. The *nerve*.

Marty Who?

Someone asked me once why I don't get into ye ole' Fat Tuesday. I had to think about it for a year or two, but I finally realized I had never even heard of Mardi Gras until I was about fourteen. Really. While in recent years the Chitimachas put on a parade the Sunday before Mardi Gras, when I was growing up I heard nothing about it. We didn't even get off of school as I remember, being a federal Indian school and all. My parents certainly never took me to any parades, and I venture to say that if my memory is faulty about the school and we did get off that Tuesday, my dad and I went fishing.

Those were pretty secluded, isolated days for me. There was still some lingering distrust between Rez residents and non-residents. I don't remember going to any kind of parade until I was in high school and started working for the Banner when I was fifteen. I've covered more than my share since then, believe me, and while I've come to enjoy them for what they're worth, well, in the long run I'd still rather be on the lake with the old man.

The first jester I ever saw, gallivanting down Main Street, scared the bejeezus out of me. Hey, gimme a break, I was a born and reared Rez boy, and I thought it was *Neka sama* or some other of the ancestral spirits my gramma told me about, the ones that would come git ya when you was bad. Nowadays, thankfully, you don't see as many frightening Mardi Gras deities. It's a good thing, too: My heart barely made it through that one!

The first doubloons I got were chocolate covered with gold foil. I gobbled 'em up like a true chocolate lover, but the next year they threw us gold-colored plastic ones, and I was highly irritated. I think it was then and there that Mardi Gras lost all meaning for me. Tootsie Rolls, even in great abundance (even if thrown by the ton), are no substitute for chocolate doubloons.

As it was, in the old days before computer systems, when the royalty was announced we had to lock up the front page in the office safe. That's how much people wanted to know who was King Sucrose, or Teche or Agmarol. Today, the page is done on computer and the files are not accessible to the general public, though I believe some Krewe members have attempted to hack into our network in desperation.

Perhaps they don't go that far, but it's funny how they'll call Monday and even as we're readying the paper Tuesday.

"I was invited to the Sucrose ball, and I forgot who the king was...?"

"This is the *New York Times* Mardi Gras editor, can you tell me who the king is this year?"

"I have the King's robes hemmed, can you tell me how I can get them to him?"

"Who is King Fructose this year?"

And so on and so forth. It's all, as I said, mysterious to me, having not experienced all this until I was an early teenager.

Soon as the parade is over, though, one of two things is going to happen with me: If the weather's good and the water's clear, I'll head off to a pond and harass the perch. If the weather's good and the water's bad, or if everything's bad, I'll head home and take a nap. Were I not a newspaper employee, I could just nap right there in my folding chair by my ice chest, until the street sweeper comes, anyway.

But as I've said every year and will continue to say for many more, it's really comforting to see folks still throwing beads after that whole Manhattan Island thing. Chitimachas now throw the beads back. Sort of like saying, "Thanks, but we want our island back, and could you please throw in the rest of the continent too? Except the Superfund sites. You can keep those."

Oddities

Here's some things I simply won't understand, for as long as I live.

Some of them involve law enforcement and criminals. One of my favorites is this: Police pull over a car on a traffic stop because the guy has a busted tail light, expired inspection sticker, no license plate light, expired license plate, and his left headlight blinks every time he makes a right hand turn—and he's carrying around fifty grand in crack cocaine.

It's perhaps a blessing to us law-abiding citizens that criminals are that stupid, don't you think? Hey, genius, you got fifty grand in crack in the car, don't bother going out in something that's street legal. Figure he's using all the profits himself, that's why he couldn't pay to fix the car with that much in drugs in his possession.

It's just like white vans and pervs. Pervs always seem to drive white vans, why is that? Think about it, you've heard it all your life. A guy is riding around trying to lure young kids into his vehicle, it's on the six o'clock news and sure enough, a white van. If a perv drove a blue van, he'd never get caught.

Jane Doe goes into Walmart and shoplifts a $1.95 lipstick. A manager sees her, calls the cops, she gets hauled downtown, where she is processed, charged and posts bond of $1,500 to get out.

What the--? The lipstick woulda been cheaper, Jane.

It's just the changing times, I guess. Times change and leave relics like me behind.

See, my dad always wore khaki pants. In his world, growing up through the Depression and so forth, blue jeans were a mark of poor folks. Pickup trucks, likewise, were for farmers. Now today jeans can cost a hundred note and a pickup truck costs more than a Caddy. Go figure.

You know what else bugs me? Pants that are purposefully made to fit just below the hips and have inseams below the knees. God help me, I've become my father and walk around in a state of perpetual amazement at the "dadgum kids these days."

Those sticky tape things they put on bags of chips and such. That bugs me. They only work for about three-quarters of the bag anyway then they don't stick well anymore, and if you go get you a handful of chips it's next to impossible to roll the top of the bag down and stick that piece of tape stuff in place with one hand, so you end up trying to hold the bag with your chin while rolling the top down with your free hand and sticking the tape with your nose. Give me a clothespin. Job over.

Cans of chips irritate me. Chips do not belong in cans. I love Pringles, but wouldn't they taste just as good in a bag, and you wouldn't have to break the bones in your hand to squeeze it down the tube to get the last third of them out? You don't want to pour them out, of course, because all the crumbs fall out and get everywhere, then you have to go get the broom or vacuum. Actually, I think chips belong in cardboard boxes like cereal, but then, they started putting cereal in bags like chips, so you know the world's really turned topsy-turvy.

Sadly enough, there's going to be a shortage of parsley one of these days. Too many restaurants just put it on plates as a garnishment and we all throw it away because garnishment rarely, if ever, tastes good no matter how much horseradish you put on it.

There are these new types of shoes called Crocs.

"Hey, what do you call those shoes?"

"Crocs."

"Excuse me?"

"Crocs. Like, you know, crocodiles."

"They look nothing like crocodiles."

"No?"

"No."

"Oh. What do you think they look like?"

"I dunno. Maybe...a crock pot?"

"Yeah! That's it!"

I'll tell you another thing that bugs me: Teflon. Teflon scares me. Sure, it makes your eggs slip off the pan easy, but when you find out that the manufacturing process of Teflon creates a byproduct carcinogen, how appetizing is your egg then? I mean, shouldn't we have known it when Teflon came out? Nothing good for you can be that slick and stickless. Eggs are supposed to stick to the pan if you don't do it right. Cook eggs in a black iron skillet like a real man and learn to get them to not stick. Then you can call yourself an egg cook. Teflon is meant for space shuttles, plumber's tape and car wax, not cooking eggs.

Add to the list one final thing for today, at least: Duct tape. Doesn't work worth pecan on ducts. Nor on ducks.

Tax Attacks

Like most other Americans, I hate tax time.

Now, most Americans hate tax time because of all the money they have to put out. I hate it for that reason, too, but I also hate it for the same reasons I hate most other modern things: Too complicated, too much turning me into just a number.

Before Internet tax filing, tax forms made no sense, and I'm not talking about the whole indecency of it. I mean they just don't make sense. Why, for instance, am I not a head of household? Because I don't have a qualifying person under my roof, I cannot claim head of household, but I am definitely the head of the household. I own it. Patches is not the head of the household, and the dog lives outside so she can't be the head of the household. According to the IRS, I cannot be the head of my household, so who is? I'd like to speak to that person, because I've been paying all the bills and tending to the upkeep around there for a long time now. Where has this invisible "head of household" been, out partying it up and living footloose and fancy free on my tax exemption?

Oddly enough, the very next tax question is if someone else can claim me as a dependent. I wonder if perhaps this mysterious, phantom "head of household" has been doing so and getting some money back from Uncle Sam off of me while I'm stuck with the utility bills and patching the roof. How do I know if someone else can claim me as a dependent? I'm dependent on the Banner for my paycheck, can they claim me as a dependent? I am dependent on the waterworks for my clean water, can they claim me as a dependent? Now, if that's true, Patches and our black Lab Daisy cannot eat unless I fill their food bowls each and every day and won't get water unless I fill their water bowls, so why can't I claim them as dependents? What's that you say? Because they're not people? You tell Patches that, you hear? Go on. I double-dog dare ya.

It gets even screwier from there. I then have to figure out if I have any taxable interest or tax exempt interest. It's really hard to say. I have an interest in fly fishing, *Star Trek*, wood working, bonsai in a twisted sort of way, fine double shotguns, Bugs Bunny and many other things, but I don't know if they're taxable or tax exempt. Who's to know? Do I get ordinary dividends or qualified dividends (I'd guess ordinary, like most everything else about me.)

No relief yet. No, I receive no alimony though I may have a capital gain around my midsection since I quit smoking, but can I get a tax credit for that? I doubt it. Other gains or losses...the cola machine at the courthouse took fifty cents from me the other day without giving me a Diet Coke, that's a loss, and I lose a lot of fishing flies to fly-eating trees, but can I claim it?

And where's the tax credit for paying more for a gallon of gas so that ExxonMobil can knock Walmart out of the top spot on the Fortune 500 list? Huh? Where on my Form 1040 is the "making big oil companies post record profits while you use all your vacation stash just driving to work" tax credit?

After several more of these odd questions, I am told what my adjusted gross income is, and yes, I'll agree that it's pretty gross with or without adjustment. It definitely needs to see a chiropractor.

Then they tell me to Add lines 23 through 31a and 32 through 35. Follow this carefully now: There is no line 31b. Why did they say "add lines 23 through 31a and 32 through 35" instead of "add lines 23 through 35"? Did they think someone wouldn't include line 31a, or must you add lines 23 through 31a in one move and then lines 23 through 35 in another move, in which case you come up with two totals, what then? Who writes these instructions, anyway, Martians?

After a few more gyrations we end up at my "taxable income" and then, at last, a line item for "foreign tax credit." I live on the reservation, which is a sovereign nation. What do I answer?

Finally we get down to the moment everyone is waiting for: Refund or payment. After doing all the kooky math, making sure you added up the lines the way they told you to, they announce you have to pay up. They say "amount you owe" and that's it, Jack, do not pass "GO," do not collect $200, that's what you owe.

If you get a refund, they ask you to fill in the "amount you want refunded to you."

Notice the disparity here?

You can choose how much you want to get back, but not how much you want to pay. And this is what your forefathers spent three months in the cramped quarters of a wooden sailing ship, risking scurvy and sea-monsters to get to America for. So you could decide if you want all of your tax refund or not.

"No, that's okay, keep half of it to go toward the national debt," you might say.

Or, "Hey, I'm feeling generous today, you take that silly old tax refund of mine and put it in the treasury to help pay for naturalizing illegal immigrants so I can further have to press '1' for English or '2' for Spanish when I call the post office."

King George must be laughing his head off right now.

All that way, across all that water, to civilize a continent that had no taxes, no exemptions, no line 31a, nothing but clean air and good fishing. And they called us savages. Hrmph.

Inclusives

Odd. Butterscotch is odd.

I might admit reluctantly that there is something mildly buttery about it, in an artificially flavored, hazy sort of way, but then only if you really concentrate hard for long, long minutes. Even then, you're really never quite sure if it's butter or margarine.

There is nothing remotely tasting like scotch about it, though. Where did the name "butterscotch" come from? Who, by the way, mixed butter and scotch in order to conceive the idea of butterscotch as a descriptive name for a candy? On the other hand, most lemon juice you buy in the store has no lemon in it and I'm reasonably sure some supermarket wines never met a grape, so there you go.

I should know about butterscotch, I used to be a devout scotch drinker, and I love butter. Scotch, that is, being a nice highland single malt or a fine blend. I also know about butter, and I do mean butter, not margarine and not a "spread." Butter by its very nature does not spread like "spreads" do and anything that does is not really butter. You do not spread butter easily, nor do you put it in a squeeze bottle and make it go *ploop!* onto your pancakes. Real butter takes work, as do most good things in life.

They make everything squeezable nowadays: ketchup, salad dressing, so-called "butter" but I draw the line at mayonnaise. I will not squeeze mayonnaise onto my sandwich. No siree Bob, thank you, uh-uh. I use Hellman's and only Hellman's and squeezing Hellman's out onto your bread and making it go *ploop!* is a death penalty in some states where the people have a little dignity left.

That's kinda like cheese, as opposed to "processed cheese food."

Though I guess American cheese is a processed cheese food. Cheese, I'm very sorry if you disagree, should not jiggle. Jello jiggles. Souffle jiggles. Cheese should not jiggle. Certainly some of it's good on nachos and the like, but then, don't call it cheese, because it ain't. Call it "jiggly cheese-like stuff" and be done. I like my cheese to be cheddar and sharp, or white Danish Havarti. I do not like it enclosed in aluminum foil packaging and when I squeeze it, it should never, ever squoosh.

I prefer pure maple syrup, too. I bought something once called "Butter Maple Syrup" that, when I read the ingredients, had neither butter nor maple syrup included. It tasted pretty good, actually, but like lemon juice with no lemon in it and vanilla concentrate with no vanilla in it, I am leery of such sleight of hand. I am particularly wary of words in ingredient lists that have more than eight syllables.

Peanut butter is another thing I'm particular—or perhaps peculiar—about. One of the greatest treats I know is to sit down with a banana, a jar of peanut butter and a butter knife (which, oddly, does not necessarily require the presence of butter, unlike butterscotch). Dab of peanut butter on the end of the peeled banana, take a bite, repeat. Peanut butter always includes peanuts, as far as I know, so that's good. Bananas are, of course, self-inclusive.

The perfect food, the one I could exist solely on, is eggs. I love eggs. Fried, boiled, scrambled, poached, you name it. Eggs are the perfect food. Even supermarket eggs, which are really mere shadows of eggs, are good. Give me eggs from chickens that eke out a living by scratching at bugs and seeds in the yard and you got a great egg. Duck eggs are even better. Pickled quail eggs? I'd get in a fight with a circular saw for good pickled quail eggs, though it's hard to find them anymore that taste right. Most producers just make them hot, and that's not what it's all about.

Eggs and Spam. Yes indeed, friends and neighbors, run screaming for the door in terror, disgust or revulsion if you like, but fried eggs and fried Spam can be breakfast of champions. I have become a fan of Treet. Fried up in a black iron skillet with three eggs gets me going for the day. Did you know that there are Spam cooking contests all over the USA? It's true. I saw one on the Food Network on the tube once. They had Spam with lobster. Spam casserole with bacon. Spam anything-you-can-think-of. I wanna go one day if my arteries can handle it.

I do not like sushi. I tried some the other night at the opening of Shorty's at Cypress Bayou Casino and *bleeeeeechhh!* You can have my share. I've been eating fish for my entire life, fried or broiled or grilled, but raw does not float my boat. I do like good raw oysters, well salted, and maybe a dash of Tabasco on a Saltine cracker. But as far as I'm concerned sushi is bait for a good catch subsequently suitable for a good fish fry. Make my catch of the day "well done."

Heat

Sure is hot, ain't it?

Surely it's just my imagination, or maybe I'm having hot flashes. It is, after all, only June 14. Everyone knows it doesn't get to be ninety-seven degrees on June 14, right? That's late July, early August weather.

Last June we weren't even reaching ninety yet. Nowadays you hear people having conversations on the sidewalk like:

"What's that smell?"

"Singed hair. On the back of my neck, I think."

"Smells terrible."

"Well, why don't you go stand somewhere else?"

"I can't."

"Why not?"

"My shoes are melted to the concrete."

It's just brutally hot, that's what it is. What little rain we get the ground soaks up like French bread soaks up roux gravy. The lack of rain is terrible, too, though it has the undisputed benefit of keeping the growth of grass slow. Unfortunately the grass also turns brown and withered. I see people watering their lawns all over the place and I certainly admire such devotion. I am far too lazy, and besides, watering it means I'd just have to cut it sooner. I hate cutting grass.

We certainly could use the rain, though, even if it does mean I have to cut the grass more often. I wouldn't mind about an inch a day, three days a week. A gulley-washer doesn't do much good because the ground doesn't have time to soak it up.

I had gotten in the habit of enjoying a cold one and watching the sunset from my patio with Suze in the evenings, but it's gotten too stinking hot for that, too. The heat of the concrete radiates upward and scalds the backs of my legs and under my chin. I put my hand to it and it's hot as the dickens, and testing reveals it really doesn't cool sufficiently until around midnight at which point the mosquitoes are too bad to enjoy a cold one on the patio anyway.

There's a big beehive in the crook of two limbs of my enormous oak tree in the back yard. Been there since I moved in years ago. This fall, a big chunk of the honeycomb fell out and I retrieved it for a keepsake, a conversation piece, so to speak. Unfortunately, I left it in the shop and noticed the other day that my dinner plate-sized piece of honeycomb had turned into a sticky puddle that smelled faintly like royal jelly. It was quite a mess to clean up and made me hungry for waffles.

The house used to be protected by many shade trees on the sunny side prior to Hurricane Andrew which took 'em all out. I've been investigating fast-growing shade trees for this zone, something on the order of twenty feet per year, but so far have not been able to locate a suitable species. I'm told cypress or red maple would be pretty good, though the maple isn't very hurricane resistant. Good shade trees make a ten degree difference in a house, especially an old one with a metal roof. The now-sunny-side of the house had several cedar trees, two pecans and a couple others I can't remember the species of, might have been chicken trees, but they were big. My grandmother had a clothesline on a post back there, one of those umbrella-style jobs that spun around. There was an old cistern back there too, and though I was forbidden to drink from it, I did steal a taste now and then when nobody was looking. The old brass faucet turned with difficulty but the water was fresh and clean and made me think of gray clouds and pattering drops on tin roofs. I miss tin roofs. My house has a metal roof, which is not the same thing. It's the new roof thing. Broad corrugations and thick. Lasts forever, but I miss tin roofs, with the little wavy corrugations and that dappled-silver kinda galvanized finish to it. Actually the garage and shop still have this kind of roof and it looks much more traditional to me. Those new metal roofs look sorta art-deco. Or maybe neo-art-deco. Who knows?

I used to ride horses in heat like this, but I don't know how I managed. Heck, I'd come home after riding Kate all day, my quarter horse that was exactly the same age as me to the day, and we'd be none the worse for wear. These days, I guess it's age, I leave the house or the office and that hot air hits my face and I think, "Which way to the bush country?"

Back in my younger days, too, I'd fish all day in my little boat in this kind of heat without thinking twice about it. Now I don't even want to think about being on the lake after about ten o'clock because I'm afraid the water will start boiling and I'll be caught in it. I used to hunt quail in the cane fields back then, right where the casino is now, and it didn't bother me, but sometimes my gun would get so hot I'd come home to find the word "Savage Fox" branded in my palm. In reverse, of course. "xoFegavaS." Whatever. Luckily I didn't shoot an Ithaca. "acahtI." Never mind.

I was never much of a duck hunter, because I hate cold worse than heat. I went one time with a pal when we were teenagers. It was something like twenty below zero (at least that's how it felt) and we were in a blind somewhere south of Nowhere, USA and did not see a single duck, not even a sparrow. I'd have shot a sparrow, believe me, with my 16-gauge Savage Fox if it meant I could go home and bathe in scalding-hot water to defrost. After six or eight hours—seemed like six or eight days—we gave up and I never went duck hunting again. Of course, the following weekend my pal told me how he had "mopped up on 'em" on his very next trip.

The old Savage Fox was a great side-by-side double barrel shotgun that I sold when I was in my early twenties and wish I hadn't. Funny about how we regret such things later in life. I still regret getting rid of my comic book collection and my Six Million Dollar Man action figures. I regret getting rid of my first Mustang, but not the subsequent ones.

I notice that since they made us change from the old Freon to the new stuff car air-conditioners really don't work as well. I had a 1976 Caprice Classic that would turn the inside into an arctic tundra. That baby blew at thirty-eight degrees. These new air conditioners with this new refrigerant you're lucky if you get it down to sixty degrees. I'm all for protecting the ozone layer, don't get me wrong, but it seems to me if we can send a guy to the moon, make cell phones the size of Saltine crackers that send e-mail and take pictures and computers faster than the Road Runner, we can make a refrigerant that gets back to thirty-eight degrees. Maybe we need to get the Swiss on that one.

Anyway. Sure is hot, ain't it?

Salad Forks

Emily Post might be the bomb when it comes to etiquette, but some of it makes no sense to me.

What the devil good is a salad fork? It's too small. It's like a baby fork. It's even too small for any baby. Why on earth would you want a short stubby fork with short stubby tines on it to try to get all those leafy vegetables and cucumbers and croutons into your mouth? Wouldn't you want something with long tines that'll really fit a good bite on it? Salad forks are ridiculous and if the state legislature wants to regulate something, it should be salad forks.

How come most refrigerators don't come with those little oval-shaped depressions at the top of the inside of the door to put eggs? Remember those? Instead, you buy an eighteen-count pack of eggs if you're like me and love eggs perhaps more than chocolate even, and when you get down to say, two eggs, you have to store this big dadgum box in the fridge because if you don't sure as shootin' those last two eggs are gonna get smashed and a horrible mess will follow.

Why don't the manufacturers of refrigerators, when they design those little doors for butter, margarine and the like on your main refrigerator door, get together with the manufacturers of butter, margarine and the like to design containers that will actually fit in those so cute little cubby holes with doors?

A personal request: A place to store my fishing worms. Fishing worms store-bought in those little white Styrofoam containers must be kept refrigerated if you want to keep them from one trip to the next, and Suze hates to find those things in the fridge. Fridges should have a special little cubby hole door marked "Fish

Bait" for me to put my packs of fishing worms where they won't turn anyone's stomach.

What's a "crisper?" Are the things you put in there not already crisp? Or can you put, say, bread in there and it comes out crispy? Shouldn't it be a "keep-it-crispy" or a "crispy-keeper" wording on those drawers at the bottom of the fridge?

(Which brings me to the irresistible urge to mention: It is NOT a "hot water heater" people, it's a "water heater." If the water's already hot, you don't need to heat it, do you?)

Explain to me what that button is that says "normal" and "energy saver" and why is it on the inside of the fridge so you have to open the door and waste energy trying to figure out which one you should turn it to?

It doesn't matter, anyway, because if it works like the temperature control in the refrigerator it'll never be right anyway. You put the temperature control on six and your milk is lukewarm. You put it on seven and the top freezes shut. You try to put it right between six and seven and it gets totally confused and the whole contraption shuts down and everything spoils including your pickles, which takes some serious doing.

My grandparents had the first fridge with ice and water dispensers on the outside of the door, and I had my own special glass near the fridge so I could go get cold water and ice if I so desired anytime I wanted. I was never a wasteful lad so I could have as much as I wanted anytime I wanted. My grandmother also had the first microwave oven I ever saw, a Montgomery Ward model that was big as a television and heavy as a load of bricks. The house lights dimmed when she hit the "cook" button and the electrical meter speeds up, but that's okay, it still worked and had plenty of room inside with a heavy, sturdy glass shelf. Most microwave ovens you see today are dinky little things that you have a hard time fitting a cup of coffee into. Hers would knock down jetliners with ray beams if she could have run it with the door open.

It had a slot where you could slide these plastic cards in the front and it would read a recipe from the cards then know what temperature to cook, maybe several ascending or descending temperatures, for how long, and so forth for say a casserole or something. That was kinda cool but I don't know if my grandmother ever used it,.

My grandmother loved gadgets, anything she thought would be "handy." Though she lived more than seventy years of her more than ninety-year life in Louisiana, she often reverted to Texan when she ran across something "handy." You know. Something like a special tool for opening stubborn jars, for example.

"Well, that's right handy," she'd say in a Texas drawl that had withstood the passing of several decades, gallons of bayou water and the best efforts of an Indian reservation to eliminate it. I miss that sound more than you'll ever know.

I found so many of those things in the house: jar openers, knife organizers, thread racks. A favorite of mine was a special multi-level clothes hanger that would hold about eight pairs of pants vertically in the same amount of space horizontally it would take to store one.

But where was I? Oh, yes. Why can't anyone design a good water hose nozzle anymore? I don't think my parents bought more than two water hose nozzles during my entire childhood and that was only because I ran over the first one with the lawnmower. I have probably bought more water hose nozzles since becoming an adult and being responsible for buying such things on my own than they did in their entire lives. Water hose nozzles today are cheap imitations of the water nozzles we used to have and you don't even have time to run over them with a lawnmower before they break. And they break in the oddest ways: You turn the dial to "stream" and you get a three-pronged shoot straight up, straight to the left and one backwards directly into your belly button. If you don't get one of those fancy-dancy selectable nozzles and just settle for your basic water hose nozzle, you squeeze the handle to shoot the water and it comes apart in your hand like a soggy gingersnap. There's nothing more irritating than a water hose nozzle coming apart in your hands. Except maybe salad forks.

Fitting In

With the weather like it's been—miserably hot for a while, then rainy every day—I have had nothing to motivate me and, consequently, spend most of my time sitting around.

I dropped 20 pounds in the month or two that I was building my pirogue, and hoped to keep it off and maybe lose a little more by paddling it around fishing. You know, they make rowing machines for exercise, right?

Well, no, not in hundred degree weather or with hundred percent humidity pouring out of the skies. Pirogues do not float well full of water.

So I'm gaining weight again, a condition I have been battling more and more since I quit smoking FOURTEEN MONTHS AGO! (Thank you, thank you very much!)

The last time I talked about this, I mentioned in this column that it's difficult to be one of only two guys on the full-time staff of the Banner, the other being the publisher who has the authority and rank to stay in his office and avoid all the brouhaha outside involving the large numbers of female employees.

I am not so fortunate. I mentioned several months ago that, while standing at the printer in the advertising room and complaining about growing larger and the ad rep nearby said, "Yeah, join the club."

Therein lies the inherent danger in working with a buncha women who complain to each other all the time about their weight, and are perfectly within their rights to say to each other, "You are starting to look like an offshore platform, girl," without raising ire. As a guy, your rights would appear to be similar, since they included you in "the club" with that statement. But no.

Luckily I'm smarter than to say something back in an example like that, such as, "Yeah, I noticed that we need more thirty-six-inch doors around the place." No, I got more sense than that, *cher.* They may say you're a member of the club, but utter something like that and you find out why women really wear those glue-on, razor-sharp fake fingernails.

So I keep my mouth shut about gaining weight around here and try to eat more healthy at lunch. We all go to lunch together here, too. It's a newspaper thing, been that way at every one I've ever worked for: Newspaper people tend to hang together, because typically, nobody else wants to. But it's impossible to be macho when you're surrounded by four giggling females.

I thought it would be more difficult to diet with a buncha guys, but I think it'd be easier. I figured it might be difficult to not be macho and order a big greasy burger and fries with the guys, opting for a wimpy salad instead. But guys are actually more accepting of such things. Girls, who complain all day about their resemblance to Buicks turn around and go to lunch for—you guessed it—greasy hamburgers and fries. Oh, now and then, sure they put on airs and have a salad, sacrificing their true cravings for the sake of appearances. I know better. I'm one of the girls, you see. An insider, and I tell you, they just do it now and then to say, "I've been eating salads," and not be lying. Challenge them on it, and you learn about those glued-on nails again.

Guys are different. A guy will order a salad and say, "Doc said I gotta watch my cholesterol," when actually he's trying to get back into his summer jeans. Guys will switch to light beer because it's "less filling. I can drink more at the camp." But really he's worried about tipping the boat too far to one side while fishing.

A guy will say he's been "working out" and girls think, "Wow, weightlifting, what a man," but in fact, he's walking the treadmill and dreaming of Miller time. A guy that is truly health-conscious jogs or something, not "works out." "Working out" is just a thinly disguised way of saying, "I'm eating salads."

The girls now...I've never seen such vindictiveness. Let some other woman pass by the table who is just slightly smaller than any of them and has in some way, shape or form given them some reason—any reason—to dislike the aforementioned passerby:

"Well. How do you like that?"

"I know. Isn't she just Miss *Thang?*"

"Sh-ee. She's a 'thang' all right!"

"I know!"

At which point they all fall into a giggling fit like you recall from Joanie's slumber parties on *Happy Days*. It's enough to make a man start eating lunch by himself, you know?

I was sitting with the Banner crew in Polito's Cafe one day and there were a couple guys in another booth from Wildlife and Fisheries. I try to be a Dudeman around law enforcement types, because I really admire and envy what they all do. I'm too dumb, blind and stupid to be a law officer, but I always wished I could have. So I'm trying my best to appear Dudemanly and the girls get this giggling fit thing going, they're all turning red in the face and having a hard time breathing, and I am wondering if the two agents can see that my lip is bleeding from biting it to keep from giggling myself.

So I finally get somewhere with a buncha the guys, and we're talking fishing and hunting and I'm not the least bit worried about anything girly, and I'm feeling like I am a Dudeman after all. Then I realize I'm having jambalaya and gumbo for supper and Mississippi mud pie for desert. And I say the girls don't make sense?

Well, we're all pals and the Banner gang remains the best gang around, bar none. I do my best to fit in, short of gluing on fake fingernails, even in self-defense.

Lunch

Lunch around here is an adventure.

It's kind of a funny thing, I guess, but we all go to lunch together, or at least, most of us. The newsroom and advertising department usually.

After the day's paper is done, when all our work is finished and it's going to press, it's lunchtime. That's not necessarily at 12 noon. That could be at 11:30. It could be at 12:30 or later. We go to lunch when we're finished, not a minute sooner.

Let me mention now that what follows is a generalization, and not necessarily the Gospel according to Stouff, nor is it intended to be reflective of every single individual in our group who may or may not have at one time not, for instance, used a napkin even though I said they did. This is a representative story, a history as recalled by the writer.

So we're finished, and we in the newsroom gather ourselves up and the three of us go stand in the advertising room at which time the Changing of the Guard at Buckingham Palace begins. No, there's no Beefeaters there and no one is forbidden to show reaction, but the point is the same procedure happens every day at the same time, without fail, with little deviation. I'm not going to do attribution of quotes because it's not important:

"So, what's for lunch?"

"What's so-and-so got?"

We look on the menus posted to the door of the advertising room for the daily lunch specials. Whatever is on the menu for Eatery A makes half of us groan and frown, and whatever's on the menu for Eatery B makes the other half of us groan and frown.

"What about so-and-so?" someone suggests.

Two-thirds of us groan, the other third nods vigorously.

"Well, what about so-and-so?" someone else suggests. One-third groans and clutches their stomachs in pain, the other nods vigorously. This is not a democratic system, so we go to the other place.

Here are the only slight variations to the Changing of the Guard: Someone doesn't have enough money this week to afford Eatery C; someone is observing Lent; someone is dieting; someone is sick of pasta; someone thought the service last time was pathetic; someone thinks they charge too much; someone wants dessert and Eatery C doesn't do dessert; someone hates Chinese; someone hates seafood, and the big winner of all, someone (or a couple of them) can't smoke there.

Then it's off to wherever the majority didn't want to go. When there were just three of us going to lunch I drove in my truck, but now there are four and most times five, and so someone else with an SUV must drive. We have never offered to chip in for gas. I don't know why. Perhaps we newspaper people are just cynical that way, or we're all just too self-absorbed with our own problems. Regardless, the person who drives never complains, so there's no sense in worrying about it, we reason. Squeaky wheel gets the grease and all that.

We get to lunch at last. We have been to any of these places a million times. How many places are there to eat in Franklin if you don't do fast food? Not many. We've been to them over and over. And over again. So what do we do when we sit down at the table?

We read the menu.

Nope, nothing new has appeared magically since we were there three days ago. Three days later, we'll read the menu again. Makes little sense, does it? If you asked me right now what Eatery D has in seafood selection, I could probably recite the whole thing by heart. But when we sit down, we look at the menu.

The waitresses know us pretty good. They come up and say, "Tea, tea, Diet Coke, root beer," and don't even wait for us to agree or disagree and if one of the "tea" persons is in the mood for, say Sprite instead, they have to yell and make a scene to get the attention of the rapidly retreating waitress.

God forbid if something is out of place or awry. If we can't get our usual table we'll stand there and half of us pouts to the hostesses and the other half glowers and stares at whoever is at our table until they hurriedly finish their meals, slam back their drinks and make a hasty retreat. It's our table, bought and paid for, ya folla?

If someone in the group wants a certain item off the menu and the waitress reluctantly—because she knows us, you see—tells us they are temporarily out of it, you'd swear a capital offense was just committed.

We are set in our ways, we newspaper people, and don't dare rock our boat.

The main course is over, then three of us order coffee while the rest smoke (back in the day when you could) Unless we went to a no-smoking eatery. Now and then we do that, and the smokers will graciously allow us to enjoy a couple cups of coffee. Sometimes we get up and drive to some place that has coffee and allows smoking. We are equal-opportunity diners, you see, but have little tolerance for abdication of our civil rights as smokers and coffee drinkers.

We may also debate dessert. This is often the most tiring part of the whole ordeal. Some of us will consider dessert. Others will complain about our weight and refuse to consider it. Some will complain about our weight, consider it, and dismiss it. Some of us will care not a rip for our weight and order two slices of cheesecake. (That would be me.)

Finally we get our tickets and we are all silent for a moment while we make sure they got it right. If they did, we all march up and pay, leaving tips. If they did not, we make them do it over. If everything's correct but the ticket is far heftier than we thought it would be, we groan and complain and wish we hadn't ordered dessert. (That would be me.)

Then we all pile into the SUV and go back to work to groan and complain all afternoon about being too full. (That would be me again, but sometimes I have company, and we sound like a symphony of seals.)

This does not include Fridays. Fridays only one person from each department has to work in the afternoon, the rest of us can stay at the eatery as long as we like, and since we just got paid, we can eat as much as we want, too. Those are the days some of us have nice entrees that we shouldn't just because we're feeling rich. By Wednesday of the following week we'll be standing around the advertising room discussing where we'll go for lunch, and the words "broke" and "cheap" will come from that person's mouth, guaranteed.

Inquiries

Friend of mine was seeing the doctor this week and before she was allowed in, she was handed five pages of questions to fill out.

Of course, most of these were your basic medical questions, but in there were some that were rather odd.

Do you use your seat belt?

Okay. Let's think about this for a moment. Sure, it's state law that you use your seat belt. Sure, it may or may not save your life in an accident or might prevent some serious level of bodily injury. But I am left to wonder why this needed to show up on a questionnaire before you see a doctor? Perhaps they're wondering if you'll freak out when they strap you down to the table? Or if you don't answer "yes" they may demand payment in advance?

It brings up all kinds of weird scenarios for warped minds such as mine. First, I wonder if the state is spying on us, somehow forcing or bribing physicians to conduct these surveys, carefully hidden inside a basic medical questionnaire. Perhaps they are simply looking for statistics, but there's maybe a more nefarious reason: Maybe, once they have your name and then can cross-reference with your license plate number they put out an APB on your car and, soon as a policeman sees you, he pulls you over because you answered "NO" on the seat belt question on the doctor's question-naire when you were going see the sawbones to get your Nexium refilled.

See, you think I'm being silly, but consider this: The next question, oddly enough, was: *Do you wear a bike helmet?*

Well, that just proves it, doesn't it? Obviously, bike helmets are not mandated by law. If it had said motorcycle helmet then you'd know that it's a clever ploy to get you to incriminate yourself legally. But you may drive a car with a seat belt and ride a bike without a helmet. Or you might not ride a bike at all, so obviously you wouldn't wear a helmet. However, if you answer "YES" to the seat belt question and "NO" to the bike helmet questions, you'll have put yourself under suspicion of fibbing because this was a "check the box" thing, yes or no being your only options and you can't explain yourself.

Clear as mud, ain't it?

It gets better. Next question on the form:

Do you own a handgun, and if so, is it locked?

Now, call me a conspiracy theorist, reprobate, ornery old curmudgeon, but just what the devil does the doctor need to know that for when I'm going in for a case of the sniffles? Or do they suspect perhaps I got that ingrown toenail by accidentally shooting myself in the foot?

But if you fill it all out, now at the very least the doctor and staff know these things about you, and at the very worst the everyone from the state police to the Secret Service know, too.

It's a pity these were only check box questions with no room to elaborate, because I probably would have to answer this way:

Do you use a seat belt?

Check "Yes." Elaborate: What, you think I'm going to say "no?" So you can track me down like a wounded animal, send out the posse and the bloodhounds? Ha! Catch me! Catch me if you can, ya filthy revuh-noors!

Do you use a bike helmet?

Check "Yes." Elaborate: I do not ride a bike, but I wear a bike helmet when fly fishing, because I am not very good at casting and it keeps me from hooking myself in my scalp on my back cast. I also find it useful for walking through bird sanctuaries, golf courses, domestic disputes and, lined with aluminum foil inside, keeping those gum'mit brain rays from brainwashing me into swimming to Cuba to assassinate Castro.

Do you own a handgun and is it locked?

Check: "Yes" "Yes" "Yes" and "Yes" and "No" "No" "No" and "No" because I have four of them and none of them are locked. Elaborate: Now, see, you've touched on a sensitive subject here, Mr. Questionnaire Writer Secretly Working For the OSI, CIA, FBI, NSA or Whatever Gum'mit Agency It Is This Week. First of all, I am not a handgun hunter, I seldom if ever target practice and I do not rob liquor stores. I keep handguns around the house for personal defense, and some of them are just old family heirlooms, though functional ones. So in answer to the questions, I must say I cannot ever envision myself acting out the following scenario:

A burglar is in the house. I wake up and hear him rummaging through my fly rods in search of the bamboo one Harry Boyd made. I call the police but he has cut the phone line, which in my case is actually the cable television line, because I have a cable phone, which also feeds the Internet, so I can't even send out an email for help.

I get my 9mm Ruger from it's hiding place but he hears me and comes at me with a fly rod tube to bludgeon me in the head since I don't wear my bike helmet when I'm sleeping (unless it's the aluminum foil lined one and the gum'mit brainwashing waves are particularly powerful that night.) So I yell:

"Wait, Mr. Bamboo Fly Rod Burglar! I have to unlock my gun so I can defend myself!"

Nope, ain't gonna happen. Now, if the question had been:

Do you own a handgun? Are there small children in the house who may not respect or understand the danger of a handgun? Is the handgun accessible to aforementioned small children? If so, is the handgun locked? Well, that'd be a different story, but the question wasn't worded as such. Just gum'mit nose-poking, that's all it is.

Or perhaps there's just a simpler reason for it, like if you show up at the emergency room having fallen off your bicycle and cracked your skull, are driving yourself to the hospital without your seat belt on and, in the process of taking your medical insurance papers out of the glove compartment accidentally shoot yourself in the knee.

Yeah, that must be it. Silly me. Sorry for making such a big deal about it.

130

Rain fell all day Saturday. I had made a vow to myself that I would not leave the house until I had written fifty pages. It was nearly noon, and the last page number was still 128. It had been 128 since I woke up and sat down with a cup of steaming coffee. It had been 128 for a month, and showed no inclination of budging.

"When you get aggravated with it, put it down," my father told me about working with wood, drawing, trying to fix something. "It'll just get worse if you don't."

Yes, that's easy to say, but I'm not getting any younger. If I walk away from something enough times, I won't ever walk back. I know myself that well, at least. I was once able to write fiction easily, but never with as much difficulty as now. Once, when I was a much younger man without so many creases in my soul and puncture wounds in my spirit, I wrote an entire short novel at white-hot pace in a weekend. *Jake Chance and the Crescent City Blues* it was called, a detective story of the Phillip Marlowe, Sam Spade variety set in New Orleans but with a rather ominous twist. Lost the only copy I had of it in Hurricane Andrew. Still, time was when I could pound out three dozen pages without a bathroom break. Now I struggle for ten pages, twenty pages being nothing short of miraculous.

Not getting any younger. Been banging out pages since I was...I don't know. Ten years old? Something like that. But on a rainy Saturday in August, they're not so easy anymore.

There's a Cary Grant marathon on Turner Classic Movies and I want to watch it instead of write. *Arsenic and Old Lace* is on, one of my favorite movies of all time. Cracks me up every time. But I switch off the television with regret and stare at page 128, the transitory paragraph. The dangling participle. The hanging indent. The edge of a precipice of white and the only signpost is a blinking cursor. I miss typewriters sometimes. There is nothing quite as satisfying as the *DING!* of getting near the end of the margin, slamming the carriage back with a mighty *WHACK!* and hammering on. Electric typewriters were okay, but manual typewriters were like martial arts training. You could, if you typed on a 1923 Underwood long enough, kill a moose with your pinky.

Frustrated, I turn off the air conditioner and throw open the doors and windows, letting the fresh scent of the rain permeate the house, and me. Hoping it will inspire me. It's a darn good story. Sometimes I wish I could feel it was junk and discard it, quit worrying over it. But it's good. Maybe too good. Maybe I'm scared I'm going to ruin it, that page 129 or 144 or 287 will destroy all the good work I've done up through page 128. It's not easy.

"You got to walk away from it," I hear dad telling me. "Put it down for awhile."

So I go outside and play with Daisy. We walk down by the bayou and the drizzle taps on my hat, wets my shoulders. Bayou Teche is brown but green duckweed floats everywhere. The dog takes a swim, lapping up water and, I'm sure, tiny green duckweeds as she goes. We spend half an hour sitting on the dock as the drizzle gets me soaked, but I head back to the house when the lightning starts again. I shower, but somehow I feel less clean than I did when I was rain-soaked. Chlorinated and chemically treated tap water can't compare with rain, and I wish I had just toweled dry and changed clothes. The rain is pouring now, God beating his wife we used to say when we were kids or, at a more genteel moment when we thought we might get a switch across the behind for the former expression, the Old Man is snoring.

It's that I'm trying to write four, maybe five stories all at once. That's what's eating me up. It's a novel, but the novel is the story of three boyhood friends, recalled from their youth through their old age, and their lives are told through stories within the novel, flashbacks leading to the conflict that the novel centers around. Four different plots, maybe five, all in one book. I'm stuck at the third. Or is it the fourth? I don't know. Rain is making me sleepy, forgetful, drowsy.

I decide to edit. I spend a few hours reading, cutting here, adding there, writing a few expansive paragraphs, adding some color, defining a character or a forest or a house. I look again. 130 pages. I feel depressed. I've added two pages, made a better story for it, I can only hope, but I'm still mired in the mud, stuck as helplessly as before.

Will these stories live on after me? Not if I don't get them down. The real ones, the imagined ones, and all the in-between ones. Harry Middleton was once asked how much of his books really happened, and Harry replied, "More than I had hoped."

More than I had hoped. Because all of it's getting blurry. So much of what's really happened finds its way into what's supposed to be imagined. So much the other way, too. It's getting harder to distinguish the two because a man tells his stories so many times he becomes them. Is it all about immortality? Yes, I guess it is. Few things sadden me more than believing they won't be gotten down. Won't be there for someone to find some decades hence. Just as a month or two ago I found Havilah Babcock's *My Health is Better in November*, first published in 1947. Just as I stumbled across W.D. Wetherell's *North of Now* which, while only a decade old, was printed small and obscure and hidden like treasures should be otherwise they become commodities, goods, products.

To hear my father tell it, every fish was a keeper in his day, every cast perfect, every day sunny within bluebird skies. He caught two bass on one lure, a floating Rapala. He caught another on his back-cast with his old fiberglass fly rod. The bass leaped out of the water to snatch the fly out of the air. A tarpon jumped over the bow of his pirogue as he was paddling around the west side of Little Pass, before the abomination of the levee was built, and he caught dog sharks in Lake Fausse Point on earthworms and spin tackle. My grandfather climbed the mast of one of Jean Lafitte's pirate ships when he was only ten years old, because all that was sticking out of the mud where it had sunk was eight or so feet of the mast. He found treasure in Peach Coulee once, but his fellow treasure-hunter cussed and it vanished right under their noses. My grandmother could understand a little mottled-brown bird named kite; and Aunt Mary's wolf came and got Aunt Mary's spirit to bring it to her ancestors late one night. Perhaps I saw thunderbirds in a lightning storm I braved to fish a little pond nobody knew about a couple years ago, or perhaps it's just a story in a short fiction collection I'm finishing up. Perhaps I never did go find another pond I saw on an old map deep in the swamp, fished it under more dark, threatening skies without getting a single bite, but when I went back to find it again that fall, it was gone. Gone, as if it never existed. Those tales become immortal if they are told for all to hear.

I sit with the computer in my lap and the cursor blinks: 130.

It's a hard thing to come by, immortality. But I plan to live forever.

Retreads

Like most rational people, there's few things I find more terrifying than visiting the dentist.

Dear Dentists: Please don't take this personally. It is a noble and heroic thing you do, taking on a job that is thankless, feared by most of the citizenry and God knows what kind of messes you see down most those mugs. However, this is a tongue-in-cheek column (Get it? Tongue in cheek? Ha!) and merely for entertainment value.

So I show up for an appointment I have waited months for. That's how it is if you only go when something is bothering you so badly you have no other choice.

Anyway, I'm filling out the questionnaire they give you now any time you see a doctor, dentist, lawyer, social worker or auto mechanic. One of the questions was:

"Are you currently using alcohol or drugs?"

Now that's about the silliest way to phrase a question as I've ever heard. Are you currently using alcohol, which is legal, versus drugs, which one would assume they don't mean the prescription kind, which are not legal. How do you answer that? Yeah, I enjoy a cold one on a regular basis. Not too regular, you understand, but regular enough that I'm no stranger to the hops. But I do not now and never have used drugs other than for the occasional headache or cold.

So I check the box that says "Yes." There is no option for clarification. There is no box to check saying "Yes, I use alcohol but not drugs." There also is no box to check, "Yes, I use drugs, but not alcohol." There is also no place to put in your address so they can deliver the arrest warrant if you answer that one in the affirmative. So I am stuck now being either labeled a pothead, crackhead, meth-fiend, boozer, gin-rummy or wino.

Next question on the sheet is, oddly enough:

"If so, do you wish to stop?"

Now what the devil kind of question is that? There's only check boxes again, "yes" or "no." So having already committed myself to a sea of uncertainty over what vices and habits I already have, their legality and frequency, I now must answer an ambiguous question regarding whether or not I would like to turn myself in to the police or join AA.

I turned to the receptionist at the office and said, "These are trick questions, aren't they?"

She nodded cheerfully and said, "Yep! Sure are!"

All suspicions confirmed, I continued the questionnaire, confirming with "no" check boxes that I do not, in fact, have hepatitis, shingles, arthritis, am not pregnant, do not have tuberculosis, bubonic plague, scurvy, curvature of the spine, skull fracture but do have flat feet.

Finally there's a question that I can answer enthusiastically:

"Is there any reason why you don't want to see the dentist" and in the blank space provided for my answer I write a single word in all capital letters:

TERROR

That clear enough? Having completed the survey, I pass the clipboard back to the receptionist and go sit down in the waiting area again to chew my nails, when finally they call me in. I follow the nurse to the room where they do the dentistry, and she sits me in a dentist's chair which is facing the wall, my back to the door. I am wondering if there's any reason for this: Is it so patients can't jump up and run? Is it so that if they try to jump up and run they'll crash into the wall and knock themselves out cold, thus saving on anesthesia costs?

I tell the kind lady about my bad tooth. Bottom left, second from last. I chipped it eating a pork cracklin' months ago, and the chip was getting bigger, so I figured if I intended to keep eating steak I'd have to get it tended to. Then the dentist came in, and noted that I had filled out a very honest questionnaire.

"Not to give my life story, doc," I said, "but I had four surgeries on my eyes before I was two years old and two on my ears before I was four years old, and when I was six I fell on a piece of tin in the back yard and you can still see the scar on my forearm, see, right there, yep, that's where I did it, no it doesn't hurt anymore but when I was ten my Shetland pony Nancy kicked me in the mouth and that's why my two front teeth are kinda crooked, and when I was twenty I fell in my dad's boat and broke a couple ribs and when I was twenty-three I had the croup really bad and I coughed so hard I broke the ribs again and then when I was thirty I stubbed my toe on the coffee table and took the nail off and when I was thirty-three I stepped on a wasp in the bathroom and when I was thirty-eight I smashed my thumb with a hammer and when I was forty I quit smoking and now I've got this bad tooth so you can see that I've had a very traumatic life when it comes to dealing with injuries and the medical profession."

So he gets to looking around in there, goes, "Oh, yeah," which I'm not sure what that means and says he's going to use his pick to see if there's any decay. I am saying, "No, you're not," and he's saying he has to, so I lean back, white-knuckled and trying not to breathe. He started picking around in there and you know what? There's no decay!

"Here's the good news," the doc says. "I think we can bond something to that little chip."

Now, you have to realize, I'm not in my right mind. Not that I'm ever in my right mind, but I am particularly not at this point. So I'm wondering: What? What's he going to bond to the little chip? A Volkswagen bumper? A cruise ship anchor?

"We'll just brush something on it first, and it smells really strong, then put something else on it and kinda shape it in place," he said and I'm starting to like this guy, especially when he says the magic words:

"You won't feel a thing."

Well, that was okay by me! Just as I was starting to feel better, at ease relaxed and had said, "Anything you say, doc," both he and the assistant donned clear plastic face shields.

"OSHA makes us," they said. "It's no big deal."

So sure enough, after adequate cleaning, drying and brushing then shaping and molding with the drill grinder thingy (that part made me a little nervous.) The brushing stuff reminded me of the epoxy I use for boat building, and I took a kind of smug satisfaction in that. I mentioned to the doc that I'd like to kinda get the rest of the ol' chompers checked out so that I could keep 'em around as long as possible and there he comes with that dadgum pick again, and taps and scrapes on every one of them while I'm lying there white-knuckled again, but nope, nothing hurt.

So I got a retread on the second to last bottom right molar in my mouth now, and we're hoping it lasts so we don't have to resort to drills, caps and that most horrid of words one hears in a dentist's office, "Spit!"

I shook the doc's hand and thanked him for not being an Inquisitor. I promised to brush on schedule, floss, cut down on the sweets and gargle with blue Listerine.

Specs

You must understand that, to begin with, I came into this world kinda messed up.

After multiple surgeries on my ears and eyes before I was two years old and corrective braces on my legs, I ended up fairly okay, though I'm still missing a vertebrae in my back for some odd reason. Doesn't bother me much, but when it flares up, boy, howdy!

The other major thing is my eyes. I have lots of problems with the ol' orbs.

Glasses are second nature to me. There are pictures of me in photo albums that I have turned over to Brinks for safekeeping. In them I am two or three, with massive horn-rimmed glasses, generally cheesing out for my grandmother's camera. I sometimes think that my eyes might be slightly better today if it weren't for all those old Polaroid flash bulbs going off in my face in my formative years, but as the only grandchild, it was my lot in life. If you look very closely into my eyes you'll see that though they're mostly brown, there's a very small speck of iridescent blue, and you'll realize after some thought that it's the exact color of an old-fashioned flash bulb, permanently imprinted on the retina like a tattoo.

Anyway, I made a recent visit to see the eye doc. I dread such visits because I know the doc is going to tell me I need a new prescription because my vision has changed again, always for the worse.

I tried to tell people that I needed to see an orthopedic doctor, a true sawbones, because it is obvious my problem was in my arms, not my eyes. That's because my arms had obviously shrunk and were shorter than they used to be. I knew this, you see, because I can no longer stretch them far enough to read a book.

But no, I was off to see the eye doc. First of all I had to take a color test and when I did, the young lady giving me the test looked very quizzical about the results. When someone giving you a medical test of any kind looks quizzical, you gotta feel a little uneasy.

"What ?" I asked. "That bad?"

"No," she said. "It's just that...last time you were here you were color blind. Now you're not."

"Hmm," I said. "Perhaps I've been chewing on my ink pens too much?"

"That's impossible," she said.

"No it isn't, I chew on my ink pens all the time," I reply, indignant.

"I mean, it's impossible to be color blind and recover," she explained.

"Oh," I said. "Well, that's okay. It's just how I am. I used to not be Indian, now I am. Go figure."

Then it was on to see the doc, who put me through the routine of reading the rows of type on the wall, then the various bars on the wall, etc. After all was said and done came the dreaded words.

"Bifocals," the doc told me.

He might as well have said:

"No more beer."

"Quit fishing."

"Transmission replacement."

"Forest fire."

"Earthquake."

"Asteroid impact."

Or any other such thing and it would have had the same effect on me. I pleaded, I begged, I threatened, but nothing worked. It was bifocals or nothing.

So then I'm off to see the optician, who is showing me wall after wall of frames. The kid who started out in horn-rimmed glasses and looked like a madcap Elton John in his early career, today hates the new trend of these tiny frames. You know, the little sliver of a lens, about half an inch wide. I can't see through that, and my eyes are not rectangular, they're round. I don't want Grandpa's old wire-rimmed glasses, but I want something with a little substance and some shape. Some of the frames were frameless. They were lenses with the arms bolted into them and a nose piece.

I finally settled on a pair I hated a little less than any of the others and ordered the lineless, graduated-type of bifocals. I then went away to grumble and fuss for a week and a half until my new specs arrived.

People are telling me all kinds of things in the meantime:

"My wife got bifocals. She was walking like she was on the moon for a week."

"Bifocals? Don't drive anymore, you'll run off the road."

"Oh, it'll be fine. Just don't try to pour coffee in a cup."

And so on and so forth. Finally my new specs arrived and, lo! They weren't so bad, actually. I got home that evening, having driven all the way without a single multi-car pileup, sat on my patio with a Harry Middleton book and after about half an hour of reading I got up and called my ophthalmologist and congratulated him on being such a fine orthopedist.

It was particularly nice when I was on vacation fishing with my cousins. If I cast into a tree or whopped a No. 6 Accardo Spook into the side of one of their heads, I could just say, "Bifocals, still getting used to them, sorry."

But a week or so into things, I started getting headaches pretty bad, and my left eye hurt like the dickens. Now, my left eye is essentially on disability, has been for years. It just doesn't get a check from the government. I can see shapes and colors, but not much else. It is, however, particular about what's known as the "focal center" of an eyeglass lens. Like a good citizen it tries to work, and even though it can't, it likes to put on good airs, so it likes the focal center of the lens to be a certain way. If it isn't, it gets persnickety. It took some dabbling to get this right, and as of yesterday I got my new lenses installed in my too-small and too-trendy frames. So far, so good!

So here I am, the bifocal-wearer at last. I am confident there are worse things in life, such as being kissed by a yak. I am grateful that the science of eye doctorin' has advanced so much. As an Indian in the old days, I would not likely have survived, or at best, been the subject of considerable ridicule for never being able to hit the broad side of a palmetto hut with my spear or bow and arrow.

42, and Counting

Having turned a year older yesterday, I am torn between wishing I was young and hale again, and desiring to become a crusty old curmudgeon.

I mean, forty-two is like some kind of netherworld between age brackets. You ain't old, you ain't young. You're old enough to know better, but too wet behind the ears still to be smart. Know what I mean?

I look forward to being an Official Old Grit. You know the person I'm talking about. Every wedding or family reunion has one. There's the Official Old Grit, or as is known in more genteel circles, the Official Old Character. My father was the last Official Old Grit in the family. He would sit at a central place in the room, just conspicuous enough to be noticed but not so obvious as to appear brazen. In this position he would draw eager ears for various stories about Chitimacha, fishing, woodwork, Texas or whatever subject was at hand, and people would in turn fetch him punch and cake. My father made quite a career out of being an Official Old Character at these types of functions, but was never greedy about sharing the limelight. If another Old Grit or Old Character ambled by, he'd gladly share the position, though his Official status remained unchallenged.

The older I get, the more I enjoy being around people I like and the less use I have for people I don't like or, at best, don't find interesting. While I was a fairly amiable fellow at thirty, I find myself paring down my group of close friends and closing the membership rolls unless an applicant is highly recommended by an existing member and comes with a lengthy resume of references. At fifty-five, I'll probably have half a dozen or so close friends and refuse to speak to anyone else except my therapist.

This is because my ability to make small talk has diminished with age. While I used to be fairly adept at passing the time of day with just about anyone I ran into, I just look at idle chatter now as taking away precious fishing time.

But about the little bracket of mine. I'm middle-aged. Middle-income. Middle-America. My middle's the only thing heading toward prosperous. My favorite author is Harry *Middle*ton. If I lived in the Midwest, I'd probably go crazy with some middling psychosis or another.

The older I get, the more I enjoy peace and quiet and the less I get of it. I regret my early years when I had hundred-watt stereos in my Mustangs, and I apologize right here to anyone that I bothered. Nowadays, when I'm sitting in my chair at home trying to write or work on a project or even just relax, a booming stereo or barking dog or passing helicopter or whatever annoys the heck out of me. I've said it before, there'll be no phones in my life at some point. That's guaranteed.

I think that one of the compensations for growing old is the right to be an old fuddy. I mean, if we have to put up with all the failing body parts, the ailments, the graying or lost hair, all that nonsense, we should have some benefits in the deal, right? One of these is the right to be cranky, tell off-color jokes at inopportune times, speak loudly and tell everyone you meet what's wrong with them. Gosh, I just can't wait!

These days I listen to people talk about their vacations to Disney or L.A., or some such, and all I can think of is how, when I take a vacation, I want to be as far away from anyone else as I can get, except the person I'm vacationing with. I want the company of wild water, wild trout, wild places and, best of all, no dadgum end table for a telephone, no hooks to hang a clock and no roads.

Gosh, I just can't wait.

Run Down

I feel run down. I don't mean by a truck or anything. Well, it sorta feels like a truck ran me down, but not literally.

You ever get that way? I woke up this morning after what I think was a good night's sleep except for a coupla weird dreams wherein gnomish creatures had invaded my house and left crayon messages all over walls, furniture and my books reading, "DOWN WITH TALL PEOPLE" and one even said "WE'LL NEVER STOOP TO YOUR LEVEL!" I have no idea subconsciously what all that was about, but I fear they're living under the sofa and Patches is bringing them food and newspapers.

Anyway, when the clock went off I was so tired I just lay there staring at the ceiling, thinking, "These covers are so heavy. I mean, it's like, a sheet and a comforter! I don't think I can lift them to get out of bed."

I tried experimentally and, sure enough, I could lift them but after flinging them off me I had to lay there for a few minutes more to recuperate, trying to figure out why I was so run down, and in the end blaming the gnomes. Or Patches. You know, in the old days they believed cats could inhale the life out of a baby's body if it got into a crib. Maybe Patches has been draining me of my spirit essence at night.

About that time she leapt up into the bed with me and nuzzled my arm for a petting, for which I didn't have the energy so she bit my index finger, which reminded me that Patches is too smart to take the life outta me. There'd be nobody there to torment if she did.

Finally I made it up and fixed coffee, though I rinsed the pot for a long, long time because I didn't feel like picking it up out of the sink. Off to the shower and it was quite burdensome to lift my feet over the edge of the tub. By the time I got back to the freshly brewed coffee, I got transfixed looking out the kitchen window at the side of my garage, and almost forgot to pour myself a cup and head for my chair in the living room.

So while I'm sitting there drinking my coffee and watching

Buffy the Vampire Slayer (What? You got a problem with Buffy?) I'm wondering absently if gnomes really do wear those long pointed hats. I like Buffy. Only on television can you find a high-school girl who is, in fact, a vampire killer, so she sneaks out of her room at night, spends the dark hours tracking down and killing vampires and all manner of other nefarious beasts...and when her mother catches her sneaking back into her room in the morning, she gets grounded for a month. I love it.

But it's all I can do to keep my eyes open. I'm so run down I feel like, I don't know...badly-set Jell-O. A souffle that fell. Over-cooked spaghetti. I drain the last of my coffee and don't feel like getting another cup.

I look at the cat lounging in my lap.

"If you were worth a plug nickel," I tell her, "you'd go get me another cup of coffee." I offer her the cup and she sniffs the handle then proceeds to ignore it.

Have you ever noticed when a cat ignores something, it ceases to exist? I mean, a cat could ignore a thousand pound grizzly tearing up a room. She'd just sit there and yawn, blinking half-closed eyelids. I swear, if you put a cat in charge of the national deficit, she could ignore it into a balanced budget in no time flat.

"The dog would go get me more coffee," I complain to her half-blinking calico face.

She opens one eye at me and then closes it again. I know what she just did. She just snapped at me. By opening that one eye and closing it again she just said, "Then get the dog to do it, fat boy, I just got comfortable." I hate it when she snaps at me.

So I get up to get more coffee, thereby disturbing her comfortable spot anyway. When I get back, she's in my chair. We go through this every single time I get up from my chair. By the time I get back, she's curled up in it and looking at me like, "Hey, use it or lose it, dough boy."

I'm too tired and run down to fight with her so I sit on the sofa to watch the end of *Buffy*. Patches can't take this, being unchallenged and ignored, so she comes over to my lap on the sofa, and I comment, "A cat with as many psychological hangups as you have could do well with the mental regiment of fetching me coffee," but she just blinks, turns around three times to the right, and settles in to rest from such a rough morning.

Just then there's a commercial on television where the announcer shouts: "Feeling tired? Run down? You aren't getting the right vitamins! That's right, you need Vitamins B, D, E, A, Z, T, S, and W along with generous doses of iron, calcium, lithium, uranium and plutonium for a well-rounded daily intake! And if you order RIGHT NOW, we'll send you not one, but FOUR bottles of Mega-Turbo-Life-Speed-Life for $19.95! That's right, and for acting in the next hour, we'll throw in a 100-tablet sample of our new product, the electric letter opener absolutely FREE!"

I'd like to turn around and go back to bed, call in sick, but I think about trying to get back under those enormously heavy covers and head off to work instead.

I don't know why I'm so run down today, but I have no energy whatsoever. It's the dadgum gnomes, I bet. The little buggers are running me ragged at night with their sign-making and political protesting. I bet in my sleep I'm trying to get all the red crayon off the sheet rock and the sofa, trying to erase it out of my copy of *Lord of the Rings*. No wonder I'm so tired. Getting crayon off is hard work.

Brr!

What's there to like about winter? I mean, sure, in Minnesota, you at least have the benefit of snow to frolic in, if you like that sort of thing. In Michigan you can marvel at the beautiful icicles. In Connecticut, you can ice skate.

In Louisiana, you can shiver and look out at a brown world.

There's no such thing as a white Christmas in Louisiana, even year-before-last when it snowed a quarter inch. Within two hours, the snow was brown.

It's all brown. The trees are brown, the ground is brown and, worst of all, the speeding transit of cane trucks and tractors either throw enough dust if it's dry or mud if it's wet to turn everything else brown from top to bottom.

Car wash owners must consider this a lean time of year, because most of us don't even bother to wash our vehicles until grinding is over. Notice I said "car wash" because who's going to wash a car by hand with temperatures in the thirties? Not I.

About that cold, though. You gotta wonder about those first European settlers to this alleged "new world." I mean, you can forgive the Indians, because we mostly came across the frozen land bridge at Beringia, chasing mastodons, from Siberia, so cold was old hat to us.

But here come the first Europeans who come in via the Caribbean, and enter this continent via Florida, Louisiana and Mexico. Slowly they began working their way north, and some began coming in at New England.

I gotta wonder how a buncha Puritans who arrived from England with little more than their buckles and top hats didn't get a taste of that first New England winter and high tail it back to King George. What, you think London was cold? Try camping on a hillside in Massachusetts starving to death while the indigenous people are eyeing your pots, pans and blunderbuss, not to be confused with a cummerbund, which does not shoot very far.

That's fine and dandy, New England can have some bad winters of course, but when the first settlers hit Minnesota in winter, and didn't promptly say, "Forget this nonsense," and catch the first frigate back to Yorkshire...well, there just wasn't a lot of good sense at work there.

All of which proves that the Cajun people were some of the smartest that ever lived in North America. Why? Because they left Nova Scotia, average mean temperature minus one hundred degrees, and didn't stop until they hit the Gulf of Mexico and warm weather. One wonders if the Acadians had veered slightly farther east on their long exodus, Miami might be named Abbeville today.

So when it gets this cold, I have to turn the water off at home, because after nine years of living there, I still haven't insulated the pipes. Which means that first thing when I wake up, before I can make coffee or take a shower, I have to put on shoes and a coat and go outside to turn the water back on. There's a few things in the world more miserable, but not many.

I also put Daisy in the workshop at night when it's freezing overnight. When I got up this morning to go to work I opened the door and said, "Come on, dearie, back to the yard."

She thumped her tail and looked up at me with those big brown eyes as if to say, "Are you kidding?"

"Come on, come on, I'm gonna be late," I say.

She gets up, walks right next to me and sits down, looking mournfully out the door. She shivers with all the drama of a 1940s character actor.

"Your ancestors are from Labrador," I say. "Average mean temperature minus two hundred degrees!"

She gives me a dismissing look, turns around and goes back to her blanket. "No, fat boy," that look seems to says, "I'm from south Louisiana and I ain't no fool."

Well, the dog's smarter than us, anyway, because we merrily throw ourselves into the cold to go to work and be miserable all day. Go figure. For this the Pilgrims almost starved to death during the winter while the Indians played stick ball in the snow and cuddled under bear skins. I really believe all the Indian wars that followed were a result of that first winter in New England: The settlers were so mad and their brains frost bitten they went postal on the indigenous people, a remarkable feat since the postal service would not be founded for another couple hundred years.

Someone told me just yesterday, "Man, they're killing the sac-au-lait at (location withheld to protect the sac-au-lait)!"

I tried to be manly and say, "Well, heck, pardner, I guess I'll just hafta load up my little bateau and head on out there Saturday morning and catch me a mess 'o them-there fishies," but in truth, I was thinking, "Forget that," and wondering if I liquidated all my assets if I could afford a shotgun house in the Keys. A quick calculation revealed I'd be hard-pressed to afford the front door, and that's throwing in a loan from the mob.

It's another hard freeze tonight, so I reckon we'll be suffering through it all again, until Monday, anyway, forecast high temperature of seventy-five degrees, low of sixty-one that night. Short pants and shirt sleeves weather.

Did I mention, I hate winter?

Restlessness

It occurs to me that I'm not thinking straight—or perhaps I'm thinking more clearly. I don't know. But I think the weather has something to do with it.

The threat of rain was imminent, but never really materialized. The wind was blowing like a banshee. It was, in short, the kind of weather that was bad for trying to do anything I enjoyed.

Too windy to fly fish, even if there had been any fish to fish for. The threat of rain didn't help, either. I usually spend sunsets at the bayou with Daisy and a cold one, it's gotten to be almost habitual with me. I love to end the day that way, over the water on the dock, watching the sunset upstream. Even if the clouds are thick, the orange glow is comforting somehow.

But Saturday and Sunday, the dog and I made three trips a day to the bayou, out of pure frustration. Sure, there were some things I could have been doing inside, but dang it, I was tired of being inside. I woke up Saturday morning, wrote a bit on my novel, but when I realized my eyes were starting to bulge, my breathing was growing more rapid and my typing was worse than normal, it was clear that I needed to be outside in the worst kind of way.

All throughout the weekend, anytime the sun peeked through the gray overcast over my neighbor's house and mine, if you had been watching, you'd have seen both our back doors fly open and two men rush outside to do...anything. Anything, something, anything at all just to get out of the dadgum house.

In fact, after my second trip to the bayou with the dog, I went and pulled the pirogue I built last fall out from under the house. It was dusty and full of rodent special deliveries, so I dragged it to the back yard where the water hose is and commenced to clean it out.

My neighbor saw this, from his tractor, and rushed over to commiserate.

"You look frustrated as I am," he said.

I threw the hose down on the ground and launched into a lengthy tirade: "Frustrated ain't the danged word for it you can't do nothing around here without the wind knocking you down or the rain about to fall on your head the dang ol' bayou side is so muddy I can't even put a chair to go cat fishing and they don't have no worms at the store anyway I know I went check and I figured I'd go paddle for a little while but then I realized I'd have to paddle against the wind coming back and I'd probably get blown to Venezuela instead of Argentina like Patagonia where there's great fishing so I figured I'd put my trolling motor on it then I realized the state makes you get a dadgum registration for putting a trolling motor on a dang piroque and canyoubelievethat???"

Luckily, I ran out of breath before the cussin' started. My neighbor admitted he was about in the same fix, and so we commiserated for a little while then both went back to our various meaningless time-killing-just-to-be-outside activities.

I cleaned up the pirogue and put it on saw horses just because it gave me something to do for a little while longer. Then I sat around and drank a Diet Coke and looked at it, admiring my craftsmanship and trying to figure out how I could set up a forward anchor system. By then it was time for my final trip to the bayou with the dog, so that ended the day.

Sunday wasn't any better. I got groceries, and bought far too much junk food, because I was in a mood. But I bought a lot of salad stuff, too, because I was in a mood, so it all equals out. Bored to tears again, I thought about doing some work inside the house, but the key word there is "inside" and, of course, I wanted no part of that. So I went to town because I forgot to get bread when I went to get groceries and came back with a new hunting knife. Don't ask me why I ended up in sporting goods when I was going for bread. All roads, eventually, lead to sporting goods for me. Doesn't matter if I'm going for socks, NyQuil, vitamins or coffee: I always end up in sporting goods and wander aimlessly down all the aisles looking at stuff. Sometimes I pick up an armful of things and head for the checkout, but usually I realize I'm being impulsive and go put it all back. This time I bought a hunting knife, just because, you know, in case I vanish one day without meaning to.

At home I spend the rest of the daylight hours honing my new knife until—you guessed it—time to go sit at the bayou with the dog, a cold one and a stogie.

Ah, spring, where art thou?

Big Bugs

I generally have a strong constitution. I don't get sick easily, with two notable exceptions: I am extremely prone to motion sickness, and I frequently have bouts of the "sick-ofs" which are, of course, pretty severe when they occur.

"I am so sick of coming home to this messy house!" a wife will say. Or a husband will note, "I am sick of you nagging at me about this house!" and so forth.

My infections of the sick-ofs tend to lean toward things like the weather. "I am sick of winter," I say, a sure symptomatic reaction to the disease. Worse-case scenarios, often requiring repeated rounds of medical treatment, include, "I am sick of everything!" These cases, while rare, often lead to the related malady, the "don't give a durns" when the "sick of everything" part just gets over-whelming.

I'm also extremely prone to motion sickness. Have been all my life, and medication helps a little but not much. I rarely ride with another person in a vehicle because that's almost guaranteed to send my stomach into somersaults. About one percent of the time even driving myself makes me ill, though I can't exactly determine what the factors are that do so.

But besides those two exceptions, I don't get your basic sick of-ten. The typical bugs that go around don't usually get me, but when they do, man, they have to be like Paul Bunyan bugs to do so. People believe that when I start whining about being sick I'm just being a big...well, whiner, I guess. They don't realize that it takes a lumberjack-sized bacteria with a big blue ox-sized attitude to get me, a contagion that would have brought a lesser man to his knees long before I even uttered the syllable, "Ugh." That is the best word for being sick. It says so much about every nuance you are feeling, every achy muscle, every churning muscle, throbbing head, stuffy nose and wheezing exhalation of breath, can all be summed up in the word "Ugh." I use it with great care, but freely, when ill.

So Saturday, long about one in the morning, I woke from a dead sleep and immediately knew that the Godzilla of all infectious bugs had latched onto me. I spent the rest of the weekend fighting off this bug and though I will spare you the sordid details, let's just say I was a pitiful specimen during that time.

It was mostly in the tummy. Also I also couldn't get warm. I'd be sitting there on my sofa or in my chair, feeling miserable, when all of a sudden I'd be wracked by these trembling, quaking shudders, freezing to death, and have to rush to the bathroom mirror to see if icicles had formed on my eye lashes.

At some point I managed to get to the store and bought a twenty-pack of NyQuil and a two-liter bottle of Pepto-Bismol, which helped a little and I got some sleep, anyway. By Sunday I was feeling about sixty percent human again, which was pretty good, since even in the best of times I seldom reach more than eighty percent anyway. I went to work Monday, and had to make a run to New Iberia that afternoon, from which I didn't return until right at dusk.

Just as I was leaving New Iberia, I started feeling hot. It was raining and the temperature outside was probably about fifty degrees, but I was burning up. It got so bad I was rushing through rain with the windows down, clawing at my shirt because I was suffocating. I also felt ill in the tummy, headache, dizzy and clammy. It was literally the longest trip home from New Iberia I have ever made in my life.

The night was miserable, and I called in sick Tuesday, spent the day recuperating and wondering absently if there was a new Indian policy in the making that we hadn't heard of. Rather than small pox blankets, I figured, they were sending me some other infectious plague in the envelopes that come from the IRS. Figures, not a medicine man in the neighborhood, either.

I'm finally feeling much better, thank you very much. Until the next King Kong virus comes along and slaps me down. Or they start sending contagions via the fly fishing supplies I order. Can you put microbes from the black plague in a fly line? The world may never know.

Shivers

Greetings from London.

That's what it feels like, anyway. Not to stereotype London, of course, but many times when you see that English city in a movie it's overcast, foggy, dreary and cold. Kinda like we've been since Christmas.

Listen, I figure it this way. My Indian ancestors likely came from Siberia across the Bering Strait and clear across North America to settle in Louisiana. My Cajun forebears left Nova Scotia and did the same. The common denominator is obvious: Both left cold, dreary climates to come to a sub-tropical paradise.

To me, if my ancestors went through all that trouble, we deserve some sorta guarantee or something.

They say not seeing sunlight and having sunshine on your skin makes people depressed, and I certainly do believe it. Given the choice right now between a) Seeing the sun again and b) Having $2 billion deposited in my checking account and never seeing the sun again, I'd have to stay destitute. Money can't buy happiness, and it definitely can't buy summertime.

They say that Phil the groundhog meteorologist didn't see his shadow yesterday, so we're going to have an early spring. Here's what bugs me about ol' Punxsutawney: If he sees his shadow, it's six more weeks of winter. If he doesn't, it's "an early spring."

Why is it Phil can be so exacting on how much more winter we're gonna get, but downright vague and shifty over when spring's coming? There's something just not right about all that.

Here it is February, for Pete's sake, and it's been wintry in Lousyana since November, at least. Oh, we've had some moments of warmth, but not many since December. Just ain't right. What's the point in living in the sub-tropics? I think we all ought to write letters to Punxsutawney and tell him to get a real job.

You know who should get Phil's job? Snoopy. That's right, Snoopy. Snoopy loved warm weather, and would be a lot more careful in the accuracy of his predictions. Snoopy would always dance a happy jig when warm weather came at last, like any self-respecting beagle should. I vote we kick Phil out on his front teeth and give Snoopy the position with extra benefits. Woodstock could be his executive secretary.

I don't know which is worse: A pure-dee, all-out downpour where it's raining like the world's ending, or these little piddling, misty, nasty rains we've been having of late. It's like, you know that feeling when you think you gotta sneeze and it just won't happen? That's what these little dinky rains have been like: You just want it to blow and get it over with it.

Those little wimpy rains are like people who can't make up their minds. Wishy-washy. I tend to be that way, but I do have a firm decisive attitude about rain: Get it over with and bring on the sunshine! It's getting close to prime sac-au-lait time (that's crappie for you Yanks, which is a ridiculous thing to call them, and for you non-fisherman, that's a fish) and I'm itching to get out there and try to fool some into biting a coupla flies I have just for them.

Dreary, nasty, dark and depressing. I spend too much time in the house, running the heater. Now, there's another thing that bugs me to no end: natural gas prices. It's one of the great failings of this country that we don't put regulations on energy prices. As soon as the weatherman predicts "a cold February" (booming voice, beating drums) the speculators drive the cost of natural gas up twelve percent.

I'm sorry, you can preach to me all you want about the free enterprise system, capitalism, the American-way, yadda, yadda, yadda, but that's not right. Just like with oil and gasoline, when someone belches in Iran and the price of unleaded goes up a quarter. It's not right to escalate the price of natural gas, especially, and put burdens on not only average Americans, but old people on fixed incomes, the poor and the like, and it's especially criminal to hike up prices based on predicted weather. If February turns out to not be as cold, are we gonna get a refund? Fat chance. Energy market speculators need to be the first ones lined up against the wall in front of the firing squad when the revolution comes.

Anyway, I'm not gonna pull the soap box out again today and preach about the sorry state of affairs these days, other than it's cold, dreary, wet and dark. I hate to get out of the house when it's like this, and when it gets too cold and dreary I let Daisy sleep nights in the workshop, which is consequently starting to smell pretty doggy. I threw an old comforter down on the concrete floor for her, and she rests comfortably there all the night. She's getting old, and I know how my bones ache in the cold, dreary, wet and dark nastiness, so I feel sorry for her and in the worst weather let her go in the shop. In the morning when I get up to go to work, I have to put her back in the yard because I'll be gone too long for her to stay inside without a tinkle break.

She comes to the door with me, looks outside, sighs in resignation and goes on out, as if thinking, "If you'd have gotten rich early in your life, like your daddy told you to, we could both stay inside today," and she's right, of course. So we trudge on out, her back to the yard where she'll find a warm spot under the house or in the woodshed, and me to work, to write columns and dream of crappie.

Winter. You can have it.

Le Chapeau

I was never really a hat person. Even in my youth, I don't ever recall wearing a hat of any kind, not even a baseball cap.

This was probably due to the fact that my father didn't wear hats, either, until later in his life when he took to wearing a straw Panama style hat when fishing. He made a silver hatband for it, with abalone and turquoise, an Indian man's hatband. Aggravates me sometimes, when people ask me what makes me an Indian and not just like "everybody else," and I can't explain to them in any way they'll possibly understand that a thousand-and-one things do, including my father's silver hatbands with turquoise. Might not seem like much to most, but like the Navajo-made ring on my right hand, it speaks worlds to those who understand.

Before he took to a straw hat, if the sun started searing his bald crown, he'd just take a handkerchief and tie it over his head, giving him a decidedly odd rock 'n roll look. He preferred Willie Nelson, actually.

I can probably count on one hand the number of times I've worn baseball caps. They aggravate me, I don't like the way they feel on my head. I started wearing fedoras a few years ago for a couple of reasons.

First, a wide-brimmed fedora protects the tips of your ears and nose from the sun in ways a baseball cap never dreamed of. Too many sportsman I know of had to have growths removed from the tips of their noses and ears, sometimes malignant.

Second, fedoras just look way cooler.

I don't like the ones you find in the department stores around here, they're kinda Panama style. I went on a search a few years ago and found my canvas-colored Country Gentleman hat at Dillard's. I wear it most of the time now, and I admit, I liked the name "Country Gentleman" a lot when I bought it. I had a straw hat rather like my dad's before that, but I retired it.

Most recently I bought a Bailey "Curtis," a brown felt fedora that is "packable." Now, that's about the coolest, yet at the same time, most unsettling thing I ever experienced. You can take a packable hat like my Bailey and roll it up into a ball in your hand, like you're wadding up a sheet of paper, and when you let it go, with just a little encouragement it resumes its original shape.

I wear the Bailey on more formal occasions, and the Country Gentleman fishing. It has taken a decidedly darker tone around the hatband from sweat, and has more than a couple of marks and scuffs, but it's still the best hat I own.

When I was in Belle Chasse a few months ago for the Saltwater Fly Rodders Expo there, Rick Pope, president of Temple Fork Outfitters fly rods in Dallas, gave me a TFO baseball cap, and I wore it most of the day out of respect and appreciation, because I have and am a big fan of TFO's rods. I also have a cap Harry Boyd, the maker of my bamboo rod, gave me, and I wear it now and then at a fly fishing get-together, but in general, I just don't wear baseball caps.

It's how I was raised, and I'm not sure how it happened. I was in my thirties before I started wearing short pants, and in my forties before I wore a pair of sandals, though you will never catch me in a pair of flip-flops or those other things that have the rope that goes between your big toe and the one next to it. That would make me crazy. It'd be like walking around with a toe-wedgie all day.

I'm particular about short pants. They must be above the knee. Below-the-knee short pants on a short person like me look like Bozo the Clown pants, or like I'm in first grade again. Must be above the knee. Not too tight, but not too baggy either, or I look like I'm wearing a single-occupant tent.

A friend of mine I've known for about most of my life years saw me the other day in a pair of shorts, tee-shirt and sandals and had to be airlifted to a hospital from the shock and trauma.

I don't know why it's that way. I've seen pics of me as a kid in shorts, but I don't remember wearing them. When I became a teenager I abandoned them for jeans exclusively. Don't know why, but my legs didn't see the sun for near-on twenty years.

When I really got into fly fishing, it was decidedly easier to wade in shorts and waterproof sandals than in jeans and hiking boots. Fishing, therefore, has once again enlightened me and made me a more fashionable person.

When I was in Montana, we wore waders to fish the first three days, but on the fourth day we were just doing some interviews on Cutbank Creek and so I didn't wear them.

I brought my fly rod, and while I was waiting I decided I'd just wet wade down the creek a ways.

Sheesh! I know now why they call it "coldwater fishing" up there! Our Blackfeet host had waded wet the whole four days, but this little Looziana native wasn't adapted to water that's the same temperature as our iced tea at lunch!

Of course, fashion is relative, and in Cajun country, land of camo pants, baseball caps and wrap-around sunglasses, I still stick out like a sore thumb no matter what I do, Bailey fedora and wading sandals included.

Becoming Our Parents

With each year that passes, I am aware that I am slowly becoming my father.

It was something I never realized before I got older. They always said it would happen. They didn't explain it well, though.

When they say, "You're going to be old one day, boy," they didn't explain, "You're going to be old like your ma and pa one day, boy."

It occurred to me when I saw myself on television fishing in Montana, and I talked to every trout I caught. "C'mere, little fella, come on, it's okay," or whatever. My father did that. He'd talk to every fish he caught. That's when I started suspecting I had begun to become my father. I do the same thing, without even realizing it.

It's not so much an individual characteristic thing, though that is part of it. When I started wearing khaki pants and losing my hair, I looked in the mirror and thought, "There's Nick." My dad wore khakis and lost most of his hair by his late twenties, early thirties. My dad never wore jeans.

More so in his day than in mine, jeans were the mark of a poor person. Dad grew up poor, so he never wore jeans as an adult. I grew up mostly in that same mindset, until my late teens, I guess, when jeans suddenly became chic and the price went into orbit.

Today, it bugs the bejeezus out of me to pay forty bucks for a pair of jeans, and that's low for some. I quit doing it after awhile and opted for fifteen-dollar models, realizing that I wasn't out to impress anyone. That's a twenty-five dollar difference I could spend on fly fishing gear. My father would not have given you two bits for any pair of jeans.

The other thing is pickup trucks. In my father's day, only farmers and working men of other trades drove trucks. Trucks were rough-and-tough, dependable vehicles that suited a certain lifestyle. They were expected to get bruised and battered, scratched and dented, and they almost always had a shotgun or rifle on a rack in the back window. They did not come with power windows, CD sound systems and dang sure didn't cost forty grand. Trucks in my dad's day had manual cranks on the windows (heck, mine still does!) huge dashboards that always got dust inside the gauges somehow and you could never get it out, and if you were lucky, an air-conditioner, which marked you as a higher-end skilled laborer. If you had a radio with more than AM band, you were uptown Saturday night.

I hate modern music about as much as my father hated rock 'n roll. My father used to complain bitterly about "all that damn noise" coming from my room, referring to strains of Steely Dan and Lynyrd Skynyrd from the stereo they bought me for Christmas. I now complain bitterly about bands called Bone Thugs-N-Harmony making albums called "Creepin OnaAh Come Up's." I don't get rap, I don't get grunge and I certainly don't get where they come off calling all this music.

I resisted and rebelled against my father's taste in music, of course. Most of us did that. I still don't particularly care for modern country, and in that regard, I realize I've become like my father, who didn't like it much, either, with the exception of Willie Nelson, who really isn't that modern anymore. He preferred older country, to which I used to pretend to gag over to demonstrate my disgust. Lately, however, I ordered a couple of Hank Williams Sr., collections and a Willie Nelson Greatest Hits. My heroes may not have always been cowboys, but the Indians always liked Willie and vice-versa.

My girl and I were watching television one night and this commercial came on with this androgynous creature kinda swaying and gyrating, and I figured it was a girl but my girl figured it was a guy, and so we both kinda figured it was just beyond our capacity to understand this entity singing, "I can give you what you want!" But by the end of the commercial neither one of us knew what the heck they were trying to sell us, much less what we wanted, other than the remote to change the channel quickly.

That happens a lot these days. We see commercials and either can't figure out what it is they want us to buy, or can't figure out how in the dickens the content of the commercial is related to the product they're trying to sell. Worst of all is car commercials. They start off seeming to be something else entirely, get your interest piqued, and then it's about a Caddy.

Makes me feel wimpy, though, when I think about what my parents saw in their lifetimes. When they were born, trans-Atlantic travel was just a dream, and landing on the moon? Insane. Talking movies were in their infant stages, and the notion of breaking the sound barrier silly. The changes I've seen in my lifetime seen minor in comparison, but I always think of my father when they happen, and how like him I've become.

What does a man dancing in the background in his underwear or a guy in a chicken suit trying to get through a revolving door have to do with telephone service? Beats me.

Dad used to talk to the television, too. When, for instance, a cop would shoot a bad guy, Dad would say something to the effect of,

"Bam! Good night Irene!" though I don't know where in the world that came from. If someone found a corpse in a detective show he'd say, "Yup! Stone-cold dead in the market, ma'am," and I certainly don't get that one, either. Dad called movies like that "shoot-'em-ups" and that's about as good a name as I was ever able to come up with for them. I catch myself talking to the television, too, criticizing the plots, snarling at the directing and you don't even want to know what I say to some of the so-called news anchors out there.

But it's really odd that, for a man I thought was so stupid when I was sixteen, how smart I realize he was now that I'm forty-two. One of his favorite jests to me was, "Dang, boy, I taught you everything I know and you still don't know nothing!"

Sometime in my twenties it occurred to me, and I said, "But pop, doesn't that mean you don't know nothing?"

He put out his hand and shook mine.

"'Bout time," he said with a grin.

Les Souliers

I never claimed to be part of the fashion scene. I'm not into much about clothing other than modesty. I try to look presentable, but I'd just as soon be comfortable.

My mother did raise me well enough to know that I shouldn't be wearing a black shirt with brown belt and brown shoes, but it happens I didn't have a pair of black shoes. So wearing a black shirt with a black belt and brown shoes just made me two thirds correct.

I found me a nice pair of black shoes I liked for twenty-five bucks. I tried one on and it was quite comfortable as I walked up and down the aisle like we do when we're testing shoes: One old shoe on one foot, one new shoe on the other foot, and we walk kinda like Groucho Marx for some reason, bow-legged and watching our feet, as if we are expecting something to happen. Are we just checking out how cool we look with the shoes, or are we expecting a jack-in-the-box to erupt from the toe?

That night, as I was lacing them up at home, I noticed that the two shoes were not identical. In fact, though the differences were subtle, they were two separate styles.

Now, I'm going to admit I thought, very briefly: "Well, maybe nobody'll notice." But I work in an office full of women. I wouldn't have made it all the way through the front door before someone would have yelled, "You have on two different shoes!" and there would have been an uproar of hilarity swelling like a fox got in the hen house.

So I headed back to the store and walked up to the service desk with my miss-matched shoes. The kind lady gave me my money back, and I went to find another pair. I was careful about inspecting them this time: Both the same style, both the same size. I put one on and did the Groucho walk again, and satisfied, took them home.

This morning I woke up, proud of my new black shoes, and put them on. Well, get this now, the other shoe, the one I didn't try on, though marked identical to the first, was at least one size smaller. By the time I got to town, my right leg was numb from the knee down because the blood couldn't find its way back up once it got in that black-leather tourniquet.

Furious, I went to another department store of the same chain limped in and bought a pair of sixteen dollar black shoes, checked the sizes, checked the styles, tried both of them on, paid for them, went out to the parking lot, sat inside the door of my truck and took off the shoes I was wearing—the right one required me to use the tire iron to pry with—and put on the new ones. The pair I took off, I'm ashamed to say, made a graceful flight across the parking lot in disgust, and I'm sure made some lucky finder very happy, providing of course his left foot is a size ten and his right a size nine, or maybe even eight.

The latest pair feel okay, but they're squeakers. You know the kind of shoes I mean: They react with certain types of floors and squeak. People can hear you coming four doors down. I hate squeakers, but I think I'm all out of options. I thought about using some kinda auto protective spray on them but figured I'd never stay vertical that way. So I'll just have to deal with sounding like I'm stepping on mice with every footfall until they wear down to silence.

When I was a kid my mom bought me blue Keds. I must be related to the great Redd Foxx, because like him, I'd wear my Keds so long the label would say "-ds" before I got a new pair. We weren't destitute, but dad worked side jobs to pay for stuff like school clothes and shoes, and he made sure I got my mileage out of them.

Later in life I got into the whole urban cowboy thing, in my teens I guess, and wore cowboy boots. I still miss a good pair of cowboy boots, with the pointy toes suitable for nailing cockroaches in corners, though they always seemed too elfin for a rough-and-tough cowboy to me.

Walls and Doors

Last weekend, I built my first wall.

I've been learning a lot about carpentry since I moved into this old house of mine. I've learned a bunch of things. But I've never built a wall before, other than metaphorically.

I have embarked on a project involving the enlarging of a small half-bath into a full-blown facility, though still not very large. This will allow me to then gut and rebuild the master bath. The current work entails taking in about sixty inches of space, thirty-six or so inches wide (I told you, it's a small bathroom). That entailed building a wall, with door frame, and a corner about seven and a half inches long to meet up with the existing air conditioner closet. Don't worry. I'm confused too.

My carpenter pal Larry gave me instructions on wall-building and corner-fitting, saving me a lot of heartache and perhaps potential disaster. I happily took off to the lumberyard that Saturday morning to pick up all the lumber I needed and five pounds of nails.

Something about fresh, uncut lumber just gets to a do-it-yourselfer such as myself. It's like...I don't know...an unsliced pie. A fresh pot of gumbo. An unread book. You get the idea. Part of me wants to leap into the job, carbide-toothed blades screaming, sawdust flying...but the other wants to just kinda admire it, pristine as it is, a neatly stacked pile of potential and imagination.

But there was a wall to be built. Part of the space was going to be a water heater closet, but that idea was nixed and the water heater will be moved elsewhere. I had picked out a door unit, so I knew the door's rough-opening size I had to build. I was ready to rock and roll.

There wasn't enough space available to do the proper thing, build the wall on the floor and lift up, so I had to built it in place. Now, in a house approaching one hundred and seventy-some-odd years old, in a back section with a decided lean toward the bayou, certain challenges are immediately evident.

I lined up the new wall with the one that I was extending by using a long straight edge and marked it on the floor, corner and all. The old adage "measure twice, cut once" does not suffice in this old house. It's more like "measure thrice, carry board out to the saw in the shop four to six times and nibble away 1/16-inch increments until it fits." I installed six studs in this wall, and their lengths varied from eight-foot ten and a half inches to eight-foot ten and three-quarters inches, in no specific pattern. Ah, me.

Luckily many years ago, realizing I have always been mathematically-challenged, I purchased a fractional calculator with a base of twelve instead of ten. Therefore I could add, subtract, multiply and divide foot-inch-fractions until I'm blue in the face, which is usually the case because I'm holding my breath hoping I hit the right keys.

At such times, when problems present themselves and I can't find my pal for advice, I take the WWND tactic. "What Would Norm Do?" of course refers to the godfather of do-it-yourself television, Norm Abrams, co-host of *This Old House* and host of his own program, *The New Yankee Workshop*. I have expanded upon the concept of WWND slightly, however, with all due respect to Norm, and converted it to "What Would Nick Do?" because my dad, Nick Stouff, was a master carpenter in his own right. Either an answer presents itself at once, or I go find something else to do until Larry can drop by.

I ended up with a wall, with a door frame, and a nicely-done corner. Came our fairly well, I think, though it hasn't been formally inspected by my mentor yet. I do have a clever tactic for getting passing grades: A fine cigar and a cold one. So far, my marks have never fallen below a "C".

Odd thing is, over the course of the last two weekends, three times I've come and found the existing door to the little bathroom open. It's latched and locked with a throw-bolt at all times. I figured maybe one of us forgot to throw the bolt the first time, so I made sure it was snug and locked in place. Sure enough, twice more, I found the old door open.

I had to stop and absorb it for a little while and a memory crept back out of the crevices of my memory where I could see it. It was back in 1997, and my grandmother, who had lived seventy years of her life in this old house, was then in a rest home. A slight mist had settled over her mind, and though she was never really inhibited, moments of clarity were never quite what they once were...or so we thought.

The last time I saw her was, I think, Mother's Day. I was living in the house by then and that morning I had cut the grass with her trusty old Snapper lawn mower. When I was a tike, she would ride me on her lap, without the blade turning, much to my delight. Later, I learned to steer, and still later, I was charged with cutting the yard myself, and a couple of generations of Snapper mowers were my tools.

My mom and dad and I went to the home to visit her, and I hugged her there in that sterile, white and stainless steel environment. She was so small and thin, but her eyes were fire.

"I saw you this morning," she said. "I saw you outside the window."

"Did you granny?" I asked, afraid the clarity was slipping again, the mist thickening to fog.

She nodded. "You were cutting the grass. You did a good job, baby."

Of course she saw. How could she not have? She rested her head on the wooden porch and listened to Papa Jack tell stories about *kich* and *Neka sama* and Grand Avoille Cove. She sat in straight-backed kitchen chairs and learned to make river cane baskets, fingers sliced and bloodied by the sharp edges of the cane. Churned butter, ground coffee, learned words and phrases and most of a language. She learned to heal with traditional medicines and learned to speak to *kich* herself, the little brown bird that would warn and advise and rejoice. There was an umbilical between her, in that antiseptic hospital bed, and that old house back on the reservation, that could never be severed.

So of course she saw me through the window, like a magic pane, like a trip through a looking glass, cutting the lawn. So of course she opened a few doors the last couple weeks, unseen, but she surely peeked her head around the corner, looking, up and down, left to right. I guess I know in my heart that she lifted her chin the way she always did, stiffened her upper lip proudly and nodded.

"You did a good job, baby."

Once More, With Feeling

But I didn't come here to tell you all that.

What I was planning on getting around to talking about was what happened when I first got into the house.

After it was clear there would be no saving the marriage I was in at the time, I prescribed and duly enacted an immediate property division and settlement: I hooked my dad's boat up to the truck, put all my clothing, books and my computer into the boat, and my English springer spaniel Shadow and my Cocker spaniel Chance into the boat as well, and headed to the old Stouff homestead. The dogs thought it was the coolest thing they had ever done.

My father allowed me to begin rehabilitating the old place. Ma Faye, my grandmother, had been in the rest home for a year and a half, and a house that had been continuously lived in since about 1840 for the first time in its existence had sat empty. Old houses don't do well. They get lonely. You can laugh all you want about that statement, but it's true. You can live in an old house ten years and lift not a finger in maintenance and it weathers pretty well inside. You leave it empty for a year and it starts warping and nails start pulling out, paint starts peeling. New houses don't really react that way, because they're usually built with far less material that was—and in many ways, still is—living.

It took me six months to get it livable. I was working at *The Daily Review* in Morgan City at the time, and worked on it every spare minute I had. I stripped two layers of linoleum off the floor in the living room to reveal a magnificent oak floor, laid diagonally to the room. I had never seen a diagonal floor before, and I inquired with my dad about it.

"The old man did that," he said. He explained that the room was so out of square my grandfather laid the oak diagonally to avoid a serious set of problems otherwise. As I worked on the place more and more, I realized there certainly was little in the house plumb, square or level. It wasn't all that obvious, it's not like the place is wavy or anything, but it's not exact by any stretch.

Maybe that's why I love it so: Neither of us are very plumb or level or exact.

But I didn't come here to tell you all of that, either.

Over the years, I've managed to do ninety-eight percent of the living room and piddling room, which are conjoined, and ninety percent of the kitchen. I never seem to be able to finish one hundred percent of anything, because I usually get fed up with it and go fishing for a couple years, then come back and start something new. I have no staying power on these projects. I predict that by the time I hammer my last nail in it some years hence, I'll stand back and proudly proclaim, "There! It's *nearly* done!"

I've had little gifts given to me along the way. When I redid the piddling room, I found an inscription on a header board inside one of the window frames reading E.A. Stouff—1947. Of course, my grandfather, Emile Anatole Stouff, left his mark there when he added that little room to the house. In the workshop, which was originally a breezeway, cookout-kinda thing, I found his initials, but no more. In both rooms I took a Sharpie and signed my own name and the year.

Once I pulled off a baseboard and a little mathematics flash card fell out. I remembered it completely. My grandmother had used math and alphabet flash cards to teach me early on. I could read before I went to grade school thanks to her efforts, but I was never very good at math despite her best intentions.

Under the house, I found a set of oars, about ten feet or more long, nicely made. One corner in the attic revealed a large Indian head penny and within a cabinet a partial set of silver engraved "C. Stouff" which, we believe, belonged to Catherine Stouff, who immigrated here from France with husband, Jean Pierre, in 1845. They were brought to Louisiana to oversee the plantation of Martial Sorrel, and did so until the Civil War was lost. One of their children married a Chitimacha medicine woman, and that's how the Stouff name came into the tribe.

While metal detecting in the back yard around that time, I found a spoon from the set, also engraved. I imagine one of the six children—Nicholas, Emile, Octave Jr., Fred, as well as Constance and David, who died as children—swiped it from the house to dig in the yard and forgot it there or lost it en route back.

Still, that's not what I wanted to tell you.

While I was working on building my wall, I recalled a day when I first moved in to the old house. Of course, I had always been here, never really left. My family's been here since it was built and I was carried into it by my mom, who married my dad in its living room, and I crawled and later teeter-tottered and finally walked and ran on its floors. I'm as umbilically linked to it as my grandmother was.

One day while I was piddling around, working on the floor or something, my dad called me on the phone.

"Say," he said, "when you get into that bathroom in the back, if you take all the paneling off the wall down to the old centermatch, you're going to find a treasure map drawn on it."

You can imagine how surprised I was. How could the old man have hid such a family secret from me for so long? I remembered then that my grandfather used to tell me how his old aunt, Aunt Clara, would lock all the kids in the house when they got short on money. They'd watch her through the window and she'd amble down to the bayou side and vanish below the ridge, returning a bit later to the house to release the kids from captivity. She'd always have a few silver coins in her hands, too.

"Really?" I asked Dad at his disclosure.

"Yeah, he said. "It's going to show a map of the property, with the house and the old oak tree and bayou on it, and a big X with the words 'This is where my money is buried' next to it."

"Really?" I blurted, shaking now.

"Sure enough," he said. "But don't pay any attention to it. The old man put that there to fun with whoever lived in the house after they did. You weren't even born yet."

I was crushed. I said, "I'm certainly glad you remembered to tell me that before you went on to the Happy Hunting Ground yourself! I'd have been out there with a back hoe digging up the whole yard!"

He just laughed and said, "Well, you know how your grandpa was. He was quite a character."

I never did get that deep into the other bathroom, the one I'll do later. But I'm anxious to see if that map is really there.

And that's what I came here to tell you.

Courtboullion Is In Session

I called my girl the other day to ask her about the redfish courtboullion someone had given me, and I had lots left over.

"How long is this stuff good?" I asked. Redfish courtboullion is worth its weight in gold, you know.

"Three days, four tops," she said.

"Hmm," I pondered. "What about potato salad?"

"Four days, five tops," she advised. "It's got vinegar that gives it a little more longevity. You can freeze the courtboullion, you know."

I didn't know that. So I decided to freeze the courtboullion. I had never liked courtboullion before, but that's probably because the only kind I ever had before was gaspergoo courtboullion. Gaspergoo, or just "goo" as we call it down here, is an oily fish, and to me, a goo courtboullion is oily fish floating in red fish-oil.

But a redfish courtboullion is pretty good stuff, odd as that may be since the redfish and the goo are first cousins once removed, so I decided to freeze it. I put it in a Ziploc bag and grabbed by Sharpie to label it. I stood there staring at the Ziploc bag for a good while then called Susan back.

"How do you spell it?" I asked.

"What?"

"Courtboullion."

"C-O-O...wait," she ventured.

"It's pronounced 'koo' so you're on the right track," I said. "How about C-O-O-B-E-E-Y-O-N?"

"Naw," she said, "it's a French word."

We bandied it about for a time and I finally looked it up: C-O-U-R-T-B-O-U-L-L-I-O-N. Ye olde coo-bee-yaw. Seafood in tomato sauce. Makes some people ill just to think about it. Admittedly, I can't eat more than ten, twelve plates of it before I get a little tuckered out myself.

So I put my courtboullion up in the freezer section of the fridge. When I was a kid, my mom bought milk in half-gallon cartons. She saved all the cartons to freeze fish in. Knowing that my dad was a far, far better fisherman than I could ever hope to be in my wildest dreams, my mom probably mooched a few cartons off her kin, too. When you opened the big chest freezer in the utility room (which I did often in search of fudgecicles, ice cream cones or chocolate swirl ice cream) you found two-thirds of it packed with milk cartons, filled with ice to a quarter-inch exactly from the top. If you looked closely enough, you could see bream tails (we called 'em perch tails) and fins and shoulders and flanks...in short, pure delicacies frozen in a milk carton.

I don't recall us having more than fried fish and shrimp. Or crawfish stews, other than the obligatory crab or mudbug boils, no courtboullion or etouffee in our house. Mom would batter up "perch" in corn meal and egg and drop them in a sizzling hot black iron skillet of grease. These "perch" you understand, were of the "stumpknocker" variety, also known as "barn doors" and "preacher perch" because they were thick as a King James version of the Bible with concordance. We always had homemade French-fried potatoes, too, and for some reason, Ritz crackers with our fried fish. To this day, I can scarcely eat a perch without Ritz crackers. And ketchup. Never tartar sauce. I don't know why. I was a teenager before I discovered tartar sauce and thought I had died and gone to seafood dining heaven...but only with shrimp.

There's a specific method of eating a bluegill (or perch, bluegill or bream, whatever you call them.) My father was specific about it. First, you get three slices of bread and put them on a saucer in the middle of the table.

Begin by nibbling off the crunchy but not overly-hard sections of tail and top and bottom fins. The best fillet mignon in the world can't be compared to fried perch fins and tail. A buddy of mine and

I considered putting them in bags and marketing them as "Perch Chips" but because bream are a game fish we weren't able to follow through on it.

Then you carefully pull the top and bottom fins of the perch from the body, along with the tail. With a fork, you can gently separate the flaky, scrumptious fillets from the bone, though it's difficult around the rib cage, just do your best.

If you happen to miss a tiny bone and get it in your throat, don't panic! Remember those three pieces of bread on the saucer? Grab hold of one and eat if fast. The bread will almost always take the bone out of your craw on the way down.

We had lots of boils, too. Crab or crawdad. Every boil started with the distribution of Jax to those eligible. Uncles, cousins, aunts, whomever. Not a single instrument of cookware was removed from storage until the Jax, or occasionally a Falstaff, was uncapped.

Then the cooking started, and a steady flow of Jax followed. My Shetland pony, Nancy, had a particular fondness for Jax, and Dad always poured some into his hand and let her lap it up through the fence.

We had an outside table where we usually dined on newspaper table cloth. It was under a couple of cedar trees. Some of my happiest moments were spent there, peeling crawfish or crabs with the old folks.

Fish fries, though, were far more common. Dad and I would fish all day and, if we had the energy left, clean the fish and fry 'em up that same evening. We'd call over the kinfolks and Mom would start the frying. If there were goggle-eye in the mix (that particular variety of panfish that is more elongated like a bass and feisty as a Tasmanian devil on amphetamines) Mom got those by default because they were her favorite. Nobody argued. My mom would, family legend had it, get in a fight with a circular saw for a fried goggle-eye.

Even today, when I have a few perch in the fridge (they'll always be perch to me, despite their fancier names) and fry them up, I wish they still made Jax. I never shared a Jax with my dad, it was out of business by the time I was legal.

But when the breaded perch drop into a crackling, spitting black iron skillet of hot grease, and that familiar scent drifts through the kitchen, I make sure there's Ritz crackers and a couple slices of bread on the table. And ketchup. For perch, it's ketchup or nothing.

My mom and Susan are usually there, but I can almost close my eyes when I take the first nibble off the crunchy end of a perch tail and imagine the whole family clamoring around the table, serving themselves fish and French fries and Ritz crackers and maybe some potato salad if one of the aunts happened to bring some.

I can almost hear the old man take his first bite and declare, as always, "Best-eating fish in the water," regarding the oft-maligned and surely misunderstood perch.

For such a small little fellow in comparison to his piscatorial peers, the bream, bluegill, perch, whatever you choose to call him, sure carries a lot of memories on his scaled but formidable back.

Crawl Spaces

One of the many things on my long list of needs to address in my old house has been the heating and cooling system.

My grandmother had central air and heat installed, bless her heart. I'm very grateful for that. Sometimes, though, it's hard to get a really efficient central system installed into an old house, especially a smaller one. One built in the 1840s. By Indians, too. I mean, *poor* Indians, at that. And still occupied by same.

When I moved in I noticed some severe deficiencies in the distribution of heating and cooling. The center of the house stayed comfy, but the front and back were either too hot or too cold, depending on the season. A good cleaning of the coils greatly increased the air flow through the system, and I later removed a large portion of the wall between the kitchen and living room to allow more even distribution. I installed a bar where the wall had been, as lagniappe so I would have a place to entertain guests with tales of my adventures and forays in home renovation over a nip.

But the back of the house never really equalized. You could put your hand over the vents and barely feel any flow. In hard winters, there'd be a fifteen degree temperature difference between the front of the house and the back. Every year I intended to try to figure out the cause of this, but invariably went fishing instead.

Well, after a spate of temperatures in the low twenties, I made up my mind that I'd go up in the attic and try to figure out what my flow problems are. So when I got home Friday afternoon I changed into some work clothes and with all the fanfare of Robert Ruark going on a safari in deepest Africa, headed out. I swear, if I had one of those really cool old safari hard-hats that doubled as a soup bowl and shaving basin, I'd have donned it along with my trusty elephant rifle, machete and knee-high safari boots, pants legs neatly tucked into them, of course, in true British explorer style.

The second story is one big room, basically the middle of the attic, with access to the rest of the attic under the roof on either side. You can walk maybe a dozen feet toward the back of the house before you have to get down and crawl. There's more junk up there than you can believe, storage space for relatives over the many years before me.

That first dozen feet you have to walk on the joists, because you'll go through the ceiling otherwise. I did that once, years ago, in the living room. Learned my lesson while patching the hole. Farther to the back, luckily, the ceiling still has one-inch cypress nailed to the undersides of the joists, and the newer ceiling over that, so you can take a few more chances, even at my generous girth.

Now, headroom is low in there, as I mentioned. About three-quarters of the attic is full of that old blown-in insulation, and the other quarter contains fiberglass insulation that I've installed as I've been remodeling. So first I have to walk over the joists and the boards placed across them for stepping on, to the rear section, and find a position to sit which does not hurt my knees, back, elbows, neck or ankles. Even then, I usually only last two or three minutes before some muscle or another starts cramping up and I waste another five minutes shifting positions, perched as I am there precariously between joist and roof. I admit with shame that this is often accompanied by a steady steam of less than gentlemanly phrases.

So I checked the connections between ducts and vents at every juncture, and found none of them askew. Hmm. I had the fan on the system running, and I did find several places where my furry invasive denizens of hell had gnawed into the flexible ducts. I fixed these with aluminum duct tape. I saw many places where the little demons might be getting into the house that I was unaware of, and reminded myself to seal those later.

I checked the flow downstairs, and it had not improved. Odd. So I went back up again, did the catwalk, and checked all the connections again. All still good. The only thing I could figure was that somehow they were blocked at the handling unit, the big sheet metal case that the ducts attach to. I couldn't imagine how that could happen, but knowing this old beloved house of mine, anything was possible.

Well, boy, was I right and wrong about that one.

Yeah, they were blocked all right. In fact, every duct leading to the back of the house was intentionally shut off at the handling unit!

There are baffles inside that flip open and closed to control the air flow. All three heading to the back of the house were closed. Must have been that way since the system was installed, probably fifteen or twenty years earlier. This led to another monologue composed almost exclusively of less than genteel expressions.

I opened them all up, put the ducts back on, and went downstairs.

Folks, we got flow now! All the vents are distributing air nicely, thank you very much, and the house heats evenly at long last, front to back. It's a small miracle, believe me.

Figured while I was up there, I'd clean up a little. Here's what I removed from the rear side of the attic Saturday:

—Six table legs. I have no idea where the tables got off too, but they're nice round and profiled legs.

—Two or three desk drawers full of junk: Screws, nuts, bolts, lighters, pencils, you name it. Nothing outstanding, nothing valuable, monetary or historical. Go figure.

—A lamp shade

—A dozen or more curtain rods, none alike.

—A kerosene stove.

—Two bedside commodes, and a walker.

—A piece of corrugated tin, five empty cardboard boxes and a pair of scissors I had been missing for a couple years. No clue how they got up there.

—The lid off an old sewing machine case, filled with electrical wiring parts.

—A headboard for a child's bed, badly dry-rotted.

—A beautiful, inlaid wooden serving tray. The bottom is shot, but I think I can restore the frame and I'm thinking of turning it into a picture frame or something.

There's more up there that I haven't gotten to yet, including some odds and ends poking out of the blown-in insulation that are intriguing and frightening all at once. The plan is to eventually either replace all the blown-in insulation with roll fiberglass, or in the more difficult spots to access at least level the former and cover it with the latter to increase the insulation factor.

I'm going to start filling all the varmint access ways soon as I can, probably with that expanding spray foam in a can stuff.

It's an undoing, really, more than a redoing. I'm undoing decades of accumulations and compounded problems. It's satisfying, too, when something actually works the way I intend it to, or I solve a puzzle like the air distribution mystery.

Well, I'll get there, and get it like I want it, eventually. I've actually accomplished more in the last six months than in the three or four years preceding. I've mentioned before, I tend to work on it at white-hot heat for a few months, burn myself out, then go fishing for a few years before I come back to it.

Oh, and let me tell you something else. I did nothing on Sunday. That was because every muscle in my body hurt, including some I didn't even know existed, from crawling around up there and wedging myself between joists and posts and trusses. I must have gone up and down the stairs three dozen times. So I spent most of the day on the sofa moaning about getting old.

An Itch In Time

About a month ago, I was just piddling along, minding my own business, when all of a sudden it hit me.

An itch.

Not a spend money itch, not a seven-year-itch, not even a palm-itch, which tends to indicate you're going to get money. I never get palm itches, dang it. No, I got an itch on my back.

I tend to have itchy skin in the winter anyway, particularly on my back. So when this one came on, it didn't faze me much. I found a likely corner in the house, scratched, and went about my business.

Well, it didn't go away.

The days that followed resulted in an increase in itches. Within a week, I was pretty much itching over every square inch of my body.

Not constantly, mind you, but when it flared up it was unbearable. I have a bamboo back scratcher Suze gave me, but of course I couldn't carry that around in a holster all the time when I go to work and such.

It was quite miserable. I'd be sitting in a restaurant for lunch, and my heel would start itching like crazy. It's hard to inconspicuously take off your shoe, vigorously scratch your heel on the table leg, and get your shoe back on and not let any of the other diners notice, who might complain and get you kicked out on your ear. Which, by the way, also itched terribly.

I changed laundry detergents and fabric softener sheets, to no avail. Meanwhile, it's just getting worse. I itch almost all the time. I changed up my meals routine, thinking it was a food allergy, but nope, no relief.

It got so crazy I had every place I regularly go to mapped out for back-scratching facilities. I know, for instance, that the corner of the brickwork in the advertising room at the Banner is the single most effective back scratching device in the whole building. I know what door frames in the house had just enough of an "edge" on the molding to suffice.

Meanwhile, I tried allergy medicines, which provided some relief but put me to sleep, so they were useless in the daytime. I tried to teach Patches to use her claws to scratch my back, but she refused. She will invariably leap onto my lap and sink them into my belly, though. Single-minded feline, that.

Sometimes I'd wake up in the middle of the night itching so

horribly I'd literally leap out of the sack and scratch wildly like some sort of crazed lunatic whose psychosis has him believing he has ants crawling all over him. The cat thought this was terribly disturbing, too, and went to hide in her secret places during these episodes.

Eventually it got to the point my skin was getting sore from all the scratching. I was no closer to finding out what was going on than when I started. I began to notice, though, that now and then I'd go half a day or so without itching too badly. This intrigued me. More intriguing was that it was usually in the afternoon.

So I considered lunch. But my lunch menu varies greatly and from various sources. I couldn't figure it out.

Meanwhile, I did all that attic work I told you about last weekend, and folks, the addition of fiberglass insulation to my skin didn't help matters at all. Little pieces of that stuff imbed in your pores, and it takes a long or a lot of showers to get them out. I was beyond miserable by then, I was starting to worry about my sanity, and eyeing the cat suspiciously, wondering if I had suddenly developed allergies to her. That would not have been good.

What would I do if I was allergic to Patches? I couldn't find a foster home for her. Who'd put up with her psychosis? Her paranoia, her bipolar disorder and her occasional unexpected outbursts of pure unadulterated sweetness?

Desperately I searched for cures. I dismissed calamine lotion and other such total-body remedies as too time-consuming and sticky. I briefly considered eye of newt and hair of bat, but there was none available at the local pharmacy.

Perhaps I could hermetically seal myself in my room away from the cat? Of course not, I still have to work. Maybe I could hermetically seal up the cat? Eh, probably not, SPCA might get upset about that.

I mean, it was getting to the point that the soles of my feet were itching like mad. Scratching the soles of your feet is a troublesome task especially if you're ticklish, and I am. My scalp was itching so bad I couldn't keep my ponytail straight, and never mind the unmentionable regions that one does not scratch in polite company. You just kinda squirm when those itch. Throughout all of this my palm stubbornly refused to itch at all, and I remain penniless.

One afternoon I was about to write a classifieds ad:

Free to a good home

Tortoise-shell calico cat, about eight years old. Answers to the name of Patches when she darn well feels like it. Litter-box trained, good with children provided they are wearing Kevlar body armor. Will require Mutual of Omaha's Wild Kingdom truck to transport to new home, buyer's expense.

When all of a sudden, I noticed, I'm not itching too badly.

I thought and I thought and I thought, trying to figure out what the devil I had done differently. It was only then I noticed the heartburn creeping into my esophagus, and it hit me like a ton of ants crawling over my skin:

Acid reflux medicine.

As in, having forgotten to take it that day.

I changed my medicine a month or so ago to another brand with another active drug. Much as I hate taking medicine, I hate my insides pretending to be a forge worse. I take one in the morning with breakfast and one—you guessed it—after lunch. Yes, and sometimes I'd come back to work after lunch and have stuff going on, so I would forget to take it. Those were the afternoons I didn't itch so bad.

Been off it two days now, and I'm doing, much, much better, and the cat has not had to be relocated to a wildlife preserve; the brick corner in the advertising room is no longer my best friend in the world, and I squirm a lot less.

So let this freshly coined albeit paraphrased adage be a lesson to you:

"No itch just in time saves the feline!"

Making the Cut

Sunday I decided that my yard had become too overgrown and I had to cut it.

It hasn't been cut since November. In fact, the last cut I intended to make was canceled. My oldest had come to borrow my gas can and the three gallons of gas it contained, to ride his friend's jet ski. That was the last I saw of it. You know how kids are. I charged him for the can, the gas and his honor when it came time to disburse Christmas money.

But the yard had, four months later, begun to look something like an alien landscape. Fire ant mounds everywhere, and strange-looking plants that might be found on another world. The old lawnmower, which I affectionately refer to as the General after that Native American folk hero Gen. George Armstrong Custer, sat on two flats and a dead battery.

After the battery was charged and the tires inflated, I braced myself for an ordeal. It's always an ordeal to get the General started after a long winter. His innards tend to gum up with caramelized egotism and excess amounts of crystallized pompousness. I dropped the bowl on the carburetor and cleaned it, then flipped the switch. Remarkably the General coughed, sputtered and hiccuped (smelling suspiciously like corn mash whiskey) and roared to life.

I've found that fighting fire ants is a losing battle. Of course, we all know that. The best thing to do is run them over with the lawn-mower. You might find this foolhardy and a sure-fire way to ruin a lawn mower blade. Does absolutely no good insofar as getting rid of the little buggers goes, but it certainly is satisfying.

The yard had also accumulated a healthy supply of fallen limbs. I have a few codes of behavior that I steadfastly abide by in life. One of those is that I won't pick up fallen limbs all winter. Gives the yard a nice, down-home cottage look. I have the same philosophy about raking leaves. Raking leaves is absolutely the biggest and most boring waste of time I ever heard of. No offense to those who rake their leaves. I admire your conviction. I rake leaves using the General. Far superior, and can be done from a sitting position.

Cutting the grass always goes in sections: Front yard east, front yard west, back yard west, back yard east. It's sorta like block scheduling without PTA involvement. By cutting the open areas first, I was able to stop and go collect all the limbs from the uncut areas and make a nice pile in the cut areas, then I go mow the rest. So I end up with three or four nice piles of limbs I'll go collect with my pickup truck later.

I learned to cut grass on a Snapper Comet. My grandmother would ride me on her old Snapper Comet without the blade engaged when I was a tyke. When I was older I was charged with the grass cutting on my own. Sort of a rite of passage I thought. Made me feel all grown up. Little did I know that the grandparents were sitting inside with cold drinks, all smug and congratulating themselves on their wisdom.

My father was not a good example to follow insofar as grass cutting goes. Nick Stouff was probably as reckless about mowing as he was enthusiastic about fishing. We had a Snapper Comet too, and when it was time to cut—meaning we couldn't see out of the living room windows anymore—he'd fire that old girl up and race around the yard in fifth gear, blades spinning, making hairpin turns that would actually till the soil until he straightened out. More than once he blazed right through my mom's prized day lilies without even noticing the rain of yellow petal fragments blowing around him. When he was done, he roared into the shed where the lawn mower was stored, which coincidentally was also where the boat was kept, and traded one for the other and was gone, leaving a yard that looked something like a corn field plowed by a chimpanzee.

My own grass cutting, though, is more to my grandmother's standards, slow and neat as I can. I have a peculiar habit, however, that I'm sure makes passersby think I'm off my rocker: I don't cut the clumps of blue wort, oxalis or spider lilies my grandmother had all over the yard and have spread ever since. I don't cut them until they've bloomed and died back in the summer heat, giving the yard a decidedly lovely cottage garden but decidedly paranoid appearance.

I love to run over those big, fleshy plants like thistles and those yellow flowers, though it depresses me a little because yellow was actually my father's favorite color, as witnessed by his close encounters with the yellow day lilies of my youth.

Biggest problem of course is clover. Clover is indestructible. You don't really cut it, you kinda just beat it into laying down with the blades. It pops right back up in a day or two and laughs at you.

It was then time to trim. We still refer to this job as "weed-eating" after the name of the first electric- and subsequently gas-powered string trimmers which quite possibly are the worst inventions in all of human history. My trimmer fired up on the first try and performed well as I chopped four-foot tall, thick, moist weeds from alongside the house, fences and around the trees. My shoes looked like soppy green elf feet by the time I was done. But that's fine, because I learned the hard way not to trim while wearing sandals.

After the cutting, I got our new puppy, Bogie, out of his kennel and put him in the truck with me to go around and collect all the limbs I had piled up. We'd drive a hundred feet or so, get out, pick up the pile, get back in, and drive to the next one, then to the burn pile in the back. He thought that was just the coolest thing ever.

After that, I sat on the patio and watched the fire ants rebuilding their mounds and laughed at them for their misery. Industrious little rascals. Gotta admire them for that.

Bugging Out

Spring, being that time of year when all manner of flora and fauna come out of their slumber, brings with it the unsavory critters, as well.

The good news is that my pecan trees are setting forth fresh green buds, which means winter is hereby duly declared officially over. So it is written, so let it be done!

The bad news is when I walk the dogs to the bayou these days the dadgum deer flies attack me like in one of those Hope and Crosby jungle movies. I mean, those speckled-hooligans are terrible right now, and I dislike the smell of DEET-based repellents so much I only use them when company's coming over that I'm not too fond of.

The Road to Chitimacha. Hey, that wouldn't have been bad, would it? Bob and Bing coulda made a great movie about traveling through the swamps of Louisiana, having hilarious misadventures with alligators, cottonmouths and Justin Wilson to reach the fabled reservation. Somewhere along the way, Gen. George Armstrong Custer could have made the requisite cameo appearance and been promptly drowned trying to cross Bayou Teche in a leaky pirogue. Or maybe Gov. Bienville. Ah, six of one, half a dozen of another, I guess. See, Bienville is to the Chitimacha what Custer was to the Sioux: A swaggering zealot who caused a whole bunch of trouble over what amounted to a really small misunderstanding. Only difference is, Bienville had no counterpart to Little Big Horn.

Anyway, the other problem we're having, every spring, is the carpenter bees. My father was a carpenter, you know, as were a couple of my grandfathers, and I have great respect for my friends who are carpenters. Carpenter bees do not deserve respect. They go in to work as unhired hands and without a contract—like illegal aliens, actually—and their hourly rate remains a mystery. They love old wooden houses, of course, but we who own them do not like carpenter bees.

They bore into the wood and make long, snaking tunnels through your joists, rafters, planks and posts. Not good. They leave tell-tale signs of their unpermitted job sites in the form of little piles of sawdust and fast-food cartons strewn everywhere, not to mention they whistle and cat-call at all the pretty ladybugs passing by.

Closing down a jobsite with caulk or the like will only work if you happen to catch them at work; otherwise they just bore another hole to create a new job. They're sometimes away from work, brawling with other carpenter bees at a neighborhood bar. Worst of all, each generation comes back to the same place year after year where they propagate more little workers until your house looks like a vinyl-sided, metal-roofed chunk of Swiss cheese just before it collapses into a pile of rubble with irritated bees swarming around it.

There's no effective poison or trap to control carpenter bees, so my girlfriend and I resort to the only proven method of carpenter bee control: Wooden paddles and sturdy fly swatters.

When I was a kid, I used to shoot them with my BB gun when they'd hover. No kidding, I really could. I probably could have ridden a wild mustang bareback at full gallop and picked off Cavalry officers with a lever-action Winchester, too, if I had been given half a chance. Now that I'm older I can't see well enough, and I'm also not quite as clever and observant and I'm afraid I'll break a window. Today we use wooden paddles and sturdy fly swatters.

Now, before you follow my lead, make sure you know what your prey is: Carpenter bees look a dang-sight like ground bees.

Carpenter bees are fairly innocuous, though they'd will sting you if you grab one bare-handed and try to kiss it. Ground bees also can be big and black and yellow, and will sting the ever-loving heck out of you with a stinger the size of a pencil lead.

The best thing about this carpenter bee hunting sport is they're smart. Once they're on to you—which is usually after three or four of their compatriots have met the paddle with the most satisfying crack!—they get pretty wise:

"Hey, did you hear about ol' Buzzer?"

"No, what?"

"Man, we was just hovering there out by the red irises, shooting the bull about the big pool game Friday, and *BAMM!!!* I saw a streak and a blur and there was this gust of wind and then ol' Buzzer was down there on the ground with head, wings and behind all backwards and mixed up!"

Well, you get the idea. They smarten up up pretty quick and get more challenging. You always gotta step on 'em, too, because even a good solid smack isn't always enough, just stuns them, then they fly off to tell the rest of the brood the giant monster is coming and he's pretty hacked off.

We have plenty of dirt daubers in the garage and such, too, and the shame of dirt daubers is they are victims of a cousin's bad rap sheet. Though they're wasps they don't sting. But your basic dirt dauber looks so much like those varieties of wasps that'll sting the hallelujah, brethren out of you just because he's having a bad day. Dirt daubers actually are good predators on spiders and skeeters and other such pests, but sure as shootin', if anything red and wasp-like comes hovering around in the shop or the house, it's got a death warrant on it no matter how goody-two-shoes it's led its life, and will promptly experience a very close relationship with either a fly swatter or rolled magazine. I admit to said prejudice. In my philosophy there are three golden rules:

1) Every gun is loaded.
2) Every snake is poisonous.
3) If it looks like a dirt dauber...it's a wasp.

Evenings are getting to be a bummer, because we like to sit and watch sunset with the puppy, but the skeeters are starting to show up en masse.

If someone could train dirt daubers to eat skeeters and then let the carpenter bees eat the dirt daubers and then move into their dauber's nest rather than chew up my joists, rafters and posts, then we'd be on to something!

Rock & Roll

I search through the radio these days desperately trying to find music I can listen to. It's almost impossible. I can't abide today's stuff, and I find myself sounding more and more like my father about "that damn noise" coming from my bedroom after I got a record player.

Nope, fact of the matter is, I'm a relic, raised on rock 'n roll. At least, mid-70s on up. It's hard to find the good stuff now. I've got a rock and roll heart, and old time rock and roll is firmly at the heart of the matter when it comes to music suitable for listening. It's not so much the peace of mind I get from rock and roll, that peaceful, easy feeling, it's also the memories resurrected from that long and winding road of my life.

But here I am, steadily reeling in the years, thinking back to the days when I was cruisin' through downtown Franklin. Seemed we were the champions of the world then, and with a little help from my friends I just knew there wasn't a mountain high enough to stop us from reaching our stairways to heaven. In those days, it was way much more than a feeling, it was a lifestyle. Eight-track, cassette and of course 45s and LPs, rock and roll was here to stay. Or so we thought.

I wore out more copies of Queen's "The Game," AC/DC's "Back in Black," Pat Benatar's "Crimes of Passion," Bob Seger's "Against the Wind" and the Eagles' "Hotel California" than I can recall. Those old albums brought me to an audible as well as visible place, a paradise theater, a grand illusion permeated by living color. There we were, all us young dudes, with mega-watt sound systems in our cars, most of the time running on empty because we couldn't afford more gas, and living life in the fast lane. What could have been better? We were at the top of our game, young, healthy and rocking in the free world. We cruised and parked with Jane,

Barbara Ann, Angie, Eleanor, Brandy, Sally, Caroline, Daisy, Gloria, Layla, Lola, Peg, Roxanne, Jenny (who's number, I seem to recall, was 867-5309), Maggie Mae...it goes on and on. Rock and roll took us aboard that long train runnin' to Chicago, Boston, Katmandu, Kokomo, Alabama, the USSR, Kashmir, Ventura, China Grove, California, Mississippi and more.

Think I've finally lost my marbles? You ain't seen nothing yet!

But the satisfaction was doomed, eventually the magic carpet ride ended and we were tied to the whipping post of jobs, car notes, mortgages or rent. Life may be a highway, but it doesn't always lead to little pink houses if you don't play by the rules. Some of us made it, became successful, followed the yellow brick road and spent our nights in white satin, dreaming of bank accounts and mutual funds. Others, like me, were a generation lost in space, and we kept our heads in the clouds, sailing, and still haven't found what we're looking for. We never amounted to much, some say, but hey, in the midnight hour when the purple haze of the past comes to visit me in dreams, they span a bridge over troubled waters that even today makes me feel like a modern day Tom Sawyer, a sharp-dressed man in cheap sunglasses who may not have much, but I got a name.

So here I am, forty-mumble-mumble years old. I'm a lucky man, by a few accounts, but a little dazed and confused sometimes by the changes I've seen. I've seen paradise by the dashboard lights, and today when I listen to the radio, I can't find a thing to make it all right now.

Being raised on rock was a journey, a wheel in the sky, living like a roundabout, a ramblin' man, a desperado, a low rider. It was all about counting the bricks in the wall, searching for the smoke of a distant fire, the Shambala of adolescence and young adulthood. In those days I thought I could see for miles and miles and could fly like an eagle.

But I've grown older, and the highway song is drawing to a close, but I still can't get it out of my head. My world isn't a vivid Kodachrome panorama anymore, it's turned a whiter shade of pale and begun to fade like dust in the wind, replaced by grunge, hip-hop and God knows what other noises pass for music these days.

It's been a long time since the music industry has produced any-thing to take us eight miles high, across the white cliffs of Dover, over the hills and far away, or since I've heard it in a love song. I've seen all good people turn their radios off and buy CDs with good music to return them to that time of the season when we did imag-ine that we could, in fact, work it out. Today's music is hopeless...rock and roll lifted us higher and higher, sent us for a walk on the wild side, made us believe in magic.

I don't know what day it was the music died, sending me and rock 'n roll into the pages of history. Abracadabra! someone said, and it was gone. If I'd known when it happened, I'd have driven a Chevy to the levee.

I'd love to change the world, make it turn, turn, turn...back into one with music that makes passersby pause, cup their hands around their ear and say, "Stop. Hey, what's that sound?" It was the sound of greatness, of young Americans, when we was fab, when we stood arrow straight, like a rock. Our music defined our generation and others, us and them, taking us from Vietnam to the dark side of the moon, leaving us wanderers, taking it on the run and riding out the storm.

But it's all over now. Rock and roll has died, oh, my sweet Lord, and I don't know how to find my way back closer to the heart, how to come together again. Day after day, I muddle through my CDs at home, seeking yesterday, comfortably numb in my aqualung. Don't look back, I remind myself. Go your own way. Don't fear the Reaper. It's not that me and modern music are at war. We just disagree.

Do you feel like I do? If so, get on the telephone line, mail me the letter, call the operator but don't lose my number. I got the deacon blues and am ready to mosey on down to Baker Street for some brass or take a stroll on Broadway for some scat. I'm lost, show me the way, carry me on, wayward son, to the point of no return. They've killed the music and the lyrics, but I still got the soul.

OMG...IDK!

When I was in grade school, I wrote on an old Underwood

typewriter.

It was one of those big, black, heavy clunkers with the keys that you had to strike so hard you got whiplash in your neck if your finger slipped off the "J" key. But I put out a lot of stuff on that old puppy.

When I was in radio, I used to haul the secretary's old IBM Selectric to the control room late at night to write behind the control board. It had one of those ball letter heads on it, and a built-in correction tape. I was in high cotton, folks.

But I don't think I'll ever be able to send text messages.

You know how I feel about phones in general, cell phones in particular. A phone should ring, you should answer it, talk, hang it up. The rest of the time it should sit there quietly, with good manners and good behavior.

When I was growing up we had one of those big black phones. The kind where the handset weighed more than a bag of sugar. Rotary dial, of course, and though we didn't have a party line by the time I came along, we didn't have to dial 923 or 828, either. Dad used to make a sandwich to eat while he dialed his brother in Ft. Worth. It took a while.

Still, all of this only took a forefinger to perform.

My first cell phone was a clam shell type that Bogie stole off the coffee table and chewed up when he was about four months old. His teeth marks are the most charming thing about it. It has a camera that I have never used, and the only text messages I ever get are from AT&T telling me I forgot to pay them, again. I've never sent an email, and it annoys me to no end that, of the four hundred ring tones built in to my phone, not one of them sounds like a phone ringing should.

I don't give a jolly rip about 3G or "the network" or any such nonsense. It has games in it that I have never looked at. About the only feature I do like is the "silent" mode.

I used it to send text messages for a short time after Hurricane Ike, and that was only because I had to, nothing else would go through. I thought my thumbs would be permanently deformed after that. I thought of myself as the Hunchthumb of Charen-Dame.

But the outside world does sometimes penetrate the veil that surrounds me, gets past the fishing daydreams and wistfulness for ice cream. Now and then something slips through. Lately it's been text-messaging shorthand.

Here's the deal. Some wise urban text messenger has learned that instead of typing "Oh, My God!" they may be able to delay the complete paralysis, loss of motor function in their thumbs and certain damnation by a day or two by simply typing "OMG."

So now, taking the Lord's name in vain is not only acceptable in polite company these days but you can abbreviate heresy as a matter of convenience and to save yourself some Advil years down the road?

Your response should be: "IDK." That means, "I don't know."

It was bad enough when I was learning e-mail. Someone sent me something with a sentence and a colon and a parenthesis at the end, like :) . I thought it was a secret code and wasted most of the morning looking for my Johnny Quest decoder ring. Turns out that :) is a smiley face. :(is a frowny face and ;) is a wink. And so on and so forth.

These evolved over the years in ways that 1950s monster movies couldn't even conceive, and became "emoticons." Icons, that express emotion. I left it there and never looked back.

For instance when I was first on a tribal peoples forum and someone said NDN, I had to sit there and scratch my head for a long, long time before I finally got so frustrated I blurted out, "What the devil does NDN mean?" and, of course, at last I got it.

Allegedly there are over one thousand text messaging abbreviations and emoticons. A quick Google search revealed the following from the hundreds and hundreds I found:

PITA: Pain in the...uhm...behind.

BOSMKL: Bending over smacking my knee laughing.

UT2L: You take too long. (Apparently someone with arthritic thumbs.)

IIIO: Intel inside, idiot outside

OMGTWSF: Oh my God that was so funny.

IYKWIM: If you know what I mean. (Uhm...no, actually.)

Some are merely numbers. There's got to be a pattern here. I mean, people couldn't honestly memorize all this. But if there is a pattern, I can't find it:

831: I love you (8 letters, 3 words, 1 meaning)

Here's some confusion in the making:

?: I have a question

or

?: I don't understand what you mean

And did the Three Musketeers have cell phones? 14AA41: One for all, and all for one.

So...

SOMY: Sick of me yet?

Well before you get to that point, let me wrap this up.

IMO TNSTAAFL IRL IOMH. I2 UNA, TBH. CM!

Which translates to:

"In my opinion, there's no such thing as a free lunch, and in real life I'm in over my head. I too use no acronyms, to be honest. Call me!"

I'm going to give Bogie my phone. He needs a new chew toy.

Characters

Resources, you understand, deteriorate with the accumulation of years. Notice I did not say "age" because soon as I do, some old curmudgeon invariably chastises me as being a wet behind the ears young whippersnapper. I look forward to the day when I can be an old curmudgeon myself, rather than just an old character.

My family has been replete with old characters. My father was quite a famous old character, so much so in fact that people came from all over world to experience and revel in his abundance of character. My grandfather, Emile Stouff, was quite the character before him, and from what I understand, I am descended from an unbroken pedigree of old characters.

I had to take on the job early, at age thirty-five, when my dad passed away. Now, my cousin Jim Ray, as the elder male Stouff is a certifiable character as well, and if he was a resident of this area, the throne would be his.

However, the Stouff kingdom falls into three realms: the Texas Stouffs, the Reservation Stouffs and the New Orleans Stouffs, but very few actually carry the name anymore due to some strange overabundance of daughters in the gene pool. Consequently, then, Jim is the elder and leader of the Texas Stouffs, myself of the Reservation Stouffs, and I'm not sure who is in charge of the New Orleans Stouffs.

There is a California detachment of Stouffs as well. These are the major units, though there are individuals scattered across the country that are direct descendants of Jean Pierre Stouff who came to this country in 1845. Consider us the four arms of the Empire, with our satellite arms everywhere. You cannot hide.

Not only that, but my grandmother's side of the family, the Rogers, were characters of considerable esteem, let me tell you. Fay Rogers Stouff was as character-ridden as any Stouff, and could hold her own against the best of them, including the old man. They came from all over the world to experience her character, too.

There was my Uncle Ray, Dad's brother, my cousins Floyd and Otis and great-uncle Luther, who was probably the chief character of the Rogers side of the family. Uncle Luther was a shrill-voiced, opinionated man who wasn't shy about sharing his wisdom with anybody and everybody, and would have been convicted of violating political correctness laws.

Cousin Otis never had a driver's license, and he lived to be quite a respectable age. He had an impressive collection of traffic tickets stored away, unpaid. My Uncle Ray once sat around at my grandparent's house during his family's summer visit to the Rez and whittled a piece of cypress knee into some bizarre creature. When done, he presented it to me and said, "That's for you, boy. Know what it is?"

"No sir," I said, staring at this big-browed, bug-eyed monstrosity he had carved.

"That's a nauga," he informed me. "A nauga. That's what they get nauga-hide from."

I was well into my twenties before I figured out he was kidding me.

Now, lest Jim call me down on that one, I admit I do get the punchline of that story confused with another one, where my grandfather did some similarly bizarre wood carving for fun and claimed it was a one-eyed, one-horned, flyin' purple people eater. I tend to get the two confused, due to my system running low on resources, so either punchline is interchangeable. My motto, adapted from the "Swamp Gravy" team in Georgia, is, "Never let the truth get in the way of a good story."

I started my boys on the road to characterdom early. I would not tolerate foolish questions from them, much to my ex's chagrin.

If either one came to me while I was, say, planting the tomatoes in the garden and asked, "Whatcha doing?" I would reply something to the effect of, "Washing the car, son, what are you up to?"

They'd furrow their brows and after a moment of deliberation say, "Nuh-uh, you're planting tomatoes!" In this way, they learned to think on their own and I could keep my few mental resources to myself.

I had the distinct pleasure, too, of explaining to them that those big orange balls on high-power electrical lines were giant tarantula eggs. Mysteriously, we never passed one as it was hatching, much as they longed to see that happen. This one lasted quite a few years before they accused me of making up stories.

Not to be out done, my cousin Jim gave his kids a salt shaker and told them if they sprinkled salt on the tail of a bird it wouldn't be able to fly, and thus they could catch it. What ensued were endless hours of peace and quiet for him and his wife while the kids were out testing his premise.

What the world is severely lacking in nowadays is characters, young or old. More often than not, folks look away from characters because their nonconformity makes people uncomfortable in this cookie-cutter world of ours.

Sweet Tea

Recently I have become infatuated with sweet tea.

I mean, it should be no surprise, right? The surprise it that's taken me so long, I guess.

See, I was a Diet Coke addict for years. When finally I gave it up, not only did my acid reflux go away, allowing me to stop that daily purple pill after too many years of taking it, but I got off the hellacious aspartame.

Unfortunately, I am also hooked on having something "bitey"

to drink when I get to the office in the morning and after lunch, and most especially after a nap on weekends, which is the slot Diet Coke used to fill. I found I could fill this void with Community Diet Iced Tea with Lemon, but unfortunately, that put me on the sucralose bandwagon, which I didn't feel was a whole bunch better.

Now, a couple months ago, Community apparently stopped making the stuff in the cans. I was furious! See, Community makes real Southern tea. The others aren't southern tea, they're Yankee tea, and don't give me that green tea nonsense, either. That's not tea, that's health food and if you take one look at me you'll know that's not my forte. Community tastes like tea. The others taste like cold brown water with lemon.

I tried Arizona. Good, but pricey. I tried Gold Peak. Very good, but pricey. And in the end, I was still getting artificial sweeteners, while conversely a two hundred-calorie bottle of sweet tea completely turned me off.

So I got to thinking to myself, am I not a Southern boy, born and reared and proud? Am I not of the same culture as Uncle Si and his blue Tupperware cup a constant fixture to his hand?

Am I not, in short, capable of making my own dadgum tea?

I thought of the noble, cultured tradition of Southern tea. A big pot of water, tea bags, sugar. Seeping, waiting, squeezing lemons (I do NOT use lemon juice, there is absolutely no lemon in that concoction!) Pour into pitchers of ice, watch it sparkle with amber goodness! Yes, this is Southern! This is as Southern as fried chicken, brown gravy and Jack Daniels!

So I bought a tea maker.

What, you think I got time for all that nonsense?

My tea maker is made by Mr. Coffee, which is kind of unsettling when it occurs to you that your coffee pot is the same thing and equally adept at making tea, save for the fact that it will taste like Community Dark Roast. So a re-branded, taller and skinnier version of a coffee pot takes the place of a big iron pot and a whole lot of time and frustration.

Well, maybe not frustration. Or time, come to that.

See, I like my tea strong. I don't want cold brown water with sweetener and lemon. I want to taste tea. And I decided that if I was going to have to consume a few extra calories to indulge my tea-sipping fascination, it would come from honey, not sugar (no offense to the sugar growers, but honeybee keepers need love too!)

Unfortunately, I also got adventurous.

I found out you could buy loose tea. I was ecstatic. My reasoning went somewhere south as a result. I thought, "Like coffee, I can regulate the strength more easily with loose cut black tea leaves than with tea bags!" So I gathered up a half-pound of loose tea leaves, my Mr. Coffee tea maker and got to work.

First lesson: Strong tea is hard to keep from getting cloudy. In fact, tea as strong as I make it—resembling the color of the aforementioned Jack Daniels—pretty much is guaranteed to get cloudy just as soon as the tea maker seeps the tea into the pitcher that they say to fill halfway with ice. I do not like cloudy tea. On this Burl Ives and I agree.

With the roots of my Southern heritage in mind and determined to master the down-home methods of making fine, strong, sparkling tea as my culture and tradition demands, I turned to the most vaulted and esteemed source of Southern tea making known to man: Google.

I read that you can prevent cloudiness by not making the tea over ice, instead letting it cool to room temperature before putting it in the fridge. I tried this. Next morning, it was cloudy. I saw that if your tea gets cloudy you can stir in a half cup or so of boiling water to the cloudy, murky mix and it clears right up. It did, but who's got the time? I may as well make it on the stove in my gumbo pot.

I stumbled on another suggestion which I ignored for two weeks before I finally got tired of producing brown, murky, bitter tea and gave it a try: just a pinch of baking soda with the brewing tea.

Know what? No more cloudy tea! And no, you cannot taste the baking soda but I suspect my tea rises beautifully in the oven.

Now, during all this, there has also been the experimentation with strength. I have brewed pitchers of tea that left me temporarily blind and unable to remember my name. I have also brewed pitchers that so marginally tasted like tea I suspected a tea tree was growing somewhere near the water plant. I have brewed tea that solidified in the pitcher and had to be removed with an angle grinder.

But I occasionally hit it just right; a dark, honey-sweetened tea with lemon in a glass (I mean a glass made of *glass*, now, not plastic...anything else is a crime and deserving of a punishment of being deported north of the Mason Dixon line) that was just pure heaven! Honey and tea are meant for each other, both with their strong, sort of earthy flavors complemented.

Then I ran out of loose tea. Now I had to learn how to brew family-size tea bags. This process is still under way, resulting so far in a three-bag tea that I stained a woodworking project to a mahogany tone with, and two-bag tea that, if there had been no honey in the brewing process, would have tasted like baking soda. Near as I can figure, I need to cut the third bag in half to get it perfect.

I'm getting better at it. Suze can tell you, when I hit a batch just right I am beyond delighted, contented and brag about it incessantly. When I get one wrong, I pour it down the sink and pray on behalf of the plumbing.

No matter. I am enjoying this manifestation of my Southerness immensely, and it even prompted me to write this increasingly-rare column on the matter!

Tea is the consummate Southern drink. It's all about drinking sweet tea while fishing with a bobber and worm alongside the pond or the creek, listening to the Allman Brothers, Marshall Tucker Band or "Foggy Mountain Breakdown" and by saying things like "Well, bless your heart!" to people that don't know it can either be a compliment or a put-down.

I have become rather proud of my Southerness, considering myself a "Southern Indian-Cajun Gentleman" to which I can find no other references in the annals of history.

The Problem With Shop Towels

So I picked up another pack of a dozen shop towels the other day.

Really, they aren't shop towels, they're terry cloth car finishing towels. But I like them for shop use because the little strands clean better.

I am rough on shop towels. My shop towels handle everything from a coffee spill to getting epoxy off my hands and the top of the table saw. I don't have a true workbench, my shop is so small, so I use the table saw and router table extension as a work bench, and sometimes I get a little drop of epoxy, varnish or glue on the top.

But I had only two badly stained shop towels left. I wash them for as long as possible, but in the case of things like epoxy, they develop hard spots all over them and don't work well anymore. I put my new shop towels on the shelf where I keep the old ones.

Invariably, when I need to clean up a mess, I grab one of the old ones. The new ones are so clean and white, I don't want to dirty them. I do this all the time, until finally the old ones are no longer viable, and with gritted teeth, I foul the first new one.

I'm like that with a lot of things. The byproduct of being raised...not poor, but not having access to anything I wanted.

When I fish my flies, I use a particular one, say a Jitterbee, until it's so ragged and near-naked it won't attract a bite anymore. Then I put on a new one. Waste not want not, right?

Not really. I just like things pretty and new and shiny and hate for them to get messed up. You know, like that first ding on your new vehicle. That's the one that hurts the most!

I tied Jitterbees in three colors, about thirty in each, some four years ago. Still have most of them, that's how long I fish a fly until it's demolished beyond use.

Normally, I don't tie flies, I buy them. This is because my eyes are getting so bad that "tying flies" can loosely be translated to "cussing, yelling, pounding the table and throwing away perfectly good fly tying materials." But the Jitterbee is not a commercial fly, so I tie my own, usually when no one else is home.

I hate writing on the first sheet in a new notebook. After that, I'm good to the end. I hate taking the first shot on a new roll of film, back when I did such things, but was eager to get to the end so I could get them developed. Interestingly, I have no such inhibitions about an empty memory card.

They say digital photography does not have the warmth and depth of film, and I disagree, I think it exceeds film. The same cannot be said of audio CDs, however. To my ear—and many others feel the same—digital audio just doesn't have the fullness and warmth of an analog recording on a vinyl record. But until they put record players in the dashboards of cars, we're pretty much stuck with CDs.

Which brings me, believe it or not, to birds.

I have recently begun to enjoy watching the birds at Suze's feeders around the yard. I even snap their photos...digitally, of course. I never much cared about watching birds. I mean, I appreciate birds, especially colorful ones, but to sit down and watch birds, well, no, that just wasn't on my itinerary.

But Suze and I sit out on the porch every evening and watch the birds on the feeders. I enjoyed it very much, and actually started getting ten-pound bags of birdseed to keep the little rascals coming.

I've got titmouse, cardinals, chickadees, house wrens, doves and others I can't really identify yet at our feeders. We even have a shy redheaded woodpecker around, but he never gets very close when we're around.

I wanted a blue bird, though. Suze had one show up briefly last winter, and she got a picture of it, but I never got to see it. My pal has blue birds galore in Cade, and makes me jealous at every opportunity by sending me photos and descriptions of them. I don't mind, I enjoy seeing them.

So I made a bluebird house according to various plans I found online, and put it on the tree in the back yard. So far, nothing. I watch it every day, hoping for a flash of color, but alas, nothing. I am feeling maligned and outcast.

One day, I looked out the back window, and saw something moving around in my bluebird house. At last! I rushed outside, sneaked quietly up to it, and looked with binoculars into the entry hole.

Looking back at me from inside was a green lizard.

I was crushed. Pete's got his bluebirds, and they actually raised a family in his back yard just thirty miles from here...I got a lizard. I feel like Charlie Brown at trick-or-treat.

But I remain hopeful. Because you see—and here's how we got from shop towels to lizards in the bluebird house, believe it or not —once a family moves in, raise some young'uns and moves on, the birdhouse won't be like a brand new shop towel sitting on the shelf anymore. And THEN I get to go build another one to put on another tree in the yard? Ya folla?

Yeah, I know. Fuzzy logic.

Downgrading

A year or so ago I fell for the slick advertising and upgraded my cellular phone to one of those fancy-dancy, gosh-wow-did-you-see-that-Ma? touch screen phones.

It wasn't an iPhone. It was Android. But this bad boy had Internet and email capability, a full touch-pad keyboard and more bells and whistles than I could count or surely comprehend.

As a self-confessed Luddite and Walden-esque follower of Brother Thoreau, I admit a certain amount of shame in its acquisition. But time always reveals that leopards do not, in fact, change their spots: I have grown to hate it and everything connected with it.

First of all, I concede that texting is a remarkably useful thing. Most of all, texting is simply divine when you just want to send a quick note or question to someone without risk of getting into a lengthy conversation on a phone call:

"Hey, who did 'China Grove'?"

"Doobies. How's the fishing?"

You know what I mean. Also, my fingers are too clumsy, calloused and thick to use the touch screen keyboard and I often hit the letter next to the one I intend, so I use whatever's handy as a stylus, an ink pen, fork, my pocket knife, straw, coffee stirrer, you name it.

I really grooved on having Internet access for the first month or so, but after a while I got tired of trying to read weather and news on it. Zooming did no good, because it makes you scroll from side to side.

Now, I realize this is not a primo phone, and there are better. I got all obsessed with a friend's new Blackberry and vowed, "Next time I'm due for an upgrade I'm getting one of those!"

But I think what annoys me most is what I pay for this rotten thing. It's insane. Cell phone charges in general are just nuts. I am paying an outrageous amount of money every month for a device that I do not like, and a service that does nothing but hack me off.

For one thing, I hate telephones. They are a necessary evil, but every time one goes off I start to cussin'. If I look at the caller ID and it's something like "unknown name, unknown number" the cussin' accelerates a notch or two in volume and caliber of chosen words. If I do not know your name or your number, I will not answer your phone calls, cellular or land line.

Here's another thing: I hardly use the Internet feature on my phone anymore and texting just as infrequently. Why am I paying the equivalent of ten six-packs of a good import beer for it?

Because I fell for the slick advertising, of course. That's why.

As it is, Suze and I can't stand the commercials on the tube. We don't understand what they're trying to sell us in half of them (and are pretty certain we don't want it) and find the other half so brain-dead stupid we wouldn't buy their products anyway, after they've insulted our intelligence so profoundly.

Like the one a few months ago where some androgynous creature—I think it was a girl but I am not sure—is gyrating on the screen and singing, "I...know...what...you...want!" It's a good thing she did, because I obviously don't have a clue and still didn't by the end of the commercial.

But back to the phone. I am also concerned about radiation. Yeah, I know, give me an aluminum foil skullcap, but there's a lot of evidence out there that those microwaves mess with your brain waves, and believe me, my brain waves are near flat-line as it is. I also have seen indications that a man wearing a cell phone on his hip causes sterility, impotence and possibly prostate cancer. While I do not plan on fathering any more children, the other two are not high on my list of "what...you...want!" either.

I worry enough about brain tumors anyway without the added threat of putting a cell phone to my ear and letting it transmit high-frequency signals through my skull. Thick as my cranium may be, it can't be good for what little cognitive ability I possess.

So I think I'm going back to a basic phone and a basic plan, which is too dadgum expensive anyway for someone who rarely uses the thing, and even then under protest. I want to keep my texting options open, even if I have to pay per use, because sometimes —don't take it personally—I just don't wanna get into a lengthy conversation. All that Internet stuff can go, though. I got a perfectly good computer or two that does Internet and yeah, it's at home or at work, but I don't carry around my microwave oven, television set, table saw, refrigerator or washer and dryer on my hip, either.

Downgrading is what I'm going to do. The problem is, when I go to the website to do so, they're going to throw all this gadgetry and gosh-wow stuff at me. iPhones and Blackberrys, watch videos on your phone, choose from four hundred zillion apps, 3G, 4G…I have to be strong. I won't fall for the slick advertising again, you hear me?

A Windshield Wash

It occurs to me that it's all about a windshield wash.

One of my earliest memories was toolin' into Chapron's Service Station in Baldwin with my mom on a grocery-getting expedition. Mom would pull that big, yellow and white Ford Galaxie up next to a pump, and the attendant would pump the gas.

While the tank was filling, he'd dip that long sponge-squeegee thing into a bucket of suds, rub the sponge side across the windshield, careful to lift the wipers out of the way. Then he'd flip it over to the squeegee side and pull the water away, wiping the rubber blade with a blue shop towel as he worked. I remember that, for some reason, vividly.

About forty years later, I pulled up at a "filling station" to get gas. You'll note that in the time expired from my memory to today, they became "filling stations" instead of "service stations." I stuck my card in the slot, entered my private information, leaned up against the truck as my gas was pumping. I noticed how dirty the windshield was.

When I was done, I hung the nozzle and got my receipt. I went home and cleaned my own windows.

Certainly you know me well enough that I constantly bemoan the fact that people do little for themselves anymore, and I'm not reversing my preachings. But it got me to thinking: A windshield wash at a service station, along with an tire air pressure check, oil check and the like, is a clear indication of what this country has lost, and what it's become.

Think back: When did they start putting garbage cans with a tray rack near the doors at fast food joints? When they stopped busing tables themselves, and decided *you* could do it instead. I had a buddy who never, ever picked up his tray and remains of the meal from a table: "I paid to eat, not bus their tables," he growled.

Rather than ask you if you'd like ketchup, mayo or mustard, they put it all out on a shelf, so they don't have to bother, but tell you it's for your convenience. The straws are there too, and since every drink comes with a lid that has a perforation for a straw, it should be automatic.

I'm as big a fan of a buffet as the next guy, but when did the buffet, or the salad bar, come into existence? They tricked us into thinking we were getting something special, but in fact, we were taking on some of their work, their responsibility, and with no price cuts; in fact most of the time with cost increases.

You have to pay a quarter or more to get air from a vending machine if you have a low tire and pull up at a gas station. They are charging you for *air*. They say you're helping pay the cost of electricity to run the compressor. But the fact of the matter is, you're paying for air, friends and neighbors.

Mom used to go to Commercial Bank with dad's paycheck, give it to the cashier and they'd fill out a deposit slip, ask her if she wanted any cash, and handle it.

I remember when Burger Chef here in town came out with a "burger bar." Me and my pals thought it was the coolest thing ever. We'd go in, pay for our bun and beef patty, then go load 'em up six inches tall with condiments. What we didn't realize then was that the price was higher, and we took on some of the employee's work, while they were sitting in the back smoking and watching *The A-Team*.

When did you start having to ask for a receipt when you make a purchase at some places? I remember when you got a receipt no matter what, because if you gave them money, they gave you proof of it. That's just what you did.

They have self-checkout lanes in some supermarkets now, so that you allegedly don't have to wait in line for a real person to check you out. Besides that, time was, you got Green Stamps, too.

See, it's all about a windshield wash. You didn't think much of it. They didn't think much of giving it. You chatted with the guy at the service station—the full-service station. I remember the kindly African-American man at Chapron's always chatted with Mom about the weather and the family.

Breaux's Foodland in Baldwin still has a person who'll take your groceries to the car and load them in most of the time when I go, but how often do you see that anymore? It's been so long, I feel guilty now when someone does it for me.

Remember when they didn't ask you to write your account number on your check and on the envelope you mail it in when paying a bill? And they didn't have computers back then. They even knew your name and face.

You could make a similar, long list. It's all about a windshield wash, and the ideas behind it: Customer service, customer loyalty, something extra, gratitude for your business.

Depression

When I started writing this I was feeling depressed, and unsure why. Sounds like an entry in a teenage girl's diary, doesn't it? But it happens. It happens now and then. Runs in the family, I guess. Practically gallops, as Mortimer Brewster might say.

People ask, "What are you depressed about?"

I say, "I don't know."

Isn't that crazy? How can you be depressed without a reason? Without knowing why? Sure, it's common these days. Clinical, even.

It starts two ways: Either as a gentle nudging, of something not quite right...butterflies in the stomach, a sense of undefined anxiety. Other than that, I might just wake up and it's just there. A companion, of sorts, because it takes on a life of its own.

I converse with it, sometimes. Yeah, I know. But I do. Discussion is better than medication. I'd rather talk things out with my depression than take pills. I hate pills. And it's cheap therapy, really. No hourly fees, and I reward myself with a cookie when I'm done.

We discuss what, exactly, it wants here, what it expects of me. It doesn't answer these questions directly. Instead, it conjures little memories for me to attempt interpretation. Memories of people I once shared this life with, who had the same blood as mine. Or didn't. It shows me dreams that never came true. Some that did. Sometimes, I can vividly see myself standing on the Beach at Charenton and there's no end to Grand Lake in sight. Sometimes, instead, I see galleons come up from the river, iron helmets flashing bright in the sun. Or myself at ten, riding my grandmother's Snapper Comet lawn mower, cutting the grass in front of her/my/our house, careful not to cut her flowers.

I don't know. What does it want with me? I'm not sure. I know that I've led a life largely comprised of loss. I've lost more already than I should have were I much older.

When I feel this way, things come to mind, but I can't be sure if they're the reason for it, or have just dropped in to crash the party. Misery loves company, after all. For instance, I think perhaps it may be because my cousin and I tried to get into Grand Avoille Cove this weekend, and it was too shallow. Slowly dying from siltation, an emphysema of water bodies. But no, I felt the tingling of it earlier last week, and knew it was there, a rough beast, as Yeats knew, slouching toward my soul to be born.

Can you imagine the party my depression might throw? It'll serve drinks in Mickey Mouse cups from a dispenser next to the toothpaste and toothbrush. And finger foods, because I'm not classy enough to serve hors d'oeuvres at any party my depression might throw. Hors d'œuvres are chips and spinach dip to me. Or maybe French onion. My depression doesn't need to impress via caviar. It's on a pizza budget, too.

So at this party for which depression sent out invitations to all my losses and regrets, some of my guilts and dreams heard about it and decided to crash, and they stand around talking like I'm not even in the room listening.

"What, you think he would have turned out any different if he had been a doctor or something?" my Regret Over Not Finishing

College queries.

"No," corrects my Dream of Digging For Native American Sites. "He was going to be an archaeologist. Ran out of money spittin' distance from his senior year, though. Tsk-tsk."

This strikes my Missing All The Old People Who Raised Me as funny and he guffaws, spilling his martini glass full of vitriol on his fly fishing vest. "You guys," he says, wiping his vest with a napkin that looks suspiciously like a five-year-old's Spiderman pajamas. I think I remember that lad, but he's been gone so, so long...

"Doesn't matter," claims Regret. "He'd still be the same."

"But he might have made some serious money as an architect," says my Fruitless Ambition.

"Ha," says my Uncontrollable Need For More Fly Rods. "He's been walking away from good money all his life, why should being a lawyer or a doctor or an astronaut matter? He'd just spend it all on fly rods anyway, and grow old and die in a cardboard box behind an Orvis store."

True, true, I nod from the corner where I'm hiding behind a vase of lovely forget-me-nots. There's a copy of *Native Waters* there on the table beside it. They know me all too well. But I chastise Uncontrollable for stealing a line from John Gierach. The one about walking away from good money, that is. I'm not that depressed, to stoop to plagiarism.

I step out from behind the vase to confront them, noticing that the flowers have somehow become snapdragons, and sure that there's an allegory there but I can't quite figure out what it is, and forget the confrontation. Beside the vase is a copy of another of my books, and it's open, and I read:

When we stop chasing thunderbirds, what else is there?

But of course none of that's real, it's just a fancy I have. In a few days, it'll pass, and I'll be back to myself, cracking wise and pontificating philosophically, rather than staring out the window at a distant line of trees, and the wisps of clouds drifting over them, somewhere I can't see but think I can smell, hear and certainly imagine.

Lots of things make me happy, like the female Northern Cardinal I saw at Suze's bird feeder early one morning, and it was bright yellow! Beautiful, beautiful creature. Sunsets make me happy. My girl makes me happy. My pets make me happy. It's no big deal. It's the things that are indefinable, I think. The weak animals the predator that is depression preys upon.

It's just a visitor, of sorts. It comes, and then it goes, and we tolerate each other's company for the duration of its stay. Like I said, it seems to be partially genetic. And when it's gone, I give a sigh of relief and continue on my merry way, and sometimes catch just the very faintest scent of gardenias wafting through the air. Then it's gone.

Happinesses

I got to thinking, after that pity-party essay, about the things that make me happy.

When my cousin from California was here last weekend and we sat on the patio with the dog discussing writing, he asked me what my new novel was about.

"Well," I said. "It's three guys, who were childhood friends, but then..."

He stopped me. "No, not the plot. What's it about. What are you saying."

The query stumped me. I had no idea I wanted to say anything at all, just tell a story. That's what I do, tell stories. Like my father did, and his father before him. I come from a long line of story tellers, you see, and it just seems to be what I do.

So I chewed on it for a time and as I stumbled over a few sentences, the light bulb went on in the darkness.

"It's about everything I think is wrong with the world today," I told him. "That's it. It's about all the things that are wrong, and how much I miss the things that were right. That's it exactly."

But if I look around, there's still remnants of that world left. They've been stashed in shadows, trampled by progress. If you look closely enough, though, they're still there, waiting to be found, caches of yesteryear.

I mentioned about the cardinal. I had never seen such a thing. Bogie and I were outside, before work one morning. Suze has bird feeders in the back by the patio which are often frequented by doves, cardinals and other feathered minions. All of a sudden, I see this yellow cardinal land on the feeder. Now, maybe I just missed it before, but in all my years I never saw a yellow cardinal before. Hereabouts, male cardinals are bright red, the females more subdued. It was beautiful, a golden-yellow with the black mask, and red beak.

Investigation proved this was the female Northern Cardinal. I was delighted. From the frozen north, a visitor I had never met. Who could be sad after such a chance acquaintance? I saw it one or two more times, but not lately. That's fine.

For a man who doesn't despise the indoors but is far happier outside, I find there are little miracles all around me, inside and out.

Here's a few:

When the bayou goes down under the push of the north wind in winter, the suddenly landlocked clams make me happy. Oh, they'll survive, the water'll come back soon enough and they can breathe for a long time that way. I like the way their shapes jut from the gray-brown mud and the little puddles they make around themselves.

I like that the clams are often surrounded by bird prints, and now and then I see raccoon tracks in the mud and long, slithering trails that must have been snakes.

Oreo cookies with the chocolate centers make me happy; add a glass of cold milk and I'm in complete nirvana.

Maps make me happy, but you knew that.

The shotgun my cousin brought me makes me happy. Trading him for a custom made by yours truly fly rod in "presentation" grade, meaning "top notch." Certainly I couldn't have done better, a Winchester 101 of 1966 vintage. You know how I love old things, and a fine double gun in twenty gauge just a couple years younger than me makes me happy. Coming from family, it makes me happier. We'll have days afield, just like my cuz did, and that makes me happy.

The way our yellow Lab puppy Bogie tucks his behind under his body and dances around in pure, unconditional joy when I come home makes me happy. You can't buy that for any amount of money.

Gumbo makes me happy. Oh, the glory of gumbo! The world's perfect food. Well, maybe not, but it should be. A dark roux, almost black, full of red onions, green onions, red bell peppers (you can keep the green ones far as I'm concerned) , okra, sausage and either chicken or seafood. File, hot sauce, rice. That right there, ladies and germs, is reason to go on living!

Trees make me happy. I do not hug them. I hug my girl, and that makes me happiest yet. Greenpeace people must not have girlfriends, so that must be why they hug trees. I recommend girlfriends for hugging; trees are for marveling over their majesty, quiet contemplation and ancient wisdom.

I think trees talk, you just have to slow down enough to listen. Tolkien taught me that. We live so dad-blamed fast nowadays—a condition which does not make me happy—that we have exceeded the speed at which we can hear the natural world speaking. Even the audible is unheard, like the words in the rolling giggle of running water or the rustling leaves in a west wind high above. I think if we'd all just slow down and listen, we'd all be happy.

Good movies make me happy. These are few and far between these days. But a good movie has the power to amuse, sadden, elate or otherwise conjure many emotions from the watcher. This is an art, and it makes me happy even if the movie is sad.

Patches sleeping on my lap—a condition for which I've been far too restless lately, poor girl—makes me happy when I'm subdued enough to enjoy it.

A golden field of slumping Johnson grass makes me bittersweet-happy, reminds me of the autumns and winters of my youth when the cold didn't bother me so much as it does now, and I knew there were quail out there waiting to be found, back before we clean-farming'd them out of habitat and out of our lives. A near-Christmas field without the sound of a cheerful *Bob-white! Bob-white!* is lonely as a funeral parlor.

Sometimes, it makes me happy to wallow in memories of things that in the present make me sad. There is a special talent in this capacity; you should admire it.

My fly rods, without question, make me happy. So do my reels. And my flies. And my lines. And...well, you get the idea.

Cypress lumber makes me happy.

Peanut butter makes me happy.

A morning, on green-black water in the back of an ancestral cove studded with cypress like old soldiers holding each other up by outstretched arms...a mist over the surface, just high enough that the bow of the boat cuts it like a bludgeon but not so high as I can't see...the whisper of spirits out there, voices speaking languages I can't intellectually understand but instinctively do...there's a world that makes me happy, to be sure.

Mechanisms

Beelzebub and the General

Though I have been grateful for the nearly daily rain to keep the temperatures down most of the time, it has had the unwanted side effect of making the grass grow like nobody's business.

I kid you not, my neighbor cut half of his yard on Friday and the other half on Saturday, and there was a good half-inch difference in the cuts. The grass had grown that much overnight!

Everyone knows how much I love grass-cutting. I have about three acres to take care of between my yard and my mom's. Thankfully, my neighbor has a big tractor with a big cutting deck and cuts the couple of acres behind the house at the bayou side for me.

I have two lawn mowers. One is a forty-two-inch department store special that I disdainfully call Beelzebub because I am certain I know exactly where it was manufactured. Beelzebub cuts a wide swath which makes the chore less time-consuming, but it rarely cuts level. It usually leaves lines on one side or the other, and there's no rhyme or reason to it. Once it caught itself actually cutting perfectly, silky-smooth level and blew out an inner tube in the back tire out of sheer meanness.

The other is a thirty-inch cut that I refer to as Gen. George Armstrong Custer. It cuts the grass very well, but like the infamous U.S. Calvary commander himself, it is sneaky, dishonest and cowardly about it. The General will approach a patch of grass and, if finding it's taller than it can chew, chokes up, sputters, coughs and shuts down in terror. The General is so much like its namesake that I often have to coax it into moving at all when it realizes it's on an Indian reservation and completely surrounded.

Well, this Sunday when I went to cut grass Beelzebub had apparently imbibed too much fire and brimstone and would not start. A little investigation revealed that the starter was shot. Since it was clear I wouldn't have one of those lying around, I put it away and retrieved the General.

The General had a bad negative battery cable but I patched that up and, since it hadn't run in awhile, I had to crank it quite some time to get it to fire. All this time, you realize, the sweat is pouring off my forehead and nose and onto the mower, and I feared the salty moisture might rust the General, but it simply sizzled and evaporated the instant it hit the red metal.

Finally the General sputtered, coughed and woke up with a hangover, another credit to its namesake. Once rejuvenated, we took off for the job at hand.

Cutting nearly two acres of land by thirty-inch swaths in ninety-eight degree weather with a heat index of one hundred and thirteen is no laughing matter. I've said it before that whoever conceived of heat indexes ought to be put in a sauna for a day without relent. It's not bad enough that the weatherman can tell you, "It's going to be ninety-seven degrees tomorrow." That's pretty depressing on its own. But no. He has to add, "With the humidity, the heat index will be one hundred and thirteen degrees." It's like wind chill, I guess, in the winter. It might be thirty degrees but with the wind chill it "feels like" twenty degrees. This is, in my book, information we as a culture lived without for centuries and don't need to know now.

Anyway, I managed to get the whole yard cut, trimmed and rather neat at last. And just as I was about to get on the General again to go do my mom's yard, it sputtered, coughed, hiccuped, called for another round of doubles, and retired for the evening.

I suspect it's a fuel filter problem from sitting up for so long, but I was too tired, cranky and suffering from heat-indexitis to pursue the matter further. My neighbor comes up on his big tractor behind me while I'm spraying some herbicide around the trees in the bayou side pasture and I say, "You be sure and let me know when it gets hot, hear?" and the look on his face told me the humor was notwithstanding at all.

I hope that in a couple months two things will happen: The heat will relent and, due to shorter days, the grass will grow less vigorously. If it was up to me, I'd let the whole yard go to nature. Throw a dozen pounds of wildflower seeds from road to bayou and call it a day. My yard could be a mini wildflower preserve on the Rez, and my neighbors on either side and across the street could look in envy (or disgust, depending) from their well-manicured, freshly-mown lawns while they mop sweat off their brows with beach towels. Eventually birds will move in and I'll have a bird sanctuary, and in even more time, I might have to declare the property an endangered species region because of its resident endangered species: Me. I'm endangered because the ostriches have built a nest next to the General and a pride of lions has made a home around Beelzebub and the male of the pride likes to sit atop its vine-covered hood and search the surrounding three-acres of wilderness for wildebeest. When you see me come home and turn into my driveway—I am now driving one of those *Mutual Of Omaha's Wild Kingdom* safari jeep-things—I vanish at once and all you see are the plants swaying as I make my way to the front door, fending off the pythons, anacondas, lions and occasional displaced Sasquatch.

Well, I hate cutting grass, anyway. That's all I was trying to say. That and it sure it is hot, ain't' it?

Lawnmowers and Bees

I was walking across the back yard toward the bayou, and I stepped right into a nest of ground bees. You know, the big, black, hairy ones that sound like a Japanese Zero when they come at you. On about two acres of property, the chances of me setting foot right on top of a two-inch hole in the ground which serves as the entrance to the nest should be unlikely, except for me. Chaos, always on the edge.

They hit me in droves. The first one got me behind the ear and I leaped about three feet into the air with no idea what had happened. Then another got me on the elbow, and again on the chin, and it was then I had finally figured out it was not in my best interests to study the problem any further, so I ran like crazy. They chased me clean to the road, a good six or seven hundred feet before they abandoned pursuit. They had stung me fourteen times.

I eradicated the nest the next day. But months later, I was mowing the back pasture, which has been an overdue venture, and I'm creeping the lawn mower through a particularly thick patch of weeds, when I suddenly realize I'm seeing spots before my eyes. Thinking I might be having a relapse of jungle fever, I do the worst thing possible: I press the brakes and stop. At that moment, a ground bee hovers right in front of my face, studies me for a moment, then dives in for the kill.

I screamed like a banshee and jumped off the lawn mower, which is supposed to have a switch that kills the engine if you leave the seat. It either did not or it no longer functioned. When I exited, the lawn mower took off toward the bayou in fourth gear. I was headed the other way, still unstung and counting my blessings when I realized there had to be a reason I was unscathed. I stopped and looked back, and there went the lawn mower, straight for the bayou, a swarm of angry bees in pursuit.

I couldn't very well let my lawn mower go swimming, of course, so I mustered all the strength and courage I could find, and doing a remarkably good imitation of Jim Thorpe, took off at full tilt. It worked well: As I dashed by the mower, I reached over and turned the key off. The engine killed but the bees continued trying to sting it. I glanced back, proud that I had emerged unstung, thinking I had beaten chaos at its own game, and ran straight into a tree.

Luckily, I hit it with my left shoulder and it left no mark, but it did knock the wind out of me and threw me back to the ground. I lay there, trying to catch my breath, looking up through the branches of the tree at a squirrel who had apparently observed the entire incident. He gave me a decidedly "what's the world coming to" look and nibbled on something. I hoped it was a bee.

And I remember lying there, as the air finally reached my lungs again, until I was finally able to roll over and get up. The bees had by then given up their attempts to execute the lawn mower, but I didn't care anymore. I left it there, walked back to the house and collapsed on the sofa. And that's where I stayed for the rest of the afternoon.

Lawn Mowing Blues

It's become all too clear that the thorns in the paw of my life are lawn mowers.

I have two lawn mowers. Neither of them work worth pecan. I have my yard to cut and my mom's yard to cut. That's about three acres of cutting. I have come to give my lawn mowers names. I won't discuss their brands, of course, but the bigger one with the thirty-eight-inch cutting deck I have deemed Beelzebub and the smaller one with the thirty-inch cut I call dubbed George Armstrong Custer.

Beelzebub—so named because I am sure I know where it was built—has a bad habit of throwing belts. It runs great, engine-wise, and cuts smooth as silk. But there I am, mowing along, singing to myself (yes, I sing to myself when I'm cutting the grass, but not in the shower) and *POW!* The belt slips off the pulley and the blade stops cutting. So I have to shut it down, climb off and remount the belt.

Now, I'm not a complete moron, only a small percentage of one, and I'm moderately mechanically inclined. I've changed the belt, changed the pulley, the guides, changed the oil, just about everything but the paint job. I'm not claiming to be a lawn mower repair expert, but there's only so much that can go wrong with a belt and three pulleys.

So I get back on and start cutting again, and somewhere in the third verse of my rendition of an Allman Brothers hit, *POW!* Sans belt again. By this time, you understand, it's a hundred degrees in the shade and I understand that Beelzebub is feeling a little homesick. So I get frustrated and put him up and go get Gen. George Armstrong Custer.

Custer runs great, its belts don't slip off, but it cuts grass about the way the U.S. Cavalry general fought Indians: Sneaks up on them at unawares, cuts down whatever it can easily without much effort and leaves the rest standing as it retreats. It is also extremely uneven in its cutting, and no matter how I adjust the deck, the left side always cuts lower than the right side by an inch. So after the cutting's done, the yard looks like an overweight cavalry soldier rode over it on a crippled horse.

Understand that while Beelzebub is a bargain department store mower, Gen. Custer is of a higher caliber. A West Point man, so to speak, and cost a few hundred dollars more. You'd expect better from a West Point grad who made it to the rank of general. Every time Gen. George Armstrong Custer and I go out to cut the grass, it's like Little Big Horn all over again, and this time, the Indians lose.

Thankfully, my neighbor kindly took pity on my eternal war with the forces of darkness and the U.S. cavalry and he cuts one acre of my two with his big tractor. Takes him about twenty minutes to cut what takes me all day, counting the time I waste putting belts back on pulleys, hammering guides back into place and failing to level cutting decks.

Having finally gotten the gas cut, it's time to trim it with the gas-powered string trimmer. Mine reminds me of a girl I used to swoon over: Sexy, curvy, loud and will cut your heart out if you ain't careful. She—the trimmer, that is—goes through monofilament line like there's no end to my pocketbook. It takes two reloads to get my yard trimmed. She also doesn't like to get going in the morning, preferring to sleep in, and she sputters, coughs and complains as I'm breaking a sweat trying to start her up.

When it's finally done, part of the yard looks silky smooth with occasional ragged patches where Beelzebub's belt slipped; the rest looks like rows of a cornfield trampled by Gen. George Armstrong Custer's regiment, and the trim looks like the remains of a frozen dinner.

I often think that when I get rich in my next life, I'll just concrete the whole yard and be done with it. Just kidding. More likely, I'll get some goats. Or sheep. Or an ostrich flock. Or an emu farm.

Lawn Mowing Shame

You really know that you've sunken to the lowest depths of pure denial when you come home and your neighbor is cutting your grass.

Friday afternoon (there's some confusion about this: I say it was Friday, everyone else says it was Thursday because I told them about it Friday. It's all a blur to me) I headed out from the office with nothing more on my mind than a good, serious, hard-timing, nitty-gritty nap. I could hear my sofa calling all the way from Wilson Street, and I was following it home like a siren's signal.

Now, you may recall that the curse of my existence is lawn mowing and lawn mowers. Add to that the fact that I tend to get distracted, and you get all the makings of one of those Hope and

Crosby jungle movies in my front yard.

My neighbor, on the other hand, is meticulous about lawn up-keep. He has, in the past, been kind enough to cut the back of my property with his big tractor with a six-foot cutting deck. I have been eternally grateful.

But out of the kindness of his own heart, he decided to cut a bit more than that, and when I got home, all set for some serious napping, my heart sank into my shoes. I went inside, where the sofa sat waiting with tempting cushions, gave it my regrets, changed clothes and went out to fire up Gen. George Armstrong Custer. As usual, he had two flats, which had to be pumped up.

So I started cutting, and within an hour, the two of us had the whole yard done. I thanked him profusely, of course, and meant it. It would have been a four-hour job without his help. I didn't mention, and neither did he, that I was a total bum and didn't deserve such kindness. I also did not mention that the rhinos no longer have a place to live and that there was an anaconda hanging from the bumper of his tractor. No use spoiling the moment.

I pulled out the trimmer then to finish up. Gasoline-powered trimmers are the greatest invention of all-time, but they still need some engineering fine-tuning. They are, nonetheless, a dramatic improvement over the electric ones, which cut more extension cord than they did weeds.

Anyway, I got maybe fifty feet done, when it suddenly belched, hiccuped and a flame shot out of the back end about three feet, scorched my Joseph's Coat climbing rose and promptly expired for good.

Now, normally I'd be fussing up a storm at such equipment fail-ure. I usually raise ten kinds of tarnation when Gen. Custer has flats, or Beelzebub refuses to cooperate and throws belts all over the place.

This time, however, I threw the trimmer into the trash and went to take a nap. There is, after all, justice in the world.

Sunday I went to get another trimmer and cut my mom's yard; the trimmer worked great. So I spent the rest of the day working on my boat, but I kept getting a really weird, uneasy feeling. I couldn't put my finger on it for hours, but it was very unsettling.

I finally realized I was having the same feeling a gazelle might have when caught on a savanna with no cover. The freshly mown grass had deprived me of my security. When the grass was high, I felt more secluded. Now, there I was, working on my boat in the garage, and everybody could see me. This is the same strange paranoia many journalists are afflicted with which results in some of us refusing to sit anywhere but with our backs to the wall at a restaurant, bar or whatever. Thusly annoyed, I picked up my tools and went to take a nap on the sofa where nobody could see me.

I think that if I had the chance, I would turn my yard into some sort of nature preserve. Have it planted with cypress trees and an undergrowth of wildflowers. I could import some hippos and maybe a saber-toothed tiger or two. No, wait, those are extinct. A Bengal tiger, then. It would look pretty, and people would pass by and "ooh" and "ahh" over my splendid landscaping.

They would not realize, of course, the truth of the matter: It requires no mowing, and nobody can see me.

Vintage Vending

Modern technological advances and scientific discovery have contributed to great leaps and bounds in the development of many things in our lives over the past several decades.

Vending machines are not one of them.

In fact, if anything, I believe vending machines are suffering from de-evolution. They are actually regressing technologically, reverting to some primitive life-form, though I'm not sure what that would be for a vending machine. You could say that, for example, a Toyota Tundra de-evolves into a Zero airplane, or a Z71 truck de-evolves into an old red pickup like John Walton drove, but what about vending machines? I don't know, but I'm sure it's something horrifying.

Sure, modern vending machines are bright and colorful and have well-lit bubble plastic graphics of tantalizingly cold-looking soft drinks on them. But they are misfits, vending machines are, the technological stepchildren of SUVs, which if you get right down to it, are nothing more than station wagons. The nation grew bored with station wagons in the early 1980s, no longer considered them hip or respectable, and the station wagon largely died. But if you look at an SUV closely, what do you see? Just a tall station wagon. No, they don't have faux wood-grain panels on their sides, nor do they kinda slink down the street like a badger on methamphetamine, but SUVs are station wagons taken to the next level. It's also interesting to note that SUVs are the only place hatchbacks still exist. The world loved hatchbacks for decades. They even put them on Mustangs, though they were far more common on Celicas and Pintos. You don't see hatchbacks anymore, except on SUVs. Sometimes I think if SUVs could wear leisure suits, Chevrolet would introduce the Tahoe "Herb Tarlek Edition."

But we were talking about vending machines. In the old days, vending machines were large and roomy inside. So roomy that the snacks inside seemed puny, and this was when a bag of potato chips weighed half a pound, not the quarter of an ounce you get now. In those days, big vending machines held big bags of chips for twenty-five cents; today small vending machines are stuffed full of small bags of chips you pay seventy-five cents or more for. Old vending machines took up half the wall of an employee lounge, while new ones are more compact, silly-looking things that the Jawas from *Star Wars* wouldn't even pick up for scrap.

Just this morning, for example, I put two quarters into a vending machine and pressed two buttons for a bag of chips. Now, there's something else I never understood. There are by my count thirty-six items in a vending machine. But you have to press like "B8" or something to get a bag of barbecue flavored chips, so they put every letter of the alphabet and the numbers 1-9 on the front as buttons so you can make thirty six different selections from an alphabet of twenty-six letters and nine digits. So which item of the thirty six never gets sold because you can't key in the right combination, and why did they put it in there in the first place? You're saying to yourself now, "But Rog, if you go from A to Z then A1 to A9 and you're one short, you just go to B1, don't you see?" Okay, fine, Mr. or Mrs. Logical-Minded. Then why do we need the numbers 1-9, huh? If you can buy twenty-six items with the letters A to Z, then all you need to add is the number 1 on a key, and press A1, B1, C1, D1, etc. until you have all items covered. It's overkill, I tell you, slovenly waste! Leave me alone, I got a headache now.

So I press the two buttons, the little twirly piece of metal moves, forcing the bag of chips to the front, where it tumbles...and gets stuck between the glass on the front of the machine and the rack. This bag was for a co-worker. The bag I wanted was directly above the stuck bag, so I fed it another two quarters, made the selection I wanted, and presto! The bag of chips directly above the stuck bag was pushed out, fell off the rack and missed the stuck bag —through some warp in the space-time continuum—by roughly half a mile.

What to do? New vending machines are so small you could easily tip them over, and I thought seriously about grabbing the top of it and pulling it toward me so the chips would fall out. But this machine was in the lobby of the courthouse, and with all the concerns about homeland security and such, I was afraid to utilize this method of chip bag retrieval.

I realized that I had two quarters left. I scrounge through my pocket and find another quarter, feed these to the machine, and choose the number for the stuck bag of chips again. The twirly thing moves, forces out another bag which, remarkably, actually hits the stuck bag and both fall to the bottom of the machine. I now have to go explain to my co-worker why rather than having one bag of chips and a quarter change, she now has two bags of chips and owes me a quarter.

None of this would have ever happened in an old vending machine, you realize. Old vending machines were like a Buick Elektra: You had enough room to do somersaults in there if you wanted to. Old drink vending machines also had another advantage: Those cool doors. They would always be damp with condensation from the cold inside, and you had to open it up to read the tops of the bottles to see what was available and if you wanted it. After you fed the machine your money, you pulled it out, and there was that satisfying snap sound after you got your bottle out. I loved that sound.

Today's vending machines do not have a door, and you cannot see inside soft drink machines to see if they have what you want.

Intermediate evolutionary machines at least had a light on the button and you could tell if it was out. Today? You feed it your money, push the button, only to find out that the machine is out of Diet Coke, and Dr. Pepper, and Sprite, and in fact, the only thing left in the entire despicable contraption is glacier water flavored with cantaloupe. I think the best thing about old vending machines was that nothing healthy was ever allowed, and if something was flavored with fruit, it was not any variety of melon and was loaded with enough pure sugar to keep you going full throttle all day and all night.

Remember the chest-type soft drink machines? Gosh, I loved those things, especially if they had root beer. Root beer tasted better in a chest-type soft drink machine, and no amount of denial, ridicule or argument from anyone is going to convince me otherwise. You lifted the lid, put in your money, then slid your bottle to the little latch area and pulled it through. Careful not to let your grip slip! If you did, your soft drink was lost forever somewhere in the bowels of the machine, but that was okay. You knew this already, and kept a firm grip. New machines keep you guessing. Old machines spelled out the rules nice and simple.

Remember cigarette vending machines? You never see those anymore. You sat there, if you were a smoker and somehow were too forgetful, busy, distracted or drunk to have remembered to stop and get cigarettes at the convenience store before you left town, so you fed anywhere from six to eight quarters into them. The slot on cigarette machines was always way up high, and all the quarters had to drop all the way down, making a big racket that announced to everyone around, "Hey! Look at the dummy who forgot to stop at the Circle K!" Then, to make matters worse, you had to pull those clear-knobbed levers which came out about three feet and dropped your pack of Marlboros into the tray, except the lever you pulled delivered Kents because some moron had loaded the machine wrong. Being out of quarters and embarrassed enough over the whole ordeal, you decide it's time to change brands anyway.

Old cigarette vending machines were not so cool as snack and soft drink vending machines, you can see, but they were cooler than station wagons with wood-grain side panels by a country mile.

The 'Net

I don't know how I survived without the Internet.

Yes, I know. This coming from the person who whines constantly about simpler days, about the maladies of modern life, the quest for a time when there weren't so many complications. You'd think I'd want to go live in a cabin by Walden Pond or something. I would, in fact, as long as it's got broadband Internet installed.

My first computer was a Commodore 64. I thought I was in hog heaven. I had a word processing program that I can't recall the name of but I think it was WordWriter or something like that. Gone were the days of black-stained fingers from threading typewriter ribbons, gone were the mounds of White-Out on the paper. The backspace and delete buttons became my best friends.

Eventually I moved up to a state-of-the-art 486 processor PC, a Packard Bell, with a whopping four megabytes of RAM, and though at first I thought I was going to need seat belts on my desk chair, I soon learned that they referred to this computer as a "Packard Bell" because the phrase "piece of junk" was already taken. Still, I hung on with that old 486 until the Pentiums came out, and have been, like everyone else, steadily upgrading ever since, due to that most dastardly of conspiracies in the computer industry known as "planned obsolescence."

But Internet didn't come along for me until that 486, and then it was AOL. I quickly outgrew that and went for a straight connection, and the whole world suddenly opened up. This led to several revelations, and pitfalls, along the way.

The Internet and an always-live connection to it is the great argument solver. You and a friend are debating whether it was Steve McQueen or Paul Newman in *Papillon*. A quick Google search wins you five bucks. Prior to the Internet, you had to argue about it all night, the argument usually growing so heated that one of you makes an emergency trip to the library, but only after calling all of your friends, half of which say one thing and the other half say the other (there's always one person who says it was neither, it was

Dustin Hoffman, but you all gang up on him and belittle him to the point of moving to Siberia to tend yaks.)

Or you can't figure out what the devil Manfred Mann's Earth Band is saying in "Blinded By The Light" so you look up the lyrics and in less than eight seconds learn that "some brimstone baritone anticyclone rolling stone preacher from the east says, 'Dethrone the Dictaphone, hit it in it's funny bone, that's where they expect it least" and still haven't a clue what in the world is going on in that wonderful tune.

Of course, I eventually discovered Ebay, and my life has been a perpetual case of kid-in-a-candy-store ever since. Make that *broke*-kid-in-a-candy-store. Many people blow their retirements on Ebay, but I have somewhat more self-control. You name it, you can usually find it on Ebay with a little time and effort. I found a center cowling, faceplate, lower unit and steering cables for a 1958 Mercury Mark 55 outboard on Ebay. In fact, I found the dadgum outboard on Ebay and had it shipped to me from Wisconsin to put on my mahogany runabout. When I was into furniture building, I bought a couple dozen board feet of quilted maple from Ebay, much to the amusement of the deliveryman who brought it to the house, who couldn't understand why I didn't just run to Lowe's.

There's plenty of other benefits to the Internet. Imagine if we had Internet in 1492. The Taino Indians could have typed up a quick email to the effect of, "Weird guys with big, ugly canoes and real macho attitudes just showed up. Send reinforcements," hit the button that addressed the email to everyone in their address book, all five hundred nations of indigenous people, and then "send." Within a split instant, every tribal nation in North and South America would have been on the offensive, and Christopher Columbus would have been relegated to some obscure footnote in history reading, "Performed an illegal operation and was shut down."

Sure, I long for simpler times, it's true. But thanks to the Internet, I can get closer to my desires for those times by finding bamboo fly rods, quilted curly maple, old outboards and vinyl albums by David Soul. Thanks to the Internet, I can read how the fishing is in Quebec, and get the weather report for Cutoff, just in case I happen to find myself that way, though I can't imagine how that would happen.

There are limitations, of course. Need a recipe for pecan duck? Internet to the rescue. Need to figure out how to wire a three-way light switch? Consult the Internet—to locate an electrician, for Pete's sake. Want to know what the population of Juno, Alaska is? Yup, it's there. Need to know how to groom a malamute? Go to the dog groomer, your dog will thank you for staying off the Internet.

Heck, I recently found the entire text of *The History Of Louisiana*, by Antoine Simone Le Page du Pratz online, and it's been out of print for decades. I also found a picture of a three headed spider monkey and that kept me awake for days.

There are things you find on the Internet, thus, that are not all that great. For instance, you investigate your family ancestry, and find that in 1873 a direct paternal relation of yours was a horse thief and was hung from a tree. So far, I have been lucky. Not only have I not found any horse thieves or any hangings at all, but I also learned that I am distantly related to Laura Ingalls of Little House on the Prairie fame. Laura's father's sister married a Stouff. I'm serious, look it up, it's all there on the Internet! Think I could get royalties?

There are other drawbacks, in that sometimes things on the Internet find you instead. Spam mail offering—well, in addition to having been the recipient of $1.8 million dollars from a kind benefactor in Nigeria, eligible for $600,000 in home equity loans (pretty good for a little house on an Indian reservation) and suddenly become the most popular guy in the world with women from Russia, Latin America and Des Moines, you know what other kinda of stuff finds you via email. We're keeping this rated general audiences.

Viruses also find you on the Internet, whether you are looking for them or not. These little boogers get into your computer system and at best destroy your hard drive, at worst get information about your credit card, bank accounts and, horror of horrors, that romance novel you started to write but thought you had deleted for fear your buddies will call you a pansy.

Every rose has its thorns, they say. I love my Internet, and I've learned to steer clear of the thorns. There's still that matter of Ebay, though. I was bidding on a town once, and got outbid at the last second. I hate it when they do that, I really do.

The General

Last weekend, I went on strike. From grass-cutting.

For two months I have cut grass every single weekend, often both mine and my mom's. With this incessant rain, the grass is practically growing before my eyes. People used to joke about "watching the grass grow" intending it to mean being utterly bored and useless. Now it's true: You can almost watch the grass grow!

As I've said before, the General cuts the grass very well, but like the infamous U.S. Cavalry commander himself, it is sneaky, dishonest and cowardly about it. The General will approach a patch of grass and, if finding it's taller than it can chew, chokes up, sputters, coughs and shuts down in terror. The General is so much like its namesake that I often have to coax it into moving at all when it realizes it's on an Indian reservation and completely surrounded.

I had another mower, a larger Murray which I called Beelzebub because I am certain I know exactly where it was manufactured. Beelzebub cut a wider swath which makes the chore less time-consuming, but it rarely cut level. It usually left lines on one side or the other, and there's no rhyme or reason to it. Once it caught itself actually cutting a perfectly, silky-smooth level and blew out an inner tube in the back tire out of sheer meanness.

Well Beelzebub's starter went out last spring, and I refuse to spend one hundred bucks for a starter for a lawn mower. I remember when starters for my 1965 Mustang (this was in the 1980s) were fifty bucks; why on God's green earth should a starter for a lawn mower be twice that? So I tuned up the General and have been using it ever since.

It is not without its quirks. It needs a carb job, and every now and then some little chunk of grit or varnish or whatever loosens up and the General sputters, gags, coughs, spits, hacks, chokes and finally sneezes then goes along nicely for a bit until another bit of debris works loose and the whole process repeats itself.

It also has the throttle in the most unfortunate of places, low on the left side of the frame, so if you pass too close to a shrub or something the limbs of the plant can actually push the lever back as you pass and the engine kills. The first time this happened to me I didn't know what caused it. I tried and tried to restart the dadgum thing, choked it, sprayed starter fluid in it, kicked the tires, changed the oil, inflated the tires evenly, everything I could think of and I was coming out of the house with a shotgun to finally put the ol' girl down when I glanced down at the throttle lever and saw what the problem was.

Now, let's be fair about this, the throttle control was designed for an idiot, and contrary to what some people around here may claim, I am no idiot. It is not labeled FAST and SLOW. No, since idiots will be operating ten horsepower lawnmowers with razor-sharp blades spinning hundreds of RPMs while a hydrostatic transmission propels them twenty miles per hour in fifth gear around the yard making hair-pin turns...because of all this, the throttle is marked with an outline of a turtle at one side and a speeding rabbit at the other.

Not only can Johnny not read, but he's all grown up now and making lawnmowers and automobiles. Think about it, there's very little writing in your car anymore because we, American people, can't read, or at best, don't want to. Your power window buttons are marked with arrows, as are your power locks. You don't have gauges marked "fuel" or "temperature" or "oil" anymore, you have pictures of a gasoline pump, a thermometer and something that looks suspiciously like Aladdin's lamp. Your headlight control has a headlight picture on it, your windshield wipers have a picture of windshield wipers, and you can't operate your radio because you can't figure out what all the little numbers mean. You can pass a written driving test, though.

In America, we're getting where we can't warm up a pizza without pictographs. We can't operate a toaster without a mouse.

So anyway, I was talking about grass cutting. My neighbor cut his grass this weekend, and after that mine was a good three inches taller. We had cut it the same afternoon the week before. Three inches, from one week's growth! I put my arms across my chest and shook my head vigorously, my upper lip stiff.

"Nope," I said, "I ain't doing it." Then promptly went into the house, closed all the blinds, locked all the doors and collapsed on the sofa to watch fishing shows until a nap overcame me.

But about the General. As lawn mowers go, it's kinda small. About thirty inches to the cut. Takes me awhile. Beelzebub had a forty-two inch cut, and that was nice, didn't take as long, but the yard ended up looking like a cornfield when I was done. The General does a nicer job, kinda near and silky like the marching field at West Point, where George Armstrong Custer finished thirty-fourth in—I kid you not—a class of thirty four. Hero, my eye.

But next weekend I'll have to buckle down and get it done, because the grass will be six inches high by then, and the General will have to set its throttle lever to (insert picture of a RABBIT here) to generate enough power to (insert picture of SCISSORS here) its way through all that (insert picture of GRASS here.)

So.

You know they found pictographs at Little Big Horn, don't you? Sure enough, near the scene of the battle, scratched into a rock were rudimentary pictures of a cross, a fish, a pair of eyes, a pile of sticks clogging a river, and two stick-figures wearing feathers.

It took years to decipher, but finally it turned out to be a message from the General himself, and translates thusly:

HOLY MACKEREL, LOOK AT ALL THE DAMN
INDIANS!

(Insert picture of ME BEING SUED BY THE ACLU here.)

Plumb Silly

Among the supposed four-letter words, which often are more or less than four letters, and in that category considered "profanity" or "cussing," let me please add the word "plumbing."

I will never complain about the money plumbers charge because plumbing has to be the worst job that's ever existed. Plumbing is worse than anything.

Last week, Tuesday I think it was (time has been a blur since then) I got a message after lunch to call the waterworks district.

"We just checked your meter," they said. "And it's spinning like crazy!"

Talk about a sinking feeling. I had noticed that my bill was higher than usual last month, but I thought that was from the time I put the hose in the dog's water bucket and walked off and forgot about it for a couple hours. But apparently not

So I went home and looked in the back yard where the main line to the house is, and sure enough, there's a big ol' puddle of clear water. I got a shovel and started digging. I've been searching for a shovel that fits my hand correctly for most of my life. Still no luck. I dug up everything from the shut off valve to the three places the water enters the house and found no cause.

Nothing left to be done. Sighing like a condemned man, I crawled underneath the house. The dog thought this was just the neatest thing ever, and she kissed my face repeatedly, as if saying, "Hey! You came over to my place this time! Want some kibble? It's kinda bland but you get used to it. Wanna play with a tennis ball?" before I found the problem: A little mud puddle, and a swirling in the center of it. I dug down with my little garden spade, and not only did I find the pipe, I knocked a chunk of rust off it when I did, and the swirling became a geyser that would make Old Faithful proud.

So I called my pal Larry, who is, among many other talents, a plumber. He arrived the next morning and, our situation being dire, I took the day off work to help out. In such an old house, we rapidly realized that nothing was what it appeared to be. The whole main line from the shut off had to be replaced, and the two tie-ins were questionable at best. The plumbing had been installed in the 1940s and remained largely original, except it had been moved around, repaired and rerouted many times over the decades. For instance, one went toward the kitchen, then made a hard right turn under the back porch and vanished somewhere out in the yard. This was the exact direction of the old well-water pump house. I assumed it was the old feed into the house, and had been capped when we tied in to what my grandparents called "city water."

You know what they say about making such assumptions,

right?

We kicked things off early, cutting pipes since we had decided to reroute rather than repair. To my pal's defense, he was working on my word about what I had seen happen up under the house in my tracings and goings about. All I can do is plead that the barrage of doggie kisses must have confused me.

We replaced the main line first, then the two tie-ins that supplied the house with water. While the glue on the main line and the tie-ins was drying, before we tied them into the house, we took a break for some ice cold tea and a coupla short cigars.

My neighbor came by then and chatted with us for a bit before getting back to work. A few hours later, we had tied in to the house and were waiting for the glue to dry on that section so we could put the system under pressure. Naturally, tea and stogies were in order, and naturally, my neighbor stopped by again to visit and catch up on our progress. He looked rather suspicious at this point and I couldn't quite figure out why.

Well, we put pressure to it and voila! We had water in the outside faucets and water in the bathroom. We congratulated ourselves on a job well-done and Larry took his leave of me.

To this day, I don't know why I didn't throw the kitchen faucet open. It's not Larry's fault, he trusted me not to be a moron, and I failed him miserably. But when I went in the house later to wash some dishes that had been piling up...no water.

It was hard to call my bud back and tell him I had mis-traced the lines somehow. It was even harder for him to tell me he couldn't make it back until Saturday. But I had water in the bathroom and laundry room, so I resigned myself to washing dishes in the bathroom sink and waited for Saturday.

I found another line, and to be certain of what I had found, I opened the valve in the kitchen, went back outside and stuck a water hose to it and held it as tight as I could for a couple minutes. When I went back in the kitchen to look, there was water in the sink. Bingo!

Saturday evening we connected that line to the main and waited for it to dry with requisite cigars and a coupla cold ones. My neighbor came by and shook his head sadly at us.

"I don't know," he said.

"What?" I asked.

"I just don't know about this crew," he said.

"Whaddaya mean?" we demanded

"How do you ever expect to get this job done? Every time I see you, you're sitting around drinking and smoking cigars!"

So I fetched him a cold one and a stogie, just to keep him quiet.

We put the pressure to it and lo! It held, and I had water in the kitchen. This time, Larry and I patted ourselves on the back and promptly knocked on wood, just to be safe.

Everything passed by nicely from then on, until that night, when I heard a weird sound I quickly realized was running water. I raced outside, and sure enough, one of the new fittings had split wide open.

If you don't think that was the hardest phone call I ever made, think again.

My pal came again, and he's still, thankfully, my pal. Unfortunately I had to be at work Monday and couldn't go assist, so I'm not sure if he and my neighbor had a cigar and tea together while waiting for the glue to dry. I can only hope something good came out of the whole mess.

You know, they say the fall of the Roman Empire was due to the plumbing. Now, the historians say it was because they used lead and it made 'em all crazy as loons from lead poisoning. I say it was just doing plumbing work. That'd bring the downfall of any civilization real quick, if you ask me.

Cellular Division

Cell phones, as I've mentioned before, will collapse our civilization.

The technology of mobile telephone communications has made us unpleasant people. It's an epidemic, and what's scary about it is we don't even seem to realize it's happening. I mean, the enlightened realize it, but we're few and far between.

The realization really came to me one morning when I'm having a conversation with someone in the office and her cell phone rings; without a word to me she answers it and starts a whole other conversation in the middle of the one she was having with me.

When she hung up, I pointed out to her how rude that was, and to her credit, she said it never really occurred to her.

There's the rub, ain't it?

Think about how often that happens. It's epidemic, if you think back and count how many times that occurs. You're at lunch with somebody, riding in a car with somebody, fishing with somebody, and even if there's a conversation going, the phone rings and they pick it up and answer it, completely dismissing you into the ether.

People weren't that rude with house phones, near as I can recall. If you had friends over and the house phone rang, even if you didn't say something like, "Excuse me a second," you at least finished your sentence and maybe added a quick point of the finger upward to indicate, "Give me a minute," before answering the phone. Chances are, you didn't hang out on it for half an hour, either, while your company waits and, in desperate boredom, starts going through the stack of mail on your kitchen table.

But somehow, cell phones have made us callous, unthinking and obnoxious. For some reason, we think if our cell phone rings, it's an ear-splitting klaxon going off signaling "RED ALERT!" and if we don't answer it now, I mean quick, right this dadgum minute, boy, it'll explode and blow our hip off.

We've all seen people carelessly walking down the aisles of the grocery or department store, chatting away on their cell phones. Now, I admit, my cell phone has come in handy when, say, searching for something my mother wants and I need clarification of what exactly it was as I stand there looking at the display shelves. But I'm on, conduct my business, and off again before someone starts putting out stadium seating around me.

And when you're standing in line to buy a pack of gum behind someone on a cell phone, and the cashier behind the register can't make the person ahead of you understand that their purchase is $14.49, not $12.29, or that they gave her a $10 and not a $20, or that their debit card isn't working because it's their library card, all because they're too busy gabbing on the cell phone while you are slowly mummifying there in front of the junk science tabloids with headlines reading *ALIENS ABDUCTED MY MOTHER AND*

GAVE HER BACK WITH TWO HEADS!

I don't understand it. My cell phone—granted, I am a relic from a bygone era when phones did three things: Ring, communicate information, hang up—is only on my hip in recent months because of health issues with other members of my family. Before that, I only wore my cell phone when I was on call for the Banner.

Now, people who want to call me for casual conversation—ask me how things are going, tell me about a nice column I wrote, ask what channel such-and-such comes on, whatever—call me on my cell phone.

Okay, let's examine the logic here: People have gotten so cell phone-addicted, they call your mobile phone before your house phone. In some cases, even before calling your office phone.

What the devil is wrong with people? If it is Monday through Friday within business hours, wouldn't it make more sense to ring my office phone if you want to talk to me, instead of this obnoxious thing on my hip that starts chiming and vibrating and demands attention like a spoiled two-year-old throwing a tantrum, even though I'm on the office phone with the mayor or something?

Same applies with the house phone. I always call people's house phone before I call their cell phone. It just makes sense. Calling my cell phone before calling my house phone at eight in the evening is like breaking a window and climbing in the house instead of using the door bell first.

People who call my cell phone are lucky I answer the thing at all these days. I used to keep it in the truck where it could ring its evil little electronic heart out, all for naught. This is because I'm in my house or my office and they got real phones in there!

And if I got into the truck and looked at the list of missed calls, and I didn't want to call you back, well, I didn't have to. That's far different than this annoying chirping, chiming, snippet of country-western song, sound byte from *The Simpsons* or whatever else harping in your ear, or the vibration mode making one hip smaller than the other like the old vibrating weight-loss machines were purported to do. Cell phones are made to demand attention, and therein is the problem.

All these silly ring tones drive me crazy. I'm walking along in the courthouse, say, and suddenly I hear a snippet of "Stairway to Heaven" from someone's purse, and just when I think I'm having an epiphany or a religious experience, they pull their phone out, flip it open and say, "Girl, where have you been?"

Or I'm having lunch somewhere and, from behind me, I distinctly hear Capt. James T. Kirk say, "Beam me up, Scotty," and I spin around but there's nobody remotely resembling Jim Kirk in the joint, no sparkling resonance of a transporter beam, and I suddenly realize I've been had again by a stupid cell phone ring tone. I hate the notion of a *Star Trek* ring tone anyway. It's demeaning. Spock would never have beeped Kirk on his communicator just to say, "Hey, Jimmy Boy, did you see *American Idol* last night?"

They're gonna be the death of us, people. The downfall of civilization, I'm telling you.

You take this device that emits ultra-high frequency, zillion-cycles-a-minute, microwave energy and stick it up against the side of your head. What you figure is happening to your brain, Einstein? It's made you obnoxious, that's what. That certain zillion-cycle frequency is the precise one that destroys the center of the brain that controls, discretion, courtesy and politeness, while enhancing as if a steroid that area of the brain dictating vocal volume, inhibition and things that seem funny to you, like a ring tone of Al Bundy belching.

Lil' Wheels

The unfortunate time in a man's life is when he's got to get a new lawn mower.

You know how I feel about cutting grass. Biggest single waste of time in the history of mankind. Why do we do it? I don't know. I'd just a soon not, but the neighbors get antsy if I go more than a couple of months without mowing. Can't imagine why.

Last March someone in my breakfast club said, "Gonna mow the yard this weekend," and I looked at him with sheer malice.

"Are you nuts?" I demanded. "I don't plan on touching a lawn mower until May."

"Oh, not, you can't wait that long!" they exclaimed.

"Possibly June, if the fish are biting," I added with appropriate disdain.

But it had gotten to the point where the clover was about to take over the yard, and I knew I had to do something before a tribe of pygmies moved in. This is sovereign territory, after all. Now, my 1998 mower the General had seen its better days. The General had its rusting cutting deck repaired four times with cloth and epoxy. The steering got to where it would go either ninety degrees left or ninety degrees right, with no in between, which made for some interesting maneuvers in the yard. It often wouldn't start at all, fearing that I was in fact a throwback from Little Big Horn and had come for another round of behind-kicking. It also ate belts like spaghetti. I overhauled the stator ring, the starter and the clutch. Sometimes it would creep along in fifth gear like a snail, other times it would be all jerky and such.

I had been saving my pennies for a long time, and figured it was now or never, before I went and bought a buncha fly rods instead. So I borrowed my buddy's trailer and went to get a new lawn mower. A grand later, I was as vehemently opposed to the entire notion of lawn mowing as I had ever been. For that I could have bought:

—Five good fly rods.
—Three really good fly rods.
—Two top-notch, Cadillackin' fly rods.
—Two canoes
—One canoe and one kayak.
—A week in Mountain Home, Arkansas fly fishing the White River for big trout.
—Or just cut to the chase and buy about five hundred pounds of fish.

You get the idea. But no. All those months of saving up, resisting the urge to bust the piggy open and let his fat belly spill out all those precious coins so that I could gleefully run off to nirvana... and I have to spend it on a stupid lawn mower.

There is no justice.

But I got it home and before I could give it a whirl, I had to pick up all the limbs that had fallen since the last time I cut grass in October. I still had my neighbor's trailer, so I commenced to picking up sticks. Now, if there's a chore I hate worse than mowing the grass, it is picking up the stupid sticks first. Besides, I am not only depriving a pygmy of a nice clover-studded home site, but denying him firewood to boot.

A couple hours of bending, picking up, throwing, repeat, and I was ready for the Advil, or Geritol maybe (is there still such a thing?) and finally I had enough debris cleared to see the clover.

I got my grass cutting fedora, a cigar and a sweet tea, then climbed aboard my new shiny steed, and sat there for about two minutes with what I'm sure was a foolish look on my face before dismounting, going in the shop and getting the instruction manual.

After a few more minutes and a better understanding of what all these mysterious switches and levers do (hey, the old one only had a couple) I fired the thing up, and the engine roared to life.

And I do mean roared. With almost twice the horsepower and cutting width, I felt like I was perched on a chariot of the gods. I figured out how to put it in gear and set the speed, starting in the first gear of seven, and then engaging the blade.

Nice. Pretty dang nice. I cut the whole front and back yard, and came within a mile or two of actually enjoying myself. That's pretty close, for me.

Just to see what this baby was capable of, I disengaged the blade, pressed the clutch and put her in seventh gear, let up the pedal and *VAROOOM!* The dang thing took off like a racehorse, and I was holding on for dear life. The g-forces pinned me to the seat, and if I hadn't held on with white knuckles to the steering wheel I would have been blown off. We were heading straight toward the bayou and with an incredible amount of effort I wrenched the wheel to avoid the five century-old oak tree, went careening on two wheels in a wide circle across my yard and two of my neighbors' yards, took a barely controlled spin through the tribal school property, passed across my mother's front porch, nearly wiped out my mail box—snatched the mail out as I flew by—and finally got my foot to the clutch brake to slow the demon down back at the house. By this time, my cigar was in my pocket, the tea on my mother's porch and the mailbox was wearing my hat.

Perhaps that's how horse and buggy folks felt when the first shanty Fords hit the market.

"Slow down!" Ma and Pa would holler at the blazing 1909 Ford, kicking up dust and gravel at an amazing, ripping speed of eight miles per hour. "Ya dag-nabbed young whipper snappers!"

"What's this world coming too, Pa?" Ma would ask

Pa would just shake his head. "Giddy up, there, mule," he'd say, and grumble all the way home how the world was going to hell in a hand basket.

Smart End of the Stick

What my goal in life has become, of late, is to graduate to the "smart end" of things.

There is of course, a "smart end" of things and a "not so smart end" of things. Let me explain.

If you are working on something that involves measuring, for instance, and you are handed the end of the tape to hold on the mark, that's the "not so smart" end of the tape. The "smart end" of the tape measure is the one where you read the results.

I learned this quite by accident, even though for my entire life my father had me holding the tape end, not the case end. He never mentioned to me that I wasn't smart enough to hold the case end and read the measurements, he was too polite for that, or perhaps didn't want to stunt my development any further than it already was. In fact, perhaps the most withering stare of complete and utter angst and fury I ever received from him was once when we were working on building Little Pass Baptist Church when I was an early-teen.

We teens used to go over to "help" construction of the inside of the church, which Dad was pretty much taking the reins of. Of course, a buncha teens trying to "help" is kinda like asking the Three Stooges to do your plumbing.

We were working on something that required level. I don't re-member what it was, but it had to be level, and though we were supplied a level by the foreman, that being my dad, we didn't get it right. Not to Dad's standards, anyway.

He chastised us, nicely but scathingly, as only Nick Stouff could do, and corrected the error himself, making a mark on whatever it was to show the appropriate position for it to be level, then setting his pencil down on a nearby joist. It was then I noticed something.

"Hey, Pop," I said. "If I'm so bad at getting stuff level and you're so good, why you gotta use a flat-sided pencil?"

I mean to tell you, that look coulda peeled wallpaper off the wall, ya folla?

So I walk out of the house Sunday and I hear, "Hey!"

I look around and don't see anyone, continue about my business, and hear, "Hey!" again, a little louder and more insistent.

I am starting to worry that the Great Spirit is calling me to Happy Hunting Grounds, but no, there's my neighbor, over on the property line in the back, with surveying gear. I am wondering if perhaps we have finally decided to dig the fishing pond I've been begging for over the last six or seven years, but of course, luck is not with me yet again. It appears that, after years of discussion between us, we've decided it's time to work on how our yards drain rainwater. With heavy equipment temporarily at his disposal, he has decided it's time to git 'er done.

Of course I'm eager to help and ask what I can do. If you've seen surveyors work, one has a tripod with a scope mounted on it, the other is holding a stick with a tape measure glued to it so the guy with the scope can read it. The stick, therefore, is the "not so smart end" of this operation.

Guess who got the stick?

It only occurred to me after a coupla minutes standing there under the trees, noticing the moss, the squirrels and the ferns, wondering absently about cloud formation, and hoping I wasn't standing in a pile of red ants.

"Hey," I said. "How come I get the 'not so smart' end?"

Then I realized it was because I have absolutely no idea how to use surveying equipment, so it was probably safest for me to hold the stick. The fact that it took me a couple of minutes to realize it also indicated my rung on the IQ ladder.

They used to give one of our buds the "not so smart" end of the stick or tape or whatever, when working on a project with the notion that, since he wasn't Indian it was probably best, recalling that

Columbus wasn't very reliable at the "smart end" of navigation and the like, while Indian people were developing sun dials and could predict the solstices, planetary alignments, build landing fields for aliens in Peru, etc., to exacting standards.

After taking elevations, my neighbor headed for the big equipment, a bulldozer. I definitely realized he was on the "smart end of the stick" in that case. I'd have mowed down both our houses and probably half the Rez with that big yeller monster.

So we spent the afternoon working on the drainage in our yards. After a little while, I figured standing around was making me feel like a gawker, so I packed an ice chest, put it in the bed of the truck, drove down to where the work was ongoing, dropped the tailgate, hopped on and pretended like some football game was going on—as if I actually liked football. Now and then I'd try to be smart and use hand signals to indicate where the trough we were dredging was too high or too low, looking more like an aircraft landing signaler without the orange flashlights, and invariably my neighbor would look at me as if I had directed him to Panama, where, of course, the trough is already complete. This is not his fault because I didn't belong there trying to needle in on the "smart end" of things, and should have just stayed on the tailgate with my ice chest and kept my uneducated opinions to myself.

But I think we did a pretty good job, all things considered. We'll know first gulley-washer we get if we were really successful.

My neighbor was probably right in giving me the "not so smart" end of the operation. I can't tell you how many times I've been working in the shop and, despite the constant warnings of my father to "measure twice and cut once," I mess up a cut and have to start over. This is particularly painful on a piece of nice curly maple or mahogany. Eventually I got myself fairly well-trained to use the WWND principle—"What Would Nick Do?"—but sometimes I falter and still blow it.

Critters

Run, Shadow

Behind the glass barrier, lonely and frightened in his little pen, a handful of black-and-white fur stared at us with sad, longing eyes. The now ex-wife and I had, a year ago, adopted a Cocker spaniel from the same store, and that was supposed to be it. No more pets, particularly since we were living in an apartment at the time.

Several hours later, all our Christmas shopping done, we were on our way out. One of us decided we wanted to see the puppy again—for years it became a center of debate exactly which one of it was, but I'll admit I made the final decision. I did so because when the store attendant brought the puppy for us to examine (too much like inanimate merchandise, I remember thinking) he handed it to her and the puppy immediately burrowed his nose into the hair around her neck and curled his legs under himself, so insecure and confused. I had to take him home, away from the glass window, the staring faces and pointing fingers. Like ours.

The puppy stayed in that position all the way home, until we brought him in to meet Chance. They got along fine at once, and the new puppy timidly began exploring a square foot or so of his new home at a time, no more. He was an English Springer spaniel, and the children named him Shadow.

Shadow grew quickly, both in size and personality. The timidity and shyness soon disappeared as he grew accustomed to his new home, and much to the then-wife's dismay, he somehow turned from a "mommy's dog" to a definite, confirmed and committed "daddy's dog" but he reserved enough space in his heart and attention for her that she still felt loved. Within six months he was as big as Chance, and by the end of that year, he was easily twice as large.

About that time, the family moved from the apartment to a house and the two dogs had a yard. Admittedly, we couldn't afford to fence in the entire back part of the property, but the adequate enclosure I made in the back and frequent romps in the pasture at my parents' home nearby confirmed they were much happier here.

Shadow, though younger, was considerably more intelligent

than Chance, but it was clear that the cocker was the unquestioned leader of their little pack. When I'd take them out to the pasture, as Chance would bound here and there, stopping to smell everything, Shadow would run.

That dog could run. He would wait, impatient but still, until I gave him permission: "Run, Shadow."

Then he'd leap into motion, belly low, legs pumping and ears flapping behind him, and he'd run like lightning across the pasture. I have never had a dog that fast, don't think I'll ever see a dog that fast again. Perhaps it just personal bias, but I'd have put Shadow up against any greyhound around.

He also had the best disposition of the two. While Chance was loving and affectionate with all of us, he tolerated little annoyance from the children, not a good quality for a family pet. My youngest got a couple of warning nips, for which I really should have taken Chance away from the family, but I did not have the heart. I tried my best to make sure he developed a respect for animals and learned how to treat dogs, which he eventually did, and there were no further incidents. Shadow, on the other hand, would put up with anything from the children without complaint.

When the separation came, I left that house with only my clothes, computer, truck and the dogs. There was never, to my ex-wife's credit, any discussion or even thought of separating the dogs. They came with me, and she and the kids could see them any time they wished. At my house, with the big fenced yard, the dogs were in heaven. Chance would bound around smelling things, while Shadow would run circles in the yard, leaping five feet into the air to swallow dragonflies and carpenter bees.

He very rarely misbehaved, but when he did, all it took was the point of a finger and a stern voice, and Shadow would do what I called the Groucho Walk. He'd hunker his head down low between his shoulders, tuck his nub of a tail down, and waddle away with his rear legs spread wide.

The months collected and slowly formed into years, and the dogs were masters of their domain. They'd chase the cats under the house, even though the cats were actually in the house, and all four would go running back to front and back again in their respective domains. Shadow rescued Chance from a couple of harrowing situations with his superior intelligence and good nature.

Despite that great disposition, I would not have liked to raise his anger. I was coming around a corner of the house one day, and he was coming around from the other way and we surprised each other. He let out the meanest, most menacing but entirely, I knew, protective growl and bark. Then he realized it was just me, and did the Groucho Walk until I called him back over and gave him a good belly rub.

In the morning, when I'd feed them before heading out for work, it wasn't unusual to see either or the other or neither. The yard was so big with so many distractions; they were often off exploring, or perhaps napping. So one morning, when I filled the food bowl, only Chance came out to greet me.

I glanced under the house and spied a white and brown shape in the gloom. I don't know why, but my heart leaped into my throat.

"Shadow!" I called. Chance came to me at once. I scratched him behind one ear and shouted again, "Shadow! Come here!"

But Shadow didn't come.

I walked to the edge of the house and knelt down. About six feet away, I could see him lying there, back to me. Chance left my side and went to sit by him, looking at me and whining.

"Shadow!" I yelled, using the tone and volume which made him listen no matter what preoccupied his attention. But Shadow didn't move.

He was only four years old. Perhaps if he had been ten, or older, I might have been expecting it. But four? He had been fine, barking and wagging his nub of a tail when I came home. He was his usual glowing, bounding self. Three years of getting used to them being off somewhere in that big yard, three years of trusting in them for they never, ever tried to escape, hadn't clued me in that there was something wrong earlier.

Investigation turned up a nest of copperhead snakes under the steps into the house. A mama and babies, which I killed.

I knew what he had done. He chased everything. This time, it was fatal.

I picked up the phone and called my ex-wife. She was as shocked and saddened as I, and she offered to come over to help me with him, but I refused. I knew her well enough to know that it was better if she didn't.

I dug a hole in the backyard. Over one hundred and sixty years, the number of pets that have been buried in that yard totals dozens. I dug, and I cried, and when it was done, I lowered Shadow into it, and just before I covered him up, I noticed that he was curled up in a ball, legs tucked under him, nose hidden under his front leg. Almost exactly the way he was when the store attendant handed him to us four years before.

It may not have been appropriate. I don't know the ways of my ancestors well enough because so much has been lost. But I placed tobacco and cedar in the grave with Shadow, and a small feather. I also placed a dog snack into the hole to sustain him on the journey to his new home. This is the way of my people, and perhaps it wasn't done that way for a dog, but it was done that way for *my* dog.

Chance walks around the yard, alone. He sometimes goes and sniffs at the mound of fresh dirt in the back. I know how he feels, and I go out to commiserate with him. Shadow was our friend for four years, but he was Chance's best friend, and I know he misses him even more than I do.

Some people, lots of people, don't understand how a person can become so attached to an animal. Some do, but after their first loss they harden their hearts against the pain and don't let the next one hurt, or they never have another pet again. There will be people who do not understand how much I miss that goofy, floppy-eared spaniel, but I do. You just don't know how much I do.

Run, Shadow. Leap forward, stretch long and powerful, and run. Like the wind, through the wind, with the wind. Wherever you are not—and I know you are somewhere, my friend—run. You were a good dog.

My Heterozygous Cat

I learned that my calico, Patches is not, in fact, just a calico.

She is, to be accurate, a "tortoise shell calico." A calico has more white in the fur, while Patches has black and orange and kinda these tan-browns.

I got interested in this distinction, so I went to the Internet and did some more research, and found the following information regarding the differences between tortoise shell calicoes and regular calicoes:

"Tortoise shells (a mix of black and yellow-orange hair) are heterozygous for a sex-linked coat color gene (XBXb). Patches of tissue where XB remains active are black; those where XB is condensed and inactive are orange. Calico cats also express a dominant gene for white spotting. Male kittens of tortoise-shell cats are either black or orange. (Klinefelters has been seen in cats)."

To which I replied in my usual intelligent manner, "Huh?"

I had no idea Patches was so complicated. I also had no idea she was heterozygous. I'm not sure what heterozygous means, though I did study genetics in college, but I'll bet my bottom dollar it has something to do with being psychotic. I must say, though, I have never noticed any Klinefelters in Patches, or any other cat, for that matter. Not that I would know a Klinefelter if it fell on me.

I almost wish I hadn't learned all this. I now seem to regard Patches not as a loving companion, but a heterozygous sex-linked coat color gene lacking Klinefelters. One day while she was sitting in my lap, I looked all over her for Klinefelters, and when she'd had enough, she bit my finger.

Anyway, the other day, I was sitting there in my chair, reclined, watching television. The lights were out because it was late, and I was just about to doze off, when Patches leaped up from behind the chair onto my arm, which was on the armrest.

She surprised me so badly I just instinctively swung my arm before I realized it was her and slung her away, along with my half-full can of Diet Coke, remote control and the book I had been reading. All went flying through the air and onto the floor. The book, Diet Coke and remote control stayed where they landed, but Patches was making tracks, not sure what the heck had just happened. Unfortunately, she made tracks right through the Diet Coke which was now puddled on the floor; her back legs went one direction while she desperately tried to maneuver the other way with her front legs, which caused her to spin in a circle three times before she caught a claw-hold on the oak floor and shot off like a rocket.

After I had cleaned up the mess, I went to find her. She was hiding behind the washing machine in the back, licking Diet Coke off her paws. I picked her up and apologized profusely, to which she replied loudly, *"MeeeeOWWW!"* which I believe translates to, *"Moron!"*

Now, as if that wasn't enough, a few nights ago a couple of my friends came by to visit. They brought with them two of Mocha's puppies, now durn-near full-grown. At least, I hope they're almost full-grown, because they're huge. They're lovable and cute, having the distinctive droopy face and skin of a Springer, but the coloration and build of their father, Bandit. Bandit is a Dalmatian who slipped under my fence one day while I was away, living up to his name.

Anyway, Patches and dogs do not get along—come to that, Patches doesn't really get along with anything that moves—so I had to put her in the back room while my visitors were there, with the dogs scampering and playing all over the place. By the time they left, I let Patches free.

Patches then went on an expedition to sniff everything in the house that the dogs had touched. This took about two days, you understand, because the dogs were everywhere. Patches sniffed every inch of the floor, every inch of the sofa, every inch of anything they came in contact with, and she was very put-out about the whole incident. I think she felt I had somehow betrayed her by allowing invaders into my house. *Our* house, I should say. She avoided me like the plague for days.

But eventually she got over it. She has learned never to jump on the chair from the back. She has learned, also, that if she jumps on the footrest, I'm much less likely to be caught at unawares, but she always looks ready to flee for a moment when she arrives, until she's sure I'm not about to go ballistic on her again.

Then she'll nuzzle up beside me, I'll scratch her ear, and she'll purr softly and rub the side of her face on my hand, blinking contentedly at me. Those are the moments that I realize I wouldn't have her personality any other way; for better or worse, she's one of a kind.

Halloween Cat

Whoever told my cat about Halloween is gonna get cuffed in the mouth.

In all the time that Patches and I have cohabitated, I have never known her to take the slightest notice of Halloween. She is, of course, predominantly black furred, and her oranges look suspiciously pumpkin in color, and while one of my friends always refers to her as "the devil cat," she has never shown one bit of give-a-durndedness about this holiday.

But a couple of days before Trick-or-Treat, Patches suddenly developed a very peculiar case of friskiness. It's not unusual for her to start feeling energetic when the weather cools. But this time, she began a new lunacy which left me dumfounded.

Without warning, she would suddenly arch her back until she looked like an upside-down U, and, running on tiptoes, bolt from one end of the house to another in a furious streak of calico lightning.

I'm telling you, I've never seen anything like it. Imagine a calico-colored, upside-down U running on tiptoes from one end of the house to the other. She'd emerge from the back while I'm sitting in the living room, stop and stare at me wide-eyed for a moment, then repeat the whole process.

But it didn't end there. Soon she started running around the back of the sofa, leaping atop the loveseat, launching herself from there and smack dab into my lap for a split instant, then rocket away to the back of the house again. This was startling enough while just sitting there watching television, but the first time she did it when I had my notebook computer in my lap was pretty interesting.

This behavior lasted for three days. I never knew when it would come. She could be napping on the sofa and then wake up, stretch, meander casually off to the food bowl, and the next thing you know, *VAAAARRRROOOMMMMM!* Round and round she goes, where she stops, nobody knows. I checked her food bag for amphetamines in the list of ingredients, but found none.

In the mornings, when my alarm clock goes off, she always comes to greet me. Patches' good morning is pretty odd: She chews my nose. Not hard or painfully, but in that adoring way some animals do to show affection. Why on earth she chose my nose, instead of a finger, for example, I'll never know. It's just one of the mysteries surrounding her.

But just before Halloween, when the clock went off, she'd leap on the bed and stare at me, an upside-down U on tiptoes. I'd reach out to pet her but before my hand could get halfway there, she'd bolt away. I could hear her ripping through the house, then she'd leap on the bed and stare at me again. If I ignored her, she'd just stay there. If I said, "Good morning," she'd take off like greased lightning.

Wednesday night was the worst. While the trick-or-treaters were out in droves, Patches was running around the house like calico lightning.

Now, here's the bizarre thing: At almost exactly eight o'clock when trick-or-treat hours officially ended, she blazed in from the kitchen, leaped onto the sofa, curled up into a nice little ball, and went to sleep. She has been completely normal ever since. Well, normal in the Patches sense of the word, anyway, which is something of an oxymoron.

I just don't know what got into her. I strongly suspect someone told her about Halloween, and how she was supposed to act, but she completely misunderstood the explanation. Maybe she was looking for a witch to get familiar with, I dunno. Either way, I'm glad it's over. Having a calico-colored, upside-down U racing through your house on tiptoes and launching sneak attacks on your lap tends to frazzle one's nerves.

Sometimes I wish I could get into her mind. When she stares up at me with those big, yellow eyes with the snakelike slits in the center, ears at attention, gaze penetrating and somehow so intelligent, I just wish I could read her thoughts. Anybody who tells you cats don't have very deep thoughts is wrong. Dogs have very deep thoughts but mostly they just want to do whatever you tell them to do and are satisfied with a pat on the head in return. Then they'll do it again, with a single-minded determination to achieve more pats on the head. If dogs had opposable thumbs, they'd mow the lawn and wash the car, all for a pat on the head.

What could she possibly be thinking in those moments, staring at me like that so intensely? Something on the order of, "You, sir, are a chump," I'm sure.

On the other hand, I'm not sure getting into her head would be a wise thing to do. I might not want to know what she's thinking.

But at least, for the moment, this crisis has passed.

My greatest concern at the moment, however, is the approach of Thanksgiving.

A Little Mocha With Your Patches?

My Cocker spaniel Chance passed away after a long, happy life. I buried him in the back yard, next to Moses and Shadow, as well many other family pets dating back some one hundred and sixty years at least.

No sadness. Chance was a good dog, and he was always a happy dog, despite a series of health problems resulting from the occasional genetic chaos that sometimes happens with purebred dogs.

His demise, however, left me with a quandary: What to do with Mocha, my two-year-old English Springer spaniel? Mocha was freaking pretty badly, having been around Chance nearly all her life and his sudden absence left her whining and miserable.

I don't want another dog right now, but I didn't like the idea of leaving Mocha outside in the yard alone from now on. So, after careful consideration, I decided to attempt making her a house dog.

Now, Mocha is a good dog. She's well-behaved, save for the hyperness that comes along with the breed. They don't call them "springer" for nothing. They have springs in their feet, like Tigger. However, I had heard that an outside dog is essentially potty-trained already, instinct being to return to the great outdoors when nature calls.

The most pressing problem, of course, was Patches.

Patches, my tortoise-shell Calico, has been mistress of her domain—the house and all who abide in it at her pleasure—since arriving there two or three years ago. Patches has never been around other animals, but I decided to give it a try.

So I gave Mocha a bath and put her on her leash, which she immediately twisted into a knot around my wrist and torso by spinning and springing wildly in excitement. After a half-hour of trying to free myself and explain to her the mechanics of dogs on leashes, she finally calmed down enough to proceed.

She did not want to go in the house. After all the times she had been forbidden to enter. So when I stood at the back door on one end of the leash and said, "Come on, Mocha," her brain went from hyperactive full-throttle forward, into neutral and to a screeching halt. You could almost see the skid marks. She just looked at me as if I had lost my mind.

"Come on, it's okay," I soothed. I gave a little tug on the leash to indicate I was serious. This caused her brain to leap out of neutral into reverse, and she backed away, attempting to retreat back under the house.

It took quite a bit of cajoling, but I managed to coax her up the steps and inside. When I closed the door behind her, she just sat there like a deer in the headlights. I led her through the house and showed her where her food and water and blanket were, and then, mustering my courage, introduced her to Patches.

Patches was sitting near the foot of the stair, and her eyes got big as saucers when I strolled in with Mocha.

Mocha looked at Patches.

Patches looked at Mocha.

I looked at Patches and Mocha.

Mocha took one step forward, timidly.

Patches took one step back, wide-eyed.

Mocha decided she wasn't very interested in Patches after all, and started sniffing the sofa.

Patches retreated to the top of the stair and stood watching.

So I let Mocha free, and she explored the house bashfully, while Patches watched her every move like a hawk.

But there was no trouble. At one point, Mocha came from the back of the house and turned the corner of the kitchen into the living room, just as Patches was heading toward the back and they came face to face with each other.

There was a frightening moment there, and my hand was already on the phone to call 911, but they simply stared at each other for a moment. Mocha's ears perked, Patches arched her back. Then, they kinda just gave each other a wide berth and went about their business.

I don't leave Mocha in the house when I'm gone. I imagine coming home and finding they've gone to war, and I don't want to place bets on who the winner will be.

On the other hand, I'm somewhat disturbed by the fact that there *hasn't* been a war. I think they're getting along entirely too well. I am starting to fear that I'll come home one day and find my key won't fit because they've changed the locks and are holed up inside eating Hot Pockets and drinking Diet Coke out of their water bowls. It's like a scene from *Animal Farm*. Maybe I watch too much television.

Come to that, I could come home one day and simply find them sleeping on the blanket I put down for Mocha, with Patches curled up under Mocha's neck like she does me. Perhaps she'll chew her nose in the morning to wake her up.

Somebody's about to lose their happy home, and I'm afraid it's me.

Flashlight Fiasco

One of my Christmas presents was a really cool set of flashlights. You know, the cobalt-blue ones. There's the big one, which weighs about twenty pounds and, once you locate the intruder in your home with the light, you can beat him senseless with it. Then there's a little penlight, which is real handy against gnats, too.

Well, I put the batteries in the penlight, turned it on, and focused it to a narrow beam on the floor of the living room.

Patches came around the corner at that point, and I tell you, she didn't know whether to die or go blind.

She saw this glob of light spinning on the floor and froze.

Now, most cats would have chased this strange invader. We've all either done this or seen it done. They swat and jump at a light on the floor or the wall, and it makes the funniest videos shows on television and somebody wins lots of money.

But not Patches. Patches did the only honorable, sensible thing she could given this new set of circumstances in her world: She ran.

Well, she tried to run. She spun around to flee, but her front end wanted to go to the stairs, her normal hideout, while her back end realized that the light was in the path to her stair so it wanted to go to the back room. What happened was that neither end managed to get anywhere for a few moments, so she spun wildly around. She couldn't get traction somehow, and merely succeeded in spinning in place as her opposite ends tried to reach an agreement on which direction was the safest to hide for eternity.

At last they seemed to reach a consensus and she shot off to the back room. I could hear her skid as she made the turn into it.

Of course, I couldn't let it alone.

When finally she emerged from hiding again, I had my trusty little penlight ready.

This time, I waited until she got nearly to the stairway and turned it on, shooting the narrow beam to the top of the stair and jiggling it a little. Then I bounced it from one stair tread to the next, up and down, like it was moving up and down the stairs, dancing. Finally, I moved it slowly down, step-by-step, closer and closer, until it was only three treads away.

All treaties and agreements between her front end and back end suddenly were null and void, and Patches proceeded to try to flee again, this time in three different directions, for her midsection had decided that neither the front nor the back ends had the sense God gave a rock and decided to find its own sanctuary. So instead of merely spinning around aimlessly, now she spun and kinda wobbled like a top losing its momentum. At last she got all her sections aligned and sped off to the back again.

Well, I left it alone after that. When she finally emerged, cautiously entering the living room, I called her over and invited her to sit by me in my chair. She didn't nap very well though, because she kept looking up for the light. I wasn't about to turn it on while she was sitting next to me, you understand. I have never had stitches, and don't want to start now.

She has, however, developed the peculiar preference for sitting beside me in the chair with her head facing the back rather than the front. This is entirely uncomfortable for me, because I keep hit-ting her in the head with my elbow, which she doesn't like very much, either. So I pick her up and turn her face-forward, which prompts an angry growl each time, and she turns right back around.

I think I know what it is. She must believe that if she doesn't face the open living room, if the light suddenly appears again, she won't see it; therefore, to a cat, it isn't there. You know how cats are. They have the remarkable ability to believe some things that are there really aren't, such as when you call them and they totally ignore you. Patches has a similar ability regarding food in her bowl that is more than six minutes old.

But I promise, I won't antagonize her any further. It is, however, a relief to get a little revenge, you know? For all the fun she has with me, it's only deserving that I get a little of my own in return, right?

What concerns me, though, is what they say about payback.

The Dogs Of Night

Please pardon me. I am very cranky today.

It comes from not sleeping well. I am not sleeping well lately, you understand, mostly because of dogs.

There has been a pack of strays running around my neighborhood, getting all the other dogs in a huff and barking all night. It sounds like the dadgum dog pound around my house. Something in my brain is programmed to wake up when I hear a dog barking. Kind of a security mechanism, I guess.

Of late I had been suspecting Mocha, my English Springer, had a tapeworm. She had been eating very much more than normal. Of course, you know where this is headed.

I came home Tuesday night from a meeting and what do I find, but four, count 'em, *four* additional dogs in my fenced back yard, all merrily eating out of Mocha's bowl. Mocha was sitting on the grass, encouraging them happily: "Eat up! Eat up! There's plenty! If it goes empty, my master will come fill it back up! It's the darndest thing! Doesn't your master fill your bowl? Is that why you're so hungry? Huh?"

"Yeah, right, that's it toots, chomp-chomp-chomp," a particularly ratty looked mutt seemed to reply.

Well, I hit the roof, I have to admit. Enough is enough, you know? I am not a violent person. Heck, I'm about the most meek, gentle, kindly person you'll ever meet, particularly toward animals. I love animals. I love dogs. And who else but me would put up with Patches?

But being sleep-deprived, finding four strays munching down on my dog's food, having them trespass on private property and just general all-around crankiness, propelled me into action.

I ran into the boat shed (this was once called the "garage" but since no automobile has occupied it in years it is now "the boat shed") and grabbed a three-foot long piece of Douglas fir. I practically leaped over the fence and commenced to chasing.

There were dogs running everywhere, and I was like Thor, the Norse god of thunder with his mighty hammer, swinging like a wild man. It was nearly dark, you understand, and since I am half-blind in one eye and can't see real well out of the other, I was having trouble finding my mark.

The four unhappy animals—all small dogs, mongrels, so I wasn't in much danger of them turning on me—didn't know what the heck was going on. There they were, happily munching on a free meal, and all of a sudden this bug-eyed, crazy man swinging a yard-long stick of Douglas fir comes after them, howling like Geronimo on General George Armstrong Custer's behind. Dogs ran everywhere, and I was hot on their trail in my dress pants, polo shirt, leather shoes and dress-up sports jacket. The dogs apparently forgot how they had gotten into the yard in the first place, so around and around we went, with Mocha running around behind, certain that we were all joining in a new game and she was just excited as all get-out.

One black mongrel let out a yelp, and the other dogs in the group suddenly seemed to think, "Okay, crazy Indian is going to murder us," and remembered where the hole in the fence was. They were like the Stooges, all pushing and shoving to get through that one little hole at the same time. I thought I heard one of them say, "Spread out!"

After they vanished, I patched the hole and Mocha, who was

sniffing merrily around while I was trying to do the fix, kept licking my hand. I refilled her food bowl, explained to her as patiently as I could about how I could not afford to feed all her friends, she was being a little tramp, and hadn't I raised her better than that? She just rolled over on her back, begging for a belly rub.

Think I'm too mean? Listen, if I come home and find *you* in my fridge eating all my groceries, I'm going to take a piece of Douglas fir after you, too. A man's gotta draw boundaries.

The next night, it all started again after midnight. They couldn't get in, but they came poking around and got all the neighborhood dogs roaring. I was to the point of madness by then. Now, I am not a cruel person. I do not want to kill or seriously injure these animals. I'm not that insane. Yet. I also did not want to run around in the dead of night with a piece of Douglas fir trying to bludgeon a dog. So I loaded my fifty-year-old air gun and gave it two pumps of the handle. Just stinging-level, you understand, just enough to let them know they aren't welcome here. It's not like I took a shotgun after them, for Pete's sake.

I spent most of the night stalking. I was the mighty hunter, under cover of darkness. I fired off about ten shots. I hit exactly zero dogs. You will recall I said I am half-blind in one eye and can't see real well out of the other? Try to hit a small dog in the dark with a low-pumped air gun. The gun is a single shot, too, so I had to reload—in the dark—and re-pump with each shot. The dogs figured this out pretty quick, and simply hid out until I got tired and went back to bed, then the chaos would erupt again. As soon as they heard the doorknob turn, quiet as I tried to be, they fled.

So I wizened up and sat in the boat shed waiting. Dogs, however, can sense you, and they apparently knew exactly what I was up to. But eventually one of them got brave and ventured toward where the hole in the fence used to be.

I rushed out, propped up the Benjamin on a corner of the house and fired. I missed by two inches. The dog jumped, looking around for the source of the noise. He didn't have to look long, because by this time I had decided that reloading was a colossal stupidity, so I spun the Benjamin around in my hand, holding it by the barrel now, and charged the hound like Teddy Roosevelt going up San

Juan Hill.

"*AAAAAAHHHHRRRRRGGHH!!!*" I screamed in the dead of night, and the dog yelped and fled. I chased him twice around the fig tree, once around the red maple tree and lost him somewhere near the live oak. I could still hear him yelping in terror in the distance.

I went back to bed. Ten minutes passed. The barking began again.

I turned the ceiling fan to high, turned the air conditioner to the fan setting, and put a pillow over my head until morning.

The next night, I think the word got out. They woke me up at two o'clock. I grabbed the Benjamin and headed to the shop. There were only two in the yard. I opened the door as quietly as I could, but they heard me anyway. I got off one good shot, which missed, of course, as they fled. I was left at peace for the rest of the night.

I think I am slowly developing a reputation in the stray mongrel mutt community as "the crazy man in the little white house." That's fine, but it's the reputation I'm garnering among my neighbors that bothers me. This would be, "The crazy man who builds boats in his garage and lets the grass get so tall there are Bengal tigers running around by the azaleas, and chases dogs around with sticks in the middle of the night screaming bloody murder."

That's fine, too, though. At least I'll get some sleep.

Mousing

My little calico kitty has been in a very good mood. I don't know what's gotten into her, but she's been extraordinarily amicable and friendly to visitors lately.

In the past, it would take Patches something on the order of four of her nine lives to warm up to someone new. She is definitely a "one man cat" and I am he.

A buddy of mine who visits every Saturday morning for coffee has attempted to make friends with Patches for months, but she generally responds to such overtures with a claw-tipped swat and then she flees. But a few weeks ago, she started to approach him tentatively, and as long as he didn't pay her too much attention, she would sniff at his arm or leg curiously.

But lately, she's been downright flirtatious. They say that when a cat rubs its head on you, there are two different reasons. If a cat rubs the flat of its forehead on you, it's a sign of affection. If a cat, on the other hand, rubs the side of its cheek on you, it's a marking of territory and/or affection.

I've never seen Patches use her forehead to rub, so she must not be solely affectionate to anyone. Even me. Or, since all I've seen her do is rub her cheeks on people, perhaps she has it in her mind that if she does like you, you therefore belong to her. That, knowing her personality, is likely the case.

The other night, another visitor was at the house and Patches was all over his legs, purring loudly. She was literally rolling over his feet, going, *Brrrrrr! Brrrrrr! Brrrrrrr!* She sounded for all the world like a cooing dove.

That's not all, either. Sometimes, she gets in the middle of the living room floor and starts rubbing her cheeks all over herself, going, *Brrrrrr! Brrrrr! Brrrrrr!* She'll flip over and over on the floor, rubbing her cheek on her front legs, on her back legs, grabbing her tail and rubbing her cheek on it.

You have to understand: Patches' mother died shortly after she was born, and she was nurtured to survival by a kindly couple. They bottle-fed her milk. Patches used to sleep under Debbie's neck, something she still insists on. I can't take that, I feel like I'm suffocating, so I put her on the side of me. As soon as I fall asleep, she climbs on my stomach, my neck or my back, whatever the case may be. When I wake up, gasping for air, she just looks at me with that half-opened sleepy-eyed look a cat gives you, like, "What?"

So Patches has no idea what it's like to be a cat and wasn't raised with other kittens. In fact, I am more than positive Patches believes she's human, having been almost solely around humans all her life.

I think she has these cat instincts, which she doesn't really know how to deal with, believing she is human and all.

One of those instincts is mousing. I have a mouse nest in the wall of the house, the first one ever since I have lived there. You can hear the little buggers squealing in the quiet of the night. I do not use poison, mostly due to the fact that I have the cat inside and Mocha outside, and the fear that the mice might die in the walls. I don't know how to get them out, or even how they got in. But Patches sits there and stares at that corner of the room for hours on end, and the moment the little mice start squealing, she leaps at the wooden baseboard and attacks it with all the ferocity of a saber-toothed tiger going after a gazelle. When the vermin fall silent, she'll go back to her sentry watch and the process repeats itself.

At least she's not rubbing her cheeks on it, so I am confident she hasn't gone completely mad.

Then there's the Springer. I decided to take Mocha for a ride to the lake, in the truck, to see if the water had cleared any.

Now, Mocha hadn't been in a vehicle since I picked her up off of Sanders Street two years earlier, but she jumped right in when I opened the door. We rode all the way to Lake Fausse Point with the windows open, and she whined the whole time. The interesting thing is that she was wagging her tail—the one that isn't there anymore—at the same time. I think she was delighted to be taking a ride but terrified at the same time.

The lake turned out to be a bust so I went home. It was dark by then, and when I got out of the truck, I said, "Come on, Mocha." She refused to get out. I said again, "Mocha, come on out," and she just whined and cowered. I didn't get it. I called her and called her, and she just whined and cowered, no-tail no longer wagging.

Finally, I had to take her by the collar and gently pull her out. As soon as she hit the ground, she laid down and cowered again.

"What's the matter with you?" I demanded and patted her head.

She looked around, and suddenly her ears perked up, she leaped to her feet, and started running in springing circles around me like greased lightning. I led her to the gate and she ran through immediately, then continued to run joyous circles around the back yard as I closed the gate.

I finally figured it out: Since it was dark when we got home, she didn't quite know where she was! She must have figured we were somewhere strange, and wasn't about to have anything to do with it, thank you very much. Once she realized, "Hey, I live here!" everything was hunky-dory.

So there you have it. I have a cat that thinks she's human, and a paranoid dog. I, by the way, am bordering on schizophrenia.

For the last few months, certain people who come into the house receive a cursory, cautious sniffing, a ready-to-flee stance for a few minutes, then are apparently considered "good enough" and the begging for an ear rub begins.

Now, this is the same feline a good friend of mine refers to as "the devil cat." She refers to Patches this way because of the cat's tendency to pounce on anything that jiggles, jerks, sways or otherwise simply exists in the same space-time continuum she does.

What started it was that this friend of mine was at my house with her little girl, who has long hair. The youngster was lying on a chair watching television, with her hair draped over the arm, and suddenly she let out a horrid scream.

The mom ran over and snatched her up to find out what was wrong. It was obvious very quickly what was wrong: There was a calico kitty hopelessly entangled by her front paws in the poor girl's hair, and the more she screamed, the more desperately Patches tried to escape, adding more drama to the situation than any of the four of us could stand with our sanity intact.

After freeing Patches from the girl—or freeing the girl from Patches, depending on how you look at it—she has thereafter been referred to by the mom as "the devil cat." Patches, I am sure, thinks of the daughter as "the screaming monster."

Patches is very small for her personality. She's a tiny cat, really, long and lanky. But in her mind, at least in a previous life, she was a saber-toothed tiger. Nothing escapes her attention in the house, and she has drawn blood on one occasion from a buddy of mine who made the fatal mistake of drumming his fingers absently on the arm of his chair. When my kids would come for a sleepover, they covered themselves up with blankets in the heat of summer as protection from Patches.

But lately, she's been downright friendly. It must be that she's about four years old now, and she's mellowing in her old age. If cat age is the same as dog age, that makes her twenty-eight. I was about twenty-eight when I finally starting making friends. I was about that age when I started getting less neurotic and more in search of a good ear rub, so I guess I shouldn't be surprised.

But the problem is, not everybody is a "cat person." Some people love cats, some people are indifferent, some people can't stand them. Patches is unable to make the distinction. Patches believes that if she deems you worthy of giving her an ear rub, then by thunder, you had better consider yourself honored and provide said ear rub without delay. Patches has gone from distrusting everyone to liking most, but without the discretionary ability. Even if you don't give her the demanded ear rub, she'll just keep preening over you until you succumb.

Her new outlook on life, that being friendliness to all, apparently extends to mice, too. When a "devil cat" suddenly turns friendly to visitors and to mice, is that a reverse possession?

I don't know how to feel about it, really. I didn't, of course, like having to worry about her when I had visitors. I didn't like having to be concerned with my liability insurance coverage. However, I was rather proud of the fact that she was a "one man cat" and I was the man.

A couple of friends dropped by one day to check out my boat, and they came inside for a bit. They had never met Patches before. Patches immediately began preening for an ear rub, eliciting the observation from the lady that I was surely telling falsehoods about my poor cat, that she was so lovable and adorable. She even reached down and *picked Patches up!* And there was neither bloodshed nor spitting, hissing nor frantic efforts at escape. Patches does not like to be picked up. I was, until then, the only person she allowed to pick her up, and then only very carefully. Now, anybody can come in my house and pick up my cat, and I think I'm jealous.

But when we're home alone, and she snuggles in beside my in my chair—she doesn't even growl at my laptop anymore, has she made friends with it too?—and she naps quietly, well, I count my blessings. This is far, far better than hanging from a screaming seven-year-old girl's hair, or drawing blood from an unsuspecting finger-drummer. I guess I can get used to it.

I just gotta figure out how to teach her about mice. Cats should not preen over mice. Mice do not give cats ear rubs. Mice and cats, she needs to understand, are natural enemies. Unless there's something going on at home when I'm not there.

I may have to install surveillance cameras.

Battling the Rodents

Maybe it's all the rain. Maybe it's just one of the disadvantages of living in a very old home. Maybe it's just my usual run of luck.

But the rodent problem around here is getting nearly as intolerable as the fact that there's still no handicapped parking behind Franklin City Hall (thought I'd forget, didn't you?)

In the nearly five years that I've lived where I do now—the family house that was built in 1860—I have had exactly two rodents. One a small mouse, one a good-sized rat, both of which were dispatched quickly by my late tabby, Moses. I never saw so much as a dropping around the house or heard a squeak.

But this summer, I've got something of an infestation. Now, most people try to keep such matters hush-hush. I do not. I understand that having an occasional mouse infestation is something that happens to everybody. Besides, it gives me something to write about.

Early in the summer, when the rains began, I started hearing the little critters in the ceiling and walls. This didn't concern me greatly, but it nearly drove Patches to a nervous breakdown trying to find them.

One night, a week or so ago, I knew that my problem had gotten worse. I knew this because I was sitting in my chair watching television, and all of a sudden something galloped across the floor of the attic.

When I say "galloped" I ain't just whistling Dixie, my friends. I mean, it was so loud I was waiting for a voice to yell, "The British are coming! The British are coming!" Patches, who was napping by my side at the time, jumped up and hid under the sofa, apparently believing a herd of rhinos had just gone through the living room.

So I bought a mousetrap. Not just any mouse trap, mind you. I bought a heavy-duty industrial mousetrap. This sucker, made of molded plastic with wicked looking jaws on the front, would catch a polar bear. I set this up in the attic and checked it a few days later. The bait was gone and the trap had snapped. That was it. Whatever I was dealing with, I realized, was not only big but also clever. This realization was not very comforting, you can imagine.

While remodeling the kitchen and installing my kitchen bar, I had the need to get into the attic to do some related work. I was a little afraid to do so. I thought about going in armed with my handgun, but decided that with my luck I'd only succeed in blowing a hole in the roof. I considered taking a long board with me, but whatever it was Patches and I heard galloping up there, I didn't think I had a board long enough. As it happens, I didn't see a sign of anything.

Over the weekend, a friend of mine and I were sitting there watching television in the living room, and Patches marched out of the back and dropped a mouse at our feet. She was so proud of herself. I was proud of her too and gave her a bowl of milk while I disposed of the mouse. You have to understand, this was Patches' first mouse, and this was a great occasion.

Tuesday morning, I walked out of the house and closed the door behind me, locked. As I was passing by the garage, I glanced up and there it was.

A rat, half as big as Patches, glaring down at me from a rafter. I mean to tell you, kiddies, this guy could have passed for a gray pillow. I eased back into the shop, unlocking the door as quietly as I could, and retrieved my pellet rifle.

I don't want to offend any animal activists. I am as kind-hearted a guy as you'll find when it comes to animals. But when a rat the size of Michael Jordan's shoe is staring down at you from the rafters of your garage, you reach for a firearm. Or a bazooka, if you have one handy. Go ahead and call PETA on me, but where I come from, rats the size of a loaf of bread are fair game.

My CO_2 powered pellet rifle has been sitting there for some time, and I wasn't sure it had any gas left in the canister. Nonetheless, I crept back into the garage, where the rat was still glowering at me, aimed, and fired.

It's pretty much a given that if you can see the pellet leave the barrel of your rifle, and watch it fly across the garage in slow motion, that you don't have much of a chance of doing any good. It's also pretty much a given that when said pellet glides across the garage, hits the rat in the side and bounces off onto the floor, you've pretty much done no good at all.

But the amazing thing is, that rat just looked at his side where the pellet had bounced off, turned back at me, shifted to where he was facing me full frontal, and glared at me.

I admit it. I was intimidated. When a rat the size of a watermelon glares at you that way, after you've shot at him with a pellet gun to no avail, you start to wonder about your personal safety. So I eased back into the shop and retrieved another CO_2 cartridge.

While I was putting it in, I glanced at the window, which looks over the back yard. I have iron bars on these windows, and there he was, hanging from the bars, looking at me, nose twitching. I think his nose was twitching with the scent of blood. My blood.

After the canister was in, I thought very seriously about shooting the monster right through the window and worrying about the repercussions later. Instead, I eased out of the shop and around back, but by the time I got there, he was gone.

This made me feel better, at first, since I wasn't quite sure even my newly-charged pellet gun would have done any good, and that I might have had to go get the .12 gauge, which would have been the end of the window, for sure. Then I realized that I didn't know where the ogre had gone. Then I didn't feel so good again.

Tuesday night, when I got home from the Franklin City Council meeting, I drove up in the driveway and turned the high beams on the truck, sitting there for a few minutes before I got out. I wanted to make sure no Doberman-sized rat was waiting for me. When I got inside, I sat down with Patches and we had a long talk. I explained to her that while I was very, very proud of her mouse-catching abilities, under no circumstances was she ever, ever to attempt to tangle with a rat that is as big as a Shetland pony. She just licked my nose and went to sleep.

I don't quite know what to do about it now. I haven't heard any galloping lately. That only makes me believe he—or they, if he has comrades—are lurking somewhere planning my demise.

All I can do is wait them out, and hope they don't have too many friends.

Mocha vs. Hitchcock

Me and my second English springer, Mocha, took a walk to the bayou the other day, just to see how things were going down there behind the house.

It's pretty often we take a walk to the bayou, where I go sit on my neighbor's wharf and relax, usually near dusk. Mocha enjoys sniffing around the bank and splashing in the water a bit, though she rarely goes for a full-fledged swim. Now and then a group of tame ducks passes by, which drives her nuts, but she so far hasn't gone out to meet them.

Anyway, we're at the bayou and I'm just walking along the bank looking at the elephant ears, when Mocha stops in front of me, ears perked up, motionless with rapt attention over something I can't see.

I stop, too, because I figure, dogs have a keen sense of sight, smell and instinct. It might, I think, be a snake, and I certainly don't like snakes.

"What?" I ask softly, but Mocha ignores me. I am nervous now. Might it be a cottonmouth? I say, "Come on, let's go around," but she continues to ignore me, attention riveted to something in a patch of Johnson grass.

She slowly creeps forward, then stops, staring at the grass. Then she inches a little more toward it. I am standing there wishing I had my gun. A few more inches, and she cranes her neck out and, ready to bolt or attack, peeks into the grass.

Then she idles off like nothing ever happened.

I walk carefully over to the grass, look down into it, and find an old rubber boot that had washed up somehow.

"You're a maroon, ya know that?" I yell at her, but she's off sniffing the base of a cypress tree now, oblivious to my insult.

Springer spaniels were bred as hunting dogs, and I guess Mocha's instinct was working right, though I doubt many English gentlemen made a sport of hunting washed-ashore rubber boots. If they did, perhaps they'd shoot it with a double-barrel shotgun? "Point!" they'd say to their Springer spaniel, the dog points, and they blast both barrels away, turning the boot into rubber bands.

Regardless, Mocha and I enjoy our walks to the bayou. I sit and watch the sunset; sometimes she sits with me and I swear she's watching the sunset, too. Most of the time she just romps around, investigating things. She is particularly fond of a bit of concrete rip-

rap near the water's edge where she can stand and stare at the minnows that congregate there. Strangely, she never tries to go after
them, but she'll watch them for a long time, ears perked, head
cocked. Once a little bluegill popped at the minnows, startling
Mocha so much she leaped backwards with a yelp.

That particular day, however, Mocha spent most of her time
with me on the dock. The water was muddy, so I guess there were
no minnows visible, or rubber boots to stalk, so she paced back
and forth on the dock, watching leaves, twigs and other debris float
by. A floating beer can caught her attention, and she followed it
from one end of the dock to the other (it was only about ten feet
out) until it drifted somewhere downstream.

Just before I was ready to head back to the house, an egret
landed on a stump not four feet from the wharf. Mocha immediately ran over to the end of the pier and stared, but the egret only
stared back. Egrets don't have stereoscopic vision, so they stare at
you sideways rather than full-frontal. I don't think Mocha understands the idea of monoscopic and stereoscopic vision and she must
have believed the egret was ignoring her, so she woofed gently. The
bird twitched a little, which made Mocha, brave soul that she is,
run back under my legs. Then she crept back to the edge of the
pier and stared back at the egret, which stared sideways at her.

This went on for about five minutes, and the skeeters were starting to get tough, so I called Mocha and we left the dock. As soon as
her feet hit the ground, she ran around to where the egret was
perched only a couple of feet from the bank and began barking her
head off.

It surprised me; Mocha is not usually so aggressive. The egret
spooked and took off, flapping wings right over Mocha's head,
which caught her completely by surprise and she went down flat
on her stomach, like a well-trained soldier in a firefight. The egret
quickly vanished, and Mocha kinda put her head up and looked
around, apparently thinking, "Is it safe now?"

We went up the ridge toward the house, and Mocha ran wide,
fast circles around me, but all of a sudden, a mockingbird swooped
out of the oak tree and made a strafing run right at her.

She went to her stomach again and the mockingbird shrieked as it passed just a couple of feet from her head.

Mocha looked around, looked at me, but refused to move. The mockingbird, apparently already irritated by a cat or something, circled the pasture and came back in again, and Mocha seemed to drop even lower. The mockingbird made three more dives at her until finally satisfied that the enemy was defeated.

Sensing the danger was over at last, Mocha leaped to her feet, and like greased lightning ran the remaining distance to the back gate, through it, and disappeared under the house. I peeked under there when I arrived, and she was curled up around a foundation block, panting.

"You," I said, "are a class act, young lady."

She just whined and put her head between her paws to nap.

I imagine I won't have to worry about the poor girl stalking egrets anymore, though I'm worried she won't be up to any further trips to the bayou. Rubber boots are safe enough, she must think. They don't fly at your head very often.

Pasta a la Mocha

Mocha, it appears, has some sense after all.

She likes lasagna.

You gotta give credit to any living creature that likes lasagna. I mean, there's probably no more perfect dish in the world. Except maybe pizza.

It remains a mystery to me, however, what folks who were living in Italy prior to 1492 considered the defining cuisine of their culture before Columbus got lost and, upon being threatened by his men to experience the delight of hanging by his neck from the yard arm, ran aground in the Americas, where tomatoes originated, thus transporting them back to Europe to eventually turn into lasagna. And pizza. But then, all pizza really is just round lasagna, sans pasta, add dough.

If the Indians had beef and cheese, lasagna surely would have been an indigenous invention. But somehow, with all due respect to my ancestors, the idea of ground buffalo and buffalo milk cheese lasagna does not appeal to me at all. So it is with great tribute that I acknowledge the accomplishments of the good folk of Italy who took that wonderful Andean gift, the tomato, and made lasagna. To those other miscreants who took the tomato and made fast-food restaurant salads with it that taste suspiciously like mummified cardboard, I have little to say.

Anyway, I like lasagna, but I can only take so much of it. I had a bit left over from a huge frozen one. Yes, I said a frozen one. I haven't the faintest idea how to cook lasagna, I'm a gumbo man at heart. I don't cook much anyway. But there's one certain brand of frozen lasagna that is pretty dadgum good, and I get it once a month or so. This time, rather than the smaller size I usually get, there was only the big family size lasagna. Desperate for a lasagna fix, I bought it and cooked it, and I did my all out best to eat it all, but even with lasagna, too much of a good thing gets old.

There were a few servings left, and I couldn't stand the thought of it anymore. Instead of wasting it, I decided to see if Mocha would like to try it.

As a rule, I don't feed my animals people food, and I forbid any of my guests to do so. I don't think it's good for them, that's just my opinion. Still, that's my rules, and I largely live by it. But I couldn't stand to think of a few more scoops of lasagna going to waste, so I put it in Mocha's bowl for her.

Unsure what this lump of beige and red stuff was, she approached it warily, ears perked and sniffed it carefully. Whoever says dogs are color blind have never seen a dog stare at a lump of lasagna in her food bowl.

"Go on," I said, standing watching. "It's lasagna. Garfield loves it."

She looked at me and cocked her head, wondering if I had, I'm sure, lost my mind. This was not her typical fare of dry dog food. It must have smelled alien and strange to her. Besides, she had no idea who Garfield is, so why should she trust his judgment?

"You eat it," I explained. "No joke. This isn't like the time with the strawberry Jello, I promise." The strawberry Jello thing was really funny to watch.

Mocha took a tentative nibble, and I swear, I've never seen anything like it. It reminded me of when a baby first starts on solid food. Well, if you can call that stuff that comes in the jars "solid food" then that's what I mean. If you give them the gross stuff, they squint and squirm, shake their heads in violent tremors of revulsion, and spit it down your shirt. Or if you give them the good stuff, like the banana one (I love the banana one!) they smile and pound on the high chair, demanding more.

The dog looked at me, perked her ears up, licked her chops and stared for a full five seconds in the most adoring, worshipful gaze you can imagine. I just knew she was thinking, "My life for thee!" and then she gobbled up the lasagna in three gulping bites.

She turned the bowl over searching for more ,and finding none, came over to sniff all around me, thinking maybe I was hiding the rest. Dismally assured that there was no more lasagna, she sat down in front of me to worship.

"That was good?" I asked.

"Burp," Mocha said, and licked her chomps again. She whined.

"Sorry, no more."

She whined again, more insistently.

"All gone!" I said, holding my arms open and hands spread wide, like you do when a baby's finished eating his jar of bananas.

Mocha frowned—no, I am serious, she really frowned—and woofed her demand for more lasagna, licking my hand.

"I could maybe locate some strawberry Jello for dessert," I offered.

At the mention of the words "strawberry Jello" she took off in a run and hid under the house. The strawberry Jello thing was really funny.

But to make it up to her, I opened the gate and took her for a walk, but after about three minutes at the bayou, she sat down and her eyes were fluttering sleepily. I understood. Lasagna is always followed by a good nap. We went back to the house, I put her in the back yard, and she yawned, rolled into a tight ball, and went to sleep. She is already an accomplished lasagna eater, you can tell.

To tell the truth, I didn't mind taking a nap either, so I retired to the sofa. Patches, who has not eaten lasagna, jumped up to meet me, sniffing at the smell of the dog, and she found the spot where Mocha licked my hand. She sniffed at this spot with the most studious, scrutinizing air about her, then lowered her ears, meowed angrily, jumped off the sofa and stalked off to the stairs to nap alone.

"What?" I said as she was leaving. She ignored me.

I suspect she was either angry with me for giving the dog lasagna and not her, or she was disgusted by the smell of it and the dog. Either way, she definitely felt betrayed.

Reminding myself to wash my hands the next time Mocha gets lasagna and gives me a lick on the hand, I went to sleep on the sofa and dreamed of long, towering tomato vines that filled the entire landscape around me, and from each flower bud grew a well-packaged, family sized box of frozen lasagna, just ripe for the picking, while Mocha ran circles around them all.

Not really. But it would have been almost as funny as the strawberry Jello thing if I had.

Spilt Milk

I got up in the middle of the night, dying of thirst, and poured myself a glass of cold milk. I love a cold glass of milk when I'm thirsty in the middle of the night.

So I sit down on the sofa in the dark to relish this. Now, over the past few months, my darling Patches has developed a love of condensation. She loves to lick the sides of cold cans, cups, glasses, mugs, whatever. Whenever one of us appears with a cola can or a frozen mug, Patches must lick the side of it.

But I'm sitting there in the dark, relishing my first long sip of ice-cold milk, and I'm about ready to take another. I haven't noticed that Patches snuck up quietly, and had taken her condensation fetish to a whole new level: Her entire head was down in the cup, and she was drinking my milk.

I didn't realize this when I raised the cup. I felt the resistance, which scared the heck out of me, and I jerked hand and cup away. This, in turn, scared the heck out of Patches, who jerked in the opposite direction to flee the sudden rush of milk up her nose as I raised the cup.

These two actions had the net result of causing the cup to move, hang on her nose, jerk free, and send milk flying everywhere.

It was all over me, all over the sofa, all over the floor, and all over Patches, who had by this time fled up the stairs. I jumped up, cussing, and turned on the light to see the huge puddle of milk on the floor, beading on the sofa, soaking my jammers, and little white milky paw prints leading up the stairs.

It took a while to clean up the mess, and even longer for me to stop raising cane. I didn't see the cat during all this. She was very well-hidden.

Lesson: Do not spoil your pets. They do not know boundaries. The condensation on the side of a cup is merely the starting gate for heading inside the cup. She's attempted this before, but a stern warning in a loud voice dissuaded her.

I think she figured that I, blind in one eye and can't see too good out the other, wouldn't notice her sneaking up for a late-night milk treat under cover of darkness.

We have new rules in the house: Patches is no longer allowed near any cups, bottles, mugs or cans. She is very put out about this. If I fuss her for it, she goes to the loveseat and gets in fights with her tail just to release pent up frustration. She's lucky I didn't make her do the laundry.

Meanwhile, she is also entirely put out by the work I have been doing in the piddling room, the little room of the house where I tie flies, work on reels, that sort of thing. Renovations make Patches paranoid. She does not like change. Patches is completely aware of every minute detail, every nuance, every slight microcosm of her world, and any discrepancy in it unsettles her deeply. It could be something so simple as leaving my shoes somewhere other than I usually do. This does not set well with her at all, and she goes about stalking them with neck-stretching, wide-eyed, ears-slanted-back paranoia.

Renovating an entire room puts her over the edge. She doesn't like it, she avoids it, and she keeps one eye on it at all times (except, of course, when sneaking to steal my milk in the middle of the night.) It has been this way any time I have made any changes in the house, and it takes her weeks to get used to it.

Cats are creatures of habit, and at this trait Patches excels. Do not mess with her routine. She won't stand for it. She is easily disgruntled and quick to anger. However, this house is a magnet for such pets.

My grandmother loved her animals more than any human being could. She was the greatest owner any pet could have, and they cherished her for it. However, there were varying degrees of their devotion to her.

B.O., for example, was a great little Chihuahua watchdog, would raise tarnation when someone drove up or knocked on the door, but was friendly once in a visitor's presence. So was Crazy Cat, and Suki, a Pekinese.

Then there was Angie.

Angie was a gray poodle. It is perhaps because of Angie that I have a strong dislike for poodles to this day. Repeated bloodshed will do that to your psyche.

If Ma Faye had a more devoted friend, companion and protector, I don't know who it was. Angie was all these things and more. Angie had a brass pet bed right near Ma Faye's chair. Nobody, and I mean nobody, got near that woman. Friends and family could forget about hugging her in welcome or departure, for Angie would remove their faces. Angie would literally leap at their chins. Bless Ma Faye's wonderful, beautiful soul, but she never knew to the end of her days how much most folks despised Angie. We didn't have the heart to say so, because she loved and adored that dog so much.

When I was in my early twenties Ma Faye spent a couple months with family in Texas. She asked a buddy of mine and me to house-sit while she was gone. We almost declined, because of Angie, but reluctantly agreed. Soon as Ma Faye was gone, Angie was our best friend.

I kid you not. Angie slept with us, Angie begged for snacks, did tricks for us, danced and whirled happily when we got home, was just the sweetest things in the world, for two whole delightful months

Until the day Ma Faye came home. Her foot was barely in the door, and Angie was trying to tear our faces off.

Crazy Cat was, by then, a few years beyond ancient, poor baby. She was a long-haired Persian mix of some sort, and in her younger days delighted in battling blue jays and mockingbirds in the front yard. By this time, though, she was getting sadly feeble.

I remember lying in bed one night, and all of a sudden, the covers started inching off my body. Now, this is in a house reputed to be haunted, stories concerning which I've heard all my life.

So I'm lying there, and the covers are sliding down my body toward my feet, so tediously, painfully, excruciatingly slowly—I was paralyzed with terror, it seemed to take hours, until finally the covers vanished over the edge of the bed beyond my feet.

Then this rickety, shaky old paw came up from below and grabbed hold of the fitted sheet. Then another. Slowly and painfully again, Crazy Cat pulled herself up onto the bed and once aboard, collapsed in an exhausted, huffing pile. She looked up at me mournfully, as if saying to me, "It was never that far up when I was younger."

So you see, the house seems to draw pets with personality, to put it kindly. Patches is somewhere between Crazy Cat and Angie in temperament. Luckily, she's still young enough to leap nimbly onto the bed. I don't think my heart could take too many scares such as that when I was in my twenties. I'm not young anymore either.

Mousing

Every spring, like the resident of almost any old house, I am beset with vermin.

No, I don't mean disreputable relatives. I mean mice. It's inevitable. Soon as spring rolls around, the little rodents start looking for a nice place to build a house and raise a family. This old house down by the bayou has all the basic utilities already connected and paid for, plenty of water nearby, lots of places to sneak in and out between the cypress framework, and a never-ending supply of places to hide.

It's a spring routine. I've been fortunate that over the last couple years I haven't had any visitors of mutant proportions, such as the one that took over my garage some time back, terrorizing me so badly I started parking the truck in the yard. But this spring, the tell-tale scurrying of little feet in the ceiling let me know the mice had returned.

The late, great mouser Moses, my gray-and-white tabby, was excellent at ridding the house of these pests, since I am reluctant to put out poison. But Moses passed away a few years ago, and Patches, thus far, had only one mouse to her a credit, a smallish one which she politely dropped at our feet while Suze and me were watching television one night.

But she's now up by two. Over just the past week, I've come home to find two little mice in the middle of the living room floor, and Patches napping on the stair. After disposing of the debris, I praised her lavishly, but she only blinked up at me like, "What? I get points for napping now?" It's true what they say about pets: You have to reward them immediately, or they forget what you are rewarding them for, and just figure you're having one of those inexplicable human moments again which completely mystifies them. Pets just can't figure humans out. We do strange things, things which they just don't understand, like closing the lid on the water bowl.

I think the thing about me which confuses Patches most, though, is why I come home with all these different smells on me. Other cats, dogs, fish, ink, fried shrimp, oil. When I come home with unfamiliar scents, she spends a great deal of time sniffing all over me, usually when I am trying to nap. Depending on what the scent is, her reaction will differ. For fish, fried shrimp or other food stuffs she'll eventually settle down and take a nap with me. But if she smells other animals she'll lay her ears back and go nap somewhere on the stairs. Patches disapproves of me fraternizing with other animals, particularly if I've had a beer or two. I think it's a trust issue. Patches has baggage.

She also does not understand one of my favorite movies, *Chitty Chitty Bang Bang*. Yes, I said *Chitty Chitty Bang Bang* is one of my favorite movies of all time, what of it? Normally, Patches ignores television, with the occasional exception of sci-fi or war movies where the planes or spaceships sound like they're flying across the living room on my surround speakers. This drives her nuts, because she can never locate the noisemaker, though she's positive she just heard it pass right over her head.

She dislikes *Chitty Chitty Bang Bang* for the same reason. The odd sounds the car makes disturb her, almost as much as Dick Van Dyke does. The *pssft! boom!* of dear Chitty's mechanics usually makes her a nervous wreck.

Anyway, she now has three mice to her credit, but I am hoping she doesn't go after any large rats. I don't think I have any in the attic this year, thankfully. But Patches is very slight, a thin, lanky cat of petite stature, and I'm afraid she'll tangle with a rat bigger than she is, since she seems to have no fear, except of brooms. Patches is terrified of brooms, and when I sweep the floor, she hides. This is why my house is always such a mess. I don't want to traumatize the poor dear.

Patches' fear of brooms probably has to do with her tortoise shell calico color. Predominantly black, she may be afraid a witch will mistake her for a familiar. Patches does not like witches, I can tell you, based on her reaction to a couple of them I dated in years past.

Lately she's been enjoying sitting at the screen door and watching the hummingbirds at the feeder hanging from the edge of the porch. Patches loves watching birds. I'm not sure what she would do if I let her out after them. My grandmother's famous feline, Crazy Cat, adored birds too. She had an ongoing war with a mockingbird in the front yard. I am sure it was the same bird because its battle strategies remained constant year-after-year. Crazy Cat would stalk the nest and the mockingbird would make strafing runs at her from behind, causing the cat to leap into the air, flip four times, and land on her feet. Meanwhile, the bird would come in again from the opposite direction while the cat was getting herself reoriented, and dive-bomb her again. This would go on for hours, until one or the other tired of the game, and Crazy Cat would sun herself on the front porch, staring at the mockingbird resting in the limbs nearby, each promising the other a return to the battlefield the next day.

I'm not sure what Patches would do in such a situation, but one day, a bright red cardinal did land right smack dab in front of the screen door while Patches was looking outside. She went still as stone, and the bird kinda flitted around, looking for bugs. Patches didn't move until they came eye to eye with each other through the screen, and the cardinal took off. Patches leaped at it as it went, ended up hanging from the screen about four feet up and unsure how to get down. I had to go retrieve her and return her safely to the floor, at which point she hissed, spit, and went off to her food bowl for respite. She sulked for days after that, staring out the screen door for hours on end, hoping the cardinal would return, but it never did.

The hummingbirds are a different matter, of course, but I think she likes them, especially the ones with a little red on them. Reminds her of the cardinal, I guess, but more bite-sized. She never leaps at them, though. One run-in with the screen door was enough, it seems.

Napping, Patches Style

Due to the recent, but improving, spate of bad weather, Patches and I have been napping a lot.

There is only one greater joy for Patches than napping with me, and that's getting an ear or chin scratching. Patches does, however, appreciate the value of a good nap as much as I do. If there's anything cats excel at, it's napping. A cat is by nature an expert napper. Dogs do not nap nearly as well as cats do. A dog will just splay out on the ground or floor, all haphazard, like somebody shot him and he fell right there.

Not a cat. Cats must first circle their intended napping spot six times. I am not really sure why Patches does this, but I suspect she is checking for sinkholes or something. Nothing upsets a nap worse than waking up in a sinkhole.

Once done circling, Patches settles in and usually starts to bathe herself. I agree, a good bath is a fine prelude to a good nap, but I seldom have the time to indulge.

When napping on the sofa, I usually prop a pillow under my head and nap on my side, my left arm under the pillow. Patches circles the spot in the crook of my arm and shoulder six times, lies down, and proceeds to take a bath while I'm drifting off.

One day last week, while I was napping and Patches was bathing in preparation for her nap, she went into one of those contortionist poses which only a cat can accomplish while bathing, back leg thrust out behind her like an exclamation point.

The only problem was, as she was situated in the crook of my arm and shoulder at the time, when she shot that back leg up and out, her foot went straight up my nose.

Now, you have to carefully follow the ensuing sequence of events to truly appreciate what happened. I was nearly in la-la land, when a furry paw went up my right nostril, close enough for a lobotomy. Since this is not my usual routine of napping, I jumped in terror, which in turn startled the daylights out of Patches, and as she panicked, she pulled her leg back. When a cat goes on the defensive, the claws come out, and well, let's just say her foot was a lot easier going in than coming out.

I jumped up like someone had stuck a cat's foot up my nose, and she jumped up like she had just figured out she was napping on a sinkhole. She went one way, I went the other, hissing and spitting and me cursing and checking for bleeding.

You have to admit: Not even Dave Barry writes columns about getting a cat foot up his nose.

Luckily, there was no serious injury, though I had to sneeze a couple times, which further confused and petrified Patches into hiding behind the washing machine for the rest of the day.

But other than such occasional disasters, Patches and I take the finest naps on my sofa in the history of classical napping. Particularly if I have a meeting or something to go to, I usually wake up before Patches does, and have to get up without disturbing her. There she is, all curled up like a fur hat, little tummy rising up and down contentedly, and I prop my whole body up with my head gently to get my arm out from under the pillow, grab the back of the sofa with one hand and push on the arm of it with the other, all the while flailing my legs for balance until at last I am sitting upright and can then stand.

All this, to not disturb a sleeping cat. What is it about sleeping cats that makes people so reluctant to wake them? I mean, normal cats, not necessarily Patches. With Patches, of course, there's always the possibility of bloodletting involved, but folks who like cats usually don't like to disturb them when they're napping. I find this highly enviable. If people showed me as much common decency when *I'm* napping, the phone would never ring, there'd never be a knock on the door, nobody would cut their grass for three houses down the road from me while I'm on the sofa, and jets and helicopters would have to heed a no-fly zone over my house.

While I was always a fairly competent napper, I admit that I have improved greatly since I have had Patches at the house with me. Patches is a great inspiration and teacher of serious napping. You could learn a lot about napping by watching a cat, particularly Patches.

Now, Patches has not figured out that I do not always lie down on the sofa to nap. Sometimes I do so to watch television, and she jumps up, begins the circle-six-times routine, and I can't see the tube.

"Patches, lay down," I say.

She turns and looks at me like I am the most incredibly stupid creature she has ever encountered. *Surely,* she seems to be thinking, *you can't expect me to nap without circling six times first?*

"Come on, I can't see the television, lay down," I order a bit more firmly.

Deciding that living with a simpleton requires certain sacrifices in etiquette, Patches lies down. Then the bath starts, and all I see is a calico leg blocking my view of the television.

"Do you mind?" I ask.

She looks at me, blinks, and continues her bath, and by the time she's done and my view of the television is clear again, the show is over.

Sometimes I come home from work, ready for a good hour-long nap, and I spy her, sound asleep at the top of the stairs, a bundle of contented snoozing as comfortable and content as any creature ever could be.

"Traitor," I mutter, but she doesn't stir, and I stalk off to the sofa to nap alone. About midway through my nap, I am vaguely, half-awake aware of her jumping on the sofa. She'll walk over my legs, up my back, sniff my hair, then cross the pillows around my head, walk all the way down the edge of the sofa to my feet again, and finally return to settle in next to me.

"What are you looking for?" I mumble. "A kitten in my pocket?"

But she never answers me. She just yawns, chews my nose, and goes to sleep.

In winter, Patches loves to sleep under the covers. Don't make the mistake of lifting your arm on a cold winter's night to scratch your cheek or something, because if you allow just the slightest opening, Patches is under the covers in a flash. Then she'll circle around six times under there, a moving hump under the comforter which looks like something out of a horror movie, bathe herself, which looks like something out of an even worse horror movie, and go to sleep. In the morning, when I throw the covers off to get up and get ready for work, she opens one eye and stares at me like I have just cussed her mother. Feeling guilty, I put the covers back over her, and standing there, staring at the lump of sleeping cat under my comforter, wonder how I could have become so downtrodden.

Then I remind myself, I'm lucky to be a fan of cats. I could have a seal in there.

Kneading Dough

Patches and I are having a row over bread dough.

Well, not bread dough as a matter of actual material, but the subject of kneading bread dough.

See, my darling little tortoise shell calico insists on kneading bread dough. She does this by flexing her claws and moving her paws back and forth, just like a baker would when kneading bread dough. The problem is, Patches has no bread dough available, so she usually does this on me.

While this might not seem like such a big deal, consider it from my perspective. Patches has needle-sharp claws. Anytime she jumps in my lap, or comes to nap next to me on the sofa, a kneading period is prerequisite. Even if I'm lying on the sofa, she will knead my arm.

As you might imagine, this is quite painful. Having a half dozen needle-sharp claws flexing in and out of your skin is not pleasant. It is likewise more of a problem if I've already drifted of to napland on the sofa before she jumps up and starts kneading my arm.

"YOWSSSSUHH!" I scream, leaping three feet off the sofa, and the cat flees in terror.

It's no fun. I don't know how to break her of this habit. She kneads everything she gets near. Me, the sofa, the bed, anything. While my furniture is not something you'd find in a New York penthouse, it is mine and it's all I've got. So are my arm and lap.

You will realize that this is a natural cat function when nursing as a kitten. Problem is, Patches' mother was killed when she was an infant, and she was bottle fed by her first co-habitators (I say "co-habitators" because no one owns Patches...the most one can hope for is that she tolerates their presence.) Thus she never got that whole kneading thing out of her system.

She's intelligent enough to understand I don't want her to do it. I know she's this intelligent, because she also knows I don't want her on the kitchen cabinets, dining room table, bar, or coffee table and she doesn't get on any of them, or so I thought. She's so intelligent, in fact, that when I turn the door knob as I'm coming home from work, I hear *Plunk!* This is the sound of Patches jumping down from wherever it is she's not supposed to be when she hears me at the door.

But if she's intelligent enough to hide her excursions into forbidden areas when I'm not home, you'd think she'd be intelligent enough to not knead dough on my arm. I think she is that smart, but she's also just that stubborn. So round and round we go. Patches jumps up, kneads my arm. I tell her to stop. She freezes like a statue, watching me out of the corner of her eye. If I do not react again, she'll start to knead in slow-motion, so painfully slowly it's like a time-lapsed documentary on PBS where they show a flower opening. I tell her to stop again, and she freezes, stone-still. Then she starts again, and I yell in pain, and that sends her running for the stairs.

No one understands cats. I don't care how many books you read with titles like *How Your Cat Sees You* or *The Secret World of Cats* or whatever. Nobody understands cats. We just want to make believe we do, because we know it's impossible. Cats are like quantum physics and relativity. If you could turn a cat into a mathematical formula, it'd be so full of variables and unknowns you'd think black holes are kindergarten stuff.

I can't leave clothes lying around if I plan to wear them, because Patches thinks these are napping spots. What, you say I shouldn't leave my clothes lying around anyway? For the first half of Patches' life I was a single man living alone. It was tradition for me to leave my clothes lying around. Don't preach, please, it's rude. If I put a shirt on the dresser or the bed to wear later, Patches naps on it, leaving friendly reminders of her presence in the form of tiny little calico hairs. Of course, Patches won't nap on the dirty clothes in the laundry basket. Her napping spots are restricted to clean, nicely-pressed clothes.

It's funny, though, her favorite place in the house is the last stair tread before it disappears up into the ceiling. Every cat my grandmother ever had, as well as my ol' pal, the late Moses, loved that spot. She lies up there, her head dangling over the edge of an eight-foot drop, staring at me while I'm in my chair. It's kinda disconcerting, having a cat stare at you all the time, those wide yellow-green eyes intent on your every move. You can't even sneak an extra slice of pie because you feel like you've been found out, that she's up there looking at you, black slits for pupils, saying, "Go ahead, fat boy...that's just more dough for me to knead."

She likes to curl up in a ball sometimes on the footrest of my recliner if I'm watching television or on the computer. She'll nap there, happy as a bug on a rug, until I need to get up. At the first hint of motion, she'll lift her head and stare at me as if I've just committed some heinous crime.

"Move, Patches," I say kindly.

She'll move, but first she has to stand, stretch, and give herself a quick bath. In other words, "It don't matter if you gotta go to the bathroom, get another slice of pie, or answer the door, I'll move when I get good and ready." Usually I just lower the footrest slowly, and it deposits her neatly on her feet, looking perturbed.

Now and then visitors will come by, those brave enough, and Patches will knead their laps.

"Don't touch her until she's ready," I warn.

"How do I know when she's ready?" they ask.

"I haven't the faintest idea," I reply. This is never good enough for visitors, who think that this adorable, tiny calico feline kneading their laps is so cute and affectionate. They start by petting her head. If, by some miracle, Patches allows this, I say, "Don't pet her past her shoulders."

Patches does not like to have anyone touch her back, even me, though she tolerates it when I do without drawing blood. With other folks, she draws blood. Of course when I warn them, they believe I am just being an old maw-maw about it, and they pet her back. She suddenly tenses, raises her hackles and razor-sharp claws prove Einstein wrong about relativity, because they swipe at light speed at the nearest flesh, and by some fluke of the space-time continuum, she has actually jumped down, raced across the floor, and found a hiding spot *before* her claws slice open their arm.

One wonders why I would tolerate such behavior in a pet. I wonder too, sometimes. But just when I start to question it, some psychic feline sense kicks in, and she leaps on my lap, no kneading, puts her front paws on my chest and rubs her head all over my chin and cheeks, purring happily, ever so loving, adoring, the epitome of the best cat one could hope for. My heart just melts again, and I pet her—just her head, not her back!—and coo and make baby-talk to her.

"Oh, that's daddy's baby, huh?" I croon. "Yes, I know that's daddy's baby, she's such a good kitty, and so pretty, yes, she is!"

To which Patches responds by licking my nose, then meows softly, almost like a dove.

Gimme a break. There are no perfect relationships, you know. It's all give-and-take. Mostly, I give, and Patches takes. That's okay. Somebody's gotta keep me on my toes.

Patches' Pride

The idea and word "finicky" surely originated with cats, and still sticks with them.

Patches, my calico kitty, is quite annoyed with me at the moment, and has been for about a week and a half. She is irritated because the store where I buy her one-and-only cat food has not stocked it recently, blaming it on back orders or something.

When I first went to get a bag and found they were out, I nearly had a conniption right there in the aisle. What in the world would I do? To come home without Patches' favorite cat food—the name of which I will not reveal because she's very private about such matters—would be disastrous. I searched the aisle for a suitable replacement, and, thinking I had found one, brought it home to the young lady.

Understand, Patches will not eat anything else, except under extreme protest. She won't even touch canned tuna. So I put a handful of this replacement variety into her bowl, and she sniffed it. She lowered her ears, sat on her haunches, and looked at me expectantly.

"What do you call this?" she looked at me.

"Gruel?" I tried, hopefully.

She jumped down from the old washing machine and proceeded to fuss loudly. I keep her food bowl on the old washing machine that's broken, because Patches also doesn't like to eat on the floor. Don't ask me why this is true or why I patronize her so, it's just the way it is.

She refused to touch it. So the next day, I bought another brand, brought it home, and tried again.

This time, Patches sniffed it. It must have smelled at least slightly more appealing, because she nibbled one tiny piece, shook her head like a baby does when you give it some of those nasty vegetables in a jar in complete revulsion. She looked at me as if I had completely lost my mind.

"And *this* is?" she seemed to be asking.

"Uhm," I tried, "Yummy, yummy for Patches' tummy?"

She jumped down and proceeded to fuss loudly again.

Day three, Option Three. This time, she sat on the floor when I opened the bag, sniffed the air, and turned around and walked out of the room with her tail up in the air like a cuss word.

Meanwhile, Mocha gets the rejects. Mocha is in hog heaven. She has never had such bounty before, nor such flavorful varieties of taste temptations such as tuna, chicken, salmon, turkey and buffalo. Okay, just kidding about the buffalo part, but Mocha has really been enjoying Patches' rejected suppers.

Patches, meanwhile, is not about to let me forget that I am badly neglecting her finer tastes. If I am sitting in my chair trying to watch television or play on the computer, she sits right where I can see her, staring at me.

If I'm using my laptop computer in my lap, I shift positions in my chair and position the screen to block the sight of her. She gets up and changes location to be in my line of sight again. Patches is nothing if not a pro at glaring.

Day four, Option Four. This time, Patches was sleeping on the sofa when I got home, surely suffering from starvation, and merely opened one eye when I said, "Look, sweetie, we've got something that's just like your favorite food, I swear it!"

She looked at the bag, yawned, and closed her eye.

"Just because the bag's a different color don't mean nothing," I grumbled. "It's great stuff, really."

Grudgingly, she got up and followed me to the dining table, i.e., the broken washer. I served up some of Option Four with grandiose flourish, she sniffed it, looked at me, sighed, and walked away. I thought I could see her ribs. Outside the house, I distinctly heard Mocha burp.

Finally, Option Five paid off. It's soft instead of crunch-soft, and made from mullet. No, not really. But she is at least eating it a little. Enough to survive, anyway. Meanwhile, she won't nap with me, won't let me scratch her ear, and never greets me at the door when I come home anymore. One day I caught her sitting on the windowsill, looking out into the yard at Mocha, who was staring back at her. The conversation appeared to go this way:

"You are a dumb, ill-bred, tasteless mutt," Patches seemed to tell the dog.

"My life for thee!" Mocha seemed to reply. "Salmon! Chicken! Tuna! Oh, for the sake of turkey, I would walk through fire!"

"Try not to slobber, peasant," the cat intimated.

I have been everywhere in the parish looking for her regular cat food. All the store managers swear to me that it's just a back order problem, that the company's not going out of business, there's no labor union problems, and it is not a conspiracy to give me a nervous breakdown. Within a week, they say, the shelves will again be stocked. I have demanded that the product be renamed "Patches' Pride."

So I'll tough it out until then. At least she's eating Option Five, though grudgingly. I can take the stare-down tactic a little while longer, I think. It's the complaining to visitors that gets me. When someone comes over, Patches wails loudly, as if in total misery and neglect, surely beseeching them, "Take me away from here! He won't feed me anything but pig slop! He treats that brick-headed dog like a queen and me like a stepchild! Oh, call the cat rescue association! Save me! Save me!"

Outside, Mocha burps. The sound carries up and into the house, as if to provide star testimony to Patches' case. I feel convicted on the spot.

Luckily, no one else can understand Patches' meaning but me. They just smile and say, "Oh, what an adorable kitty," reach down to pet her, and draw back a puncture wound.

"Cretin," Patches' tail says to the visitor as she stalks off, unrescued, a princess held captive in a castle tower by a mean, ugly ogre with a brick-headed dog for company.

Soon as it hits the shelves again, I'm going to buy two dozen bags of Patches' favorite cat food and freeze it. I won't be left in the lurch again. This is like stocking up for the big balloon. If there ever is a nuclear war, make sure to have plenty of fresh water, canned and dry goods, batteries, flashlights, a radio and two dozen frozen bags of Patches' Pride.

Bees, Oxalis and Mockingbirds

So if April showers bring May flowers, what do May flowers bring?

Pilgrims. Hee-hee.

Indian humor, sorry.

I love this time of year! Every season has a different feel, every month is good for something different. October is the time for dancing in the dark, for rhythms and movements and visits. December is the time for quiet melancholy, for introspection and wonder. April, though, is jubilation and celebration.

April is my kinda season. The trees are budding, the fish are biting (theoretically, at least) and the cat is so frisky she's climbing the walls. My biggest problem with spring is carpenter bees. You know the ones I'm talking about: Big, yellow and black suckers that bore into your wood on the house and swarm all over the place.

Now, the carpenter or "wood bee" is not to be confused with the ground bee that looks almost the same but will sting the bejeezus out of you. The carpenter bee does not attack easily though it will sting if you grab one. The ground bee has a stinger like pencil lead.

But the carpenter bees have infested my garage and front porch. The thing about this critter is that every generation comes back to the same nest. Nothing gets rid of them, except one thing I've found: A piece of cypress, about two-foot long and five inches wide, one end of which is carved into a hand grip like one of my high school teacher's paddles.

Each evening, I grab my Bee Paddle and lurk in the front yard near the garage or front porch. The bees have a wonderful tendency to hover around your face and a good, firm swipe with the Bee Paddle does 'em in. You have to be fast and aim good! But they give the most satisfying crunch when a piece of inch-thick cypress impacts at maximum velocity with their exoskeletons and you say in triumph, "There! Eat *that* piece of wood, ya bum!"

It never occurred to me how foolish I must look standing stone still in the front yard waiting for a bee to come by me, or slowly stalking one I see hovering near the porch. Not that I worry about looking foolish anyway: I am, after all, a fly fisherman, wooden boat enthusiast and balding Indian. Mocha and Daisy sit there by the fence and watch me in transfixed fascination, wondering just what in the world has happened to their usually only mildly lunatic master. Patches sits inside on the window sill and watches, too, obviously believing her worst fears about me have been confirmed: I'm truly mad as a hatter.

But one day while I was busy crunching carpenter bees with my Bee Paddle, my neighbor yelled over at me, "You had better be glad I don't have a video camera!"

He's probably right. On the other hand, I'm sure it would have won the grand prize.

My porch is so riddled with bee holes I'm afraid it's going to collapse when someone comes to visit. With any luck it'll be one of the ne'er-do-well kinfolk it collapses under.

I'm told that if you squirt WD40 into the holes the bees inside die. I am also told you can use a caulk gun to plug up the holes and they die inside. I may have to try these methods, but so long as my neighbor doesn't have a video camera, the Bee Paddle is a lot more fun. Some folks use tennis rackets for the same purpose, I hear, but that would look really silly.

At this point you're probably going to call PETA because of my cruelty to the poor bees. Well, lemme tell you, I never abuse honey bees, I never bother ground bees if they don't bother me, and I fully understand the beneficial acts of bees to the natural world. However, I am not going to let them chew my house into Swiss cheese. I have all the respect for the right to live of termites, too, but you think I'm gonna give them a free supper? Forget it.

Bees should be more like hummingbirds. I put up a feeder on the porch and the little darlings come regularly to sip at the sugary stuff inside. Drives Patches bananas watching them from inside. Now and then the mockingbirds get hacked off at the humming-birds and dive-bomb them, but mockingbirds are no match for hummingbirds in terms of speed, agility and stealth. A humming-bird can fly circles around a mockingbird eight times before the mockingbird can say, "Nanny-nanny boo-boo!" That's what mock-ingbirds do, you know: They mock. All those sounds you hear them making? Translated they amount to:

"Roses are red! Violets are blue! You've got a nose like a B-52!"

"Your mama wears combat boots!"

"Hey! Your ears stick out from your head so far and your nose is so big you look like a Mac truck coming down the road with the doors open!"

"Yo! I would argue with you, but you can't have a battle of wits with an unarmed person!"

Mockingbirds are good at mocking, they just haven't figured out how to do it in English yet.

I love the little wild onions that pop up in the yard, with the delicate white flowers with yellow centers. Also the oxalis, the little lavender flowers whose stems are the source of oxalic acid, and biting one is rather like taking a sip of battery acid. Don't ask me how I know this. The mockingbirds had a field day with that one.

Hmm. Now if I could get the oxalis to grow in the holes the carpenter bees bored and get the mockingbirds to stand around and shout, "Yo, Bee! You look like a Pipi Longstocking on crack! Your mama gets nectar from hummingbird feeders! You need to get a Bowflex!" Then maybe the carpenter bees would get burned by the oxalic acid and get tired of the verbal abuse and get fed up and leave.

Where's that video camera?

The Great Patches Hunt

I don't know whether it's the changing of the seasons or something I did to her, but Patches has been acting very mysteriously.

Perhaps its October, being the month of Halloween and all. She's perhaps starting to feel the need to be a Halloween Cat. Her tortoise-shell calico (all colors but white) has shades resembling pumpkin, you know.

She's been suspiciously absent the last week or so. In fact, when I first realized I hadn't seen her in a day or two, I panicked. Patches has never since the day she moved here eight or nine years ago, been out of the house. She's strictly a house cat. There was one time she slipped into the attic and I searched and searched until I finally heard her mewling and let her out, but that's her only foray beyond the rooms inside.

When I first realized I had not seen her for a while, you see, the weeks before had been a period of permanent attachment. She goes through those phases, too. As long as I am standing up, everything is fine. But the minute I sit down or lie down *zzzzooooooommmm!* There's Patches, beseeching either an ear rubbing, chin scratching or seeking to perch precariously on my belly. Or all of the above. For weeks, I felt like I had a calico growth.

So when she was absent, I started looking. I searched all her usual hiding spots: The piddling room, between my tackle bag and the wall. Nope. Up at the top of the stairs, where my girlfriend put a little pet bed for her to lounge around in the sun from the window up there, but no, not there. Behind the loveseat. Uh-uh. On the various windowsills, hidden behind curtains, blinds or shades. No Patches. I checked to make sure I hadn't left my sock drawer open. Nope, Patches is not sleeping in my sock drawer. She was, once, and it was half-dark and I was half-awake getting ready for work in the morning, and when I reached in to grab a pair of socks I grabbed a Patches butt instead and got bloodied for my mistake.

She's so tiny she can hide easily. She really is a little cat, lithe and long-legged. Not an ounce of fat on her, wiry as a snake and slippery as an eel. She can hide in the tightest places. I searched under the bed, under the sofa, under the broom, magazines on my coffee table and books on the bookshelf. Okay, maybe she's not that tiny, but she is remarkably adept and hiding when she doesn't want to be seen.

I even checked in the bathroom I'm remodeling, but she wasn't in there. I noticed the eight-inch drain pipe in the floor, and peeked into it, just to make sure she hadn't tried to crawl in there chasing a dust bunny or something. I immediately felt foolish, then corrected myself: There's no telling, with Patches.

I got my flashlight and checked in the "junk room," i.e., that room where I've moved everything from the rest of the house while renovations have progressed, insofar as the word can be used to describe the snail's pace at which I'm accomplishing anything. There's so much stuff in there it's hard to search it all, but I did my best.

"Patches," I said, sweetly. "Come out and see me."

No reply, not even a little meow. I remembered belatedly that Patches is terrified of flashlights so I hastily turned it off.

"Paaaaaattccccccchhheeeeessssss," I cooed, as sugary-sweet as I could. "Where's my baby, hmmmm?"

Not a peep. I put some dry food into her bowl, purposely making it rattle noisily as it poured. This usually sends her running to the bowl. But not a sound, not a sign of her.

At this point I'm really getting worried that she somehow escaped into the yard. I go look around outside near the house, but there's no Patches. It's dark and I can't search very far. I'm getting a sinking feeling in my stomach, but I convince myself that I've been careful for all these years about closing doors and making sure she doesn't get out. She never even tries to get out; most she'll do is peek around the corner of an open door curiously and flee if she even notices me noticing her. Nobody's been to the house all week, so nobody else could have left an open door.

I go inside and check the clothes closets. Maybe she sneaked in there while I was getting out my day's wardrobe? Nope, no Patches. I check the other closet, a miscellaneous one for anything I can't find a proper place for. No cat to be found.

I check the refrigerator. Hey, stranger things have happened. Just check the television news. I check the washer and the dryer, the bathroom cabinets and the toilet tank. Okay, I went overboard, but worry makes you crazy.

It was nearly midnight by then, and I was exhausted and depressed. I had to get up and go to work in the morning so I reluctantly called off the search and lay down on the sofa, miserable.

Eventually I dozed off, and woke up sometime in the early morning hours. The first thing that popped in my mind was Patches, and I decided I just had to go search again, maybe I hadn't looked everywhere, like in the desk drawers and all my fly rod cases.

I turned over to roll off the sofa, opened my eyes, and there, all curled up in the most contented and unknowing calico ball you ever saw, was Patches, nuzzled up against my side.

I sighed. I wasn't angry. I wasn't even relieved. I was kinda like you know, "Well, there you go." Sorta numb resignation, I guess.

"Thanks for dropping in," I whispered. She opened a yellow eye I could barely see in the dim light, and blinked at me. She lifted her head, yawned widely, and tucked her head back down over her back legs and closed her eyes.

"Pathetic," I whispered, but I wasn't referring to the cat. "Just plain pathetic."

More Than An Archangel

We were on vacation last week.

Didn't go anywhere. Last week seems distant already. A lifetime ago. Half-forgotten, almost dreamlike.

Except one thing.

We lost our old dog last week.

Her name was Daisy. She had just passed her fourteenth birthday. That's a long life for a Labrador retriever. And she lived it happily and to the fullest.

I met her ten years ago. Muscular and black, Daisy immediately charmed me completely. Her otter-like tail would thump like a drum against the door of the car when her "girl" or her "boy" came home, that being Suze and her son. She'd stand there waiting for them to open the car door, *Thump! Thump! Thump!*

Daisy was built like a classic Lab, broad and husky. I'm told she was the queen of Centerville in her day. Knew everybody, and everybody knew her. She was a regular at the little convenience store, an unofficial greeter, and a receiver of pats on the head and the occasional treat.

She came to live with me about seven years earlier when Suze asked me to care for her for a little while. I remember when we tried to get her into the back of my truck, Daisy would have no part of that idea at all. It took the better part of an hour to cajole her in. She hated it.

I settled her in to her new home and she adapted well. That was the thing about Daisy: She was adaptable. But more than anything, Daisy was the epitome of charm and sweetness.

They tell me in her younger days, Daisy could run like the wind, that she was amazingly fast, a spot of midnight there one moment and gone from sight the next. She had slowed when she came to stay on the Rez, and I never actually saw her go at more than a brisk trot.

But true to her breed's reputation, Daisy could put on the charm. Her facial expressions were of complete endearment. She could look worried sick and completely delighted all at the same time. When Daisy walked up to someone for attention, she sat and waited for them to pet her. She had been taught well.

She was beautiful. Suze says people used to always remark how gorgeous she was. Jet-black and with a sheen that almost seemed iridescent, Daisy was indeed a looker. She carried herself with great dignity, too, something too many dogs completely lack.

For a long time, she was my best fishing buddy. Daisy didn't like the boat much, but she loved pond fishing with me. It only took a couple of trips to instruct her that swimming in the spot I was fishing was a no-no. After that, as I made my way along a pond bank casting and at times even catching, Daisy followed behind me. She knew.

We'd often sit at the bayou tight-lining for catfish, back in my bait-fishing days. Daisy would sit there and watch the line with me. I kid you not, she'd watch the line intently, and when it twitched, her ears would perk and her behind would start to wiggle. If I set the hook on a catfish, she would instantly leap to her feet, waiting to see what I hauled in.

If the fish was small enough, I'd dispatch it with a sharp blow and then clip the fins off. Then I'd give it to Daisy, and she'd make a huge fuss over it, rolling on it for a while then with a hearty chomping noise, take it down as a snack. Next thing I knew, she'd be sitting by me again, watching the line...

As the months and years passed, Daisy didn't try to jump into the back of the truck anymore, but I could tell she still wanted to go. So I started picking her up, put her in the back of the truck and took her out, and she'd wander and sniff around the pond, swim a little—never where I was fishing!—and eventually just plop down to preen in the sun happily.

Eventually, we could tell arthritis was setting in with the advance of her age, and we quit going fishing in the truck, though we made quite a few more catfishing trips at the bayou behind the house.

Daisy had a close call once. When that rash of contaminated dog food thing happened she got some of it. She had a terrible time of it, and I am sure we almost lost her. But with our care and close attention, she snapped out of it. It took a lot out of her, though, and she was never quite herself again.

She ran into a UPS truck once. No, I don't mean a UPS truck ran into her, she ran into it. Put quite a knot on her head, and for the rest of her life, she knew the sound of a UPS truck before it even got close, and would growl low and menacing.

Oh, I could go on and on about her. She hated baths. Just the sight of a water hose sent her into hiding for the rest of the day. She hated to smell good, too, and would find anything to roll in to restore a good funk. She had bright, clever and so, so gentle and joyful brown eyes. Eyes that would melt your soul if you looked in them too long.

Her joints stiffened, and getting to the bayou and back became a hardship. She was content to lie in the yard, soaking in the sun. Her muzzle grayed and her toes did, too. But her eyes always remained joyous.

We knew she was living the last of her days, and that the time would come. It's something you know, but when it does arrive, takes you by surprise. I guess you really don't want to believe it. It's always going to be tomorrow, or next week, next year...

The way and the how of what transpired that day are too hard to relate, so I will pass them. Suffice it to say, we knew it was time, and I think she did, too. We took her to our veterinary clinic and they were so kind and sympathetic, not just to her, but to us, too.

"You can stay if you want to," the kindly doctor said to us. "But we don't recommend it."

There was no way we would have done that. Fourteen years for Suze, seven for me...who could leave her alone, among strangers, no matter how kind, when she needed us most?

There are three kinds of dog people, I believe: Those who see them as entertaining though just animate objects; those who cherish and treasure them as possessions and care for them as they would a prized car or boat, and those of us who find true feelings and friendship.

When she took her last breath we were there, hands upon her, telling her it was going to be all right, what a good, good girl she was, and how much we loved her.

Then she was gone. I kissed her forehead.

We cried, on an off, the rest of the day. But more for us than for her. She is in a place where her legs are not stiff and sore, her body hale and strong, and she can run, run like she used to, fast as the wind.

"If there is a heaven," Pam Brown wrote, "it's certain our animals are to be there. Their lives become so interwoven with our own, it would take more than an archangel to detangle them."

And that's really what I remember most about my vacation last week. I'm glad we were there, in the end. It was hard. Oh, so hard. But it could not have been any other way. I miss her mightily. The day is sadly unfilled without my trip to her food bowl; I look to the back yard, expecting to see her lounging in the sun, and I keep closing the gate, even though she's not there.

So this is Daisy's eulogy. This, her epitaph.

We loved you, old girl. We still do, and won't stop.

You were a good, good girl.

Mr. Bogart

It's been an eventful, and rewarding, almost three months since Mr. Bogart came to live with us. I call him that when I'm displeased, you see. Kinda like your mom would use your proper name when she found out you skipped out of school and were smoking cigarettes back of the neighbor's tomato garden. "Roger Emile Stouff!" It's required to put an extra emphasis and volume on the final word in the series, usually the surname. As if, somehow, that makes more of an impact. So he's Mr. Bogart when he steals my left sandal and runs off with it. Rest of the time, he's Bogie.

Thankfully, I'm rarely displeased with the little fella. Bogie has proven to be remarkably intelligent, well-behaved and obedient. He has learned to SIT, STAY, COME and FETCH and is pretty reliable on all of them. I am teaching voice command and whistle command at the same time. It's pretty hilarious to see him bounding ahead of me on some trail somewhere, full-throttle, when I blow one long staccato blast on my whistle and that blonde behind hits the deck and he skids another three or four feet before coming to a complete halt, turning toward me as if to say, "What?"

We have a wonderful time together, exploring the bayou side and some of the wide-open spaces I take him to. No way our Bogie will be afraid of anything or anyone! Last week he made his first water retrieve. He has, since he came to live with us, loved water, but dared no deeper immersion than his chest. Well, we were at a pond one day and he got to playing with an old clear plastic water bottle some idiot had left as litter. He galloped through the edge of the water—three or four inches deep—and I thought, "Hmm."

I had him bring me the bottle and threw it about five feet into the pond.

The little streak of yellow lightning hit the water before he realized what he had done, and when it touched his chin he froze like a statue. He kinda stood there, staring at the bottle just a few feet away, and you could see the mental processes going on as the fear left him and he just seemed to think, "What's the big deal?" and swam out to the bottle, took it in his jaws, and brought it back to me. Bravo! We played fetch several more times in the pond, and I realized I had indeed a true water dog.

He's just a pup, of course, and sometimes he'll get distracted and not hear his commands. Of course I insist he do what I tell him, not harshly, and he's coming along nicely with understanding that I Am The Boss, and more importantly, I Am He Who Takes You Fun Places With Interesting Smells and Critters.

I always heard Labs were a handful, bundles of unbridled energy and destructive tendencies if bored. He's surprisingly good with Patches, who's extremely curious about the little fellow, but Patches has the same dysfunction with Bogie as she does people. Patches wants to be sociable, wants to play, but when you interact with her, she panics and swipes. She's the same with Bogie. There's been no bloodshed, thankfully, and I can usually hold Bogie back just by voice. I think Patches thinks he's just a big lumbering oaf with no dignity. She ain't seen nothing yet. Wait till he's seventy pounds or so!

I spend an hour with Bogie in the morning while drinking my coffee, and he gets a brief outside break before Suze leaves for work. He is kennel-trained and quite content in his "safe place." When I get home, we spend three, sometimes four hours gallivanting across the countryside, checking out all the neat smells and chasing all the funny critters. I let him rest for a few hours in the evening, then give him a half-hour or so before bedtime.

He loves us both like the world centers around us two. We're working on DOWN at the moment, having failed miserably at resisting the temptation to let him on our laps when he was oh, so cute and adorable. Well, he's doing pretty well with it, though I had to enlist the aid of the neighbors to help insist with a gentle knee to the chest that he doesn't jump on them, either. He's getting there!

I have taught him that when I am out in the yard practicing my fly casting he must absolutely, positively leave my fly line alone. Sinking his sharp teeth into a forty dollar fly line would not be good.

One day, standing out there practicing, I noticed a smell. I looked down and Bogie was chewing happily on something I couldn't quite make out. I took it from him and reeled in disgust to find it was a squirrel head!

I was confused and nauseous. Did my little man chase down and kill a squirrel while I wasn't looking? I threw the thing away, and watched him. He ambled over to the corner of the yard where an old boat trailer sits, sniffed around, and came back with a squirrel tail. Ah-ha! I take this away from him as well and he gives me that, *Aww, man*, look then I go to investigate. I find no more squirrel body parts so I figure it was the leftovers of a stray cat or something that feasted on tree rat a few days earlier.

Another day he came prancing up to me with something dark in his mouth and I ordered him to DROP IT at once, and soon as he opened his mouth to comply, a toad leaped free, bounded across the patio with Bogie in hot pursuit and managed to escape into the garden. Bogie looked at me with a gaze of, *Nice going, Ace*.

His favorite part of the day is when the lady of the house comes home. He perks his ears up when he hears the car coming down the drive, and waits by the door with his behind wagging uncontrollably. When she comes through the door, his ears lay back and his behind-wagging becomes a spiraling, spinning cyclone like his tail is a propeller and he's about to launch into orbit. Hey, I don't blame him. I feel the same way when she comes home. I just don't have a tail.

My favorite times are dusk. Twilight, and a dragon-fire sunset is spreading like wind-fanned flames across the tops of browned cypress along Bayou Teche. I lean my back against a live oak. Bogie comes to me and, in an uncommon moment of calm, sits and looks out over the conflagration to the west. I rest my hand on his back.

He whines, and it may have just been because he's had a long, exciting day, but I'd like to think it's an exhalation of wonder at the glorious sunset before us, and the sharing between us.

I stroke his little back, but it feels strong, and will only grow stronger. The things he'll see, and learn and experience! The things we both will. Takes my breath away now and then, when I dream of it...when I glimpse it there in the sunset at the close of his seventeenth week of life on this rare and wonderful old world, bathed in amber and saturated with eventide. He'll see it all for the first time, and I envy him for that.

We watch the light fade and wait for the tomorrow of an uncertain world unfolding before us one sunset at a time.

The First Year

Our yellow Lab, Bogie, celebrated his first birthday between Christmas and New Year's Day. I say "celebrated" but there was no real party or anything. It occurred to me one day and I told Suze, "Hey, Bogie's a year old now," and we patted him on the head and he wagged his tail. End of celebration.

When dogs are registered with the AKC, they are usually given fifty-cent names such as "Grayshire's Pearl Mistress Languishing Annie" or something like that. Bogie's not AKC registered, though both his parents were, and since their backyard rendezvous under a starry, starry night of autumn amour resulted in Bogie and ten siblings, well, we figure Mr. Humphrey Bogart Esq. is about all we can afford.

He's grown into quite the lad. At about sixty pounds, he's far smaller than his puppy feet indicated he might become. That puppy had big feet, and I swore he'd be a hundred, maybe more. They say Labs reach their full height at a year or maybe a little longer, but put on their final weight in the second year. I expect he'll top out at no more than seventy.

And let me tell you, friends and neighbors, that dog is just lousy with personality. Keeps us in stitches He's a beautiful golden-brown with whiter flanks and deep brown eyes that'll pierce right through you if he wants them to. He's extraordinarily well-behaved on almost all counts (greeting visitors and chasing anything from cats to wind-blown leaves being the leading exceptions) and even is starting to get along with Patches, my calico cat.

At first, Bogie's frenzied enthusiasm sent Patches into a hair-on-end, tail-straight, hissing, spitting, growling ball of calico terror. Over time, though, she's gotten more used to him, and his own calming with maturity has helped. Still, it's funny as all get-out to see Bogie notice Patches, rush to her, drop on his front legs, behind in the air, tail spinning like a helicopter and begging Patches to play with him. Meanwhile, the cat is sitting there a couple feet away with a look of complete disdain. "Simpleton," she seems to be saying. "Go chase a tree stump."

When Bogie realizes his pleading is not working, he'll try to play with her physically. He's finally gotten it through his head that Patches may resemble the furry, animal caricature toys we bought him when he was a little puppy, but Patches is not a chew toy. Unlike his puppy-hood chewables, Patches bites and scratches back. No bloodshed has resulted; she has shown amazing restraint.

I thought she was petrified and overwhelmed by him—and at first she was—until one day Bogie had tired of trying to get her to play when all she'd do was arch her back and feign indignation. He went to lie down on his mat, and don't you know, that dang cat peeked around the corner, saw the dog lying there dozing off, walked over and sat right next to his nose, as if saying, "Quitter!"

One day Bogie was in the workshop. I had gone in the house for another cup of coffee or something, and when I came out he was halfway down the steps and frozen like a statue. I saw the white toe and heel of one of Suze's outside shoes from my vantage point at the back of his head.

"Bogie," I said, "what do you have?"

He stood stone-still, one leg on each step of the descent.

"Bogie, is that Suze's shoe?"

And at once he dropped it, hit the concrete running and vanished out the back door. He knew good-and-well he had performed a dreaded "No!" action.

Last night I noticed him staring at my living room chair, tail spinning. I throw an old blanket over the chair, and it has this cool

Native American design of a turtle or a beetle or something on it. Bogie was staring at it cautiously and tilting his head from side-to-side.

"Come see this," I told Suze. "He thinks it's alive!"

We had a little chuckle over it, and I walked off but in a minute or two Suze tells me our pup isn't quite as dense as I thought he might be.

"Why's that?" I asked.

"Because Patches is under the blanket," she said. Sure enough, Patches—who might weigh five pounds soaking wet, which I can't prove because nobody's got the nerve to get her soaking wet—suddenly realized she had been found out and retreated behind the chair, with Bogie in hot pursuit.

Around Christmas, when there was just stuff scattered everywhere in usual holiday rush and disarray, Bogie came walking into the living room with a small red and white stocking in his mouth. I looked at him and he looked at me and froze, staring at me, trying his best to express silently that *Suze gave it to me, honest,* but of course, I knew better.

"Give it to me," I said. He brought it to me, put it in my hand gently and sat. This, you understand, is completely opposite of what he does when we are playing fetch and training for bird retrieves, when he'll bring the dummy back to me and whirl around my feet, dancing happily, pitching the dummy in the air so he can catch it and ignoring my repeated pleas of, "Bogie! Give! Release! Drop! Give me the damn thing! Hey! Give! Drop! Relinquish! Abandon! Surrender! Dangit! Bogie! Come back here!"

We don't give our dogs enough credit, I think. Now, I've known some genuinely USDA-inspected A-Number-One Certified Dumb Dogs in my time, but they are few and far between.

They say that every bird hunter will inevitably face one of the most humbling and miserable moments of his life when his dog flushes a quail or a grouse or whatever, the bird takes flight, the hunter shoulders his shotgun, fires, and...misses. They say that at such a time, the dog, just then a-quiver with anticipation of the retrieve, will drop his ears, turn around and look at the hunter. "Nice shootin', ace," they seem to relate, and many a wing-shooter has withered under their own dog's disgruntled gaze.

But that moment's yet to come, I guess, if Bogie and I ever get afield. Meanwhile, I'm just taking immeasurable joy out of watching him grow up into a fine dog, and a good friend.

Contrition

Somehow, I stood at the edge of an expanse of corn stubble. I felt confused, not quite sure of myself or my eyes. But the shotgun, cracked open, lay in the bend of my elbow and there was a low mist of fog over the rows, and it was just all so right.

A golden arc crested the horizon and, like dragon's breath, set everything ablaze, golden and auburn, ocher and wheat. I thought I had never seen anything more beautiful, and when I looked behind me the few scattered houses at the edge of the reservation were distant. I could just make out the little white schoolhouse. I was... what...? Fourteen?

I dug two shells out of a leather bag on my hip and dropped them into the chambers of an old Savage Fox for which I had saved Christmas and chore money a whole year to buy. The nagging at the nape of my neck was slight, but persistent. I knew that off in the broadening dawn was Baldwin, but I could not see it. Corn and sugar cane fields and the errant patch of trees were all I could discern in mist slowly burning off, dropping, to brown earth and withering stalks.

I closed the Fox and it latched up tight, as it always did. The straight-stock in my right hand and the barrels over my left elbow, I worked slowly along the third row of corn stubble, wary, hoping I'd react sanely when the maddening burst of brown and white wings erupted at my feet. I reminded myself to be cool and, there in a corn row seeded with doubt, I looked for Bob yet again.

Comes the near-silent pads behind me, if not for the crackling of brittle leaf and husk, and the dog has caught up, trotting by me, sure of his duty and his intent.

"Hunt 'em up, Shadow," I said, and there was a sting in my temple. Not much, just a pang of sadness that I couldn't quite take a bead on.

Flawlessly, the Springer went to work, quartering the field despite the rows, and within moments he had found and pointed a covey. I crept up on it and, when they launched skyward in crazy, dipping and ascending flight, I dropped one with the left barrel and, after a split second to let the quail gain some distance, took it from flight with the tighter choke. Shadow retrieved one at a time and I put them in my old bag, a carpenter's bag my father had donated to my pursuits afield.

He stopped, looked at me, and the tuft of hair on his bobbed tail wiggled delightedly, then he shot off to find the other bird. And in his dark brown eyes I saw the reflection of myself, wondered at my size and my build and my thinning hair. But he didn't give me long to ponder before he was on the hunt again.

I was in awe of him. He was perfect. Immaculate. With all the love and spoiling I had poured on him the old timers would have said he wouldn't be worth a plug nickel as a bird dog. But he had succeeded and excelled despite my flawed training.

There were oddities in that memory, oddities in the field as the shroud of mist diminished, but I couldn't determine why. Why it seemed the treeline along the ditch bank where we flushed four birds and I got one (missed the other as cleanly and inexcusably as you could hope for) was thick and the trunks within so big around, and why that bothered me at all. Why, when we crossed a dirt headland road I paused, and told Shadow, "Whoa" and looked left and right, when I certainly knew the harvest was over. There'd be no tractors out that early. The farmers were resting, readying for the next planting. But Shadow sat, and waited, and when we crossed the road, for a moment, the vanishing mist seemed to obscure him, fade him somehow.

We hunted for about an hour and then, with a full bag of quail —I could already smell them cooking with onions in a gravy on my mother's stove top—Shadow and I sat on a small mound where farmers had cleared a large ditch and deposited the dirt. Out to the south were woodlands and more fields and I wished I had brought Kate, my quarter-horse, for the hunt, but then I remembered Kate could be very skittish, especially around guns.

I put my hand on Shadow's head, felt the panting warmth of him, and he swallowed once and sighed. "You did good, buddy," I said. "Haven't been birds like this since…" Then it was my turn to swallow, because I wasn't even sure what I was going to say then.

The dog lay beside me, head up, and together we watched the morning continue to unfurl. I reached into my shirt pocket and found a Punch, bit off the cap and lit it. The heady, pungent aromas of maduro leaf surprised me, and I looked at it, thinking how much trouble I'd be in if my parents caught me. But then, I was old enough, after all, to smoke a little cigar if I wanted. I had to remind myself of that, feeling surreal, confused.

Shadow leaned over, and nudged my knee and I laughed. Those eyes sparked with such intelligence. I took my water bottle off the strap over my shoulder and let him drink from the stream that I squeezed out. He slurped it up and tipped his head at me when he was done in thanks, a wiggle of his nubby tail for good measure.

"Come a long way from a pet store in the mall, haven't we?" I asked, stroking his shoulder and he glanced at me, tipped his head again, and a chill ran up my spine. I shuddered it away. For all the bad things, and probably some true ones, they say about pet-store dogs from puppy mills, here was a liver-and-white bundle of the most extraordinary canine intelligence, gentle calm and at once atomic-powered energy the species had until then produced. While Chance, his buddy, would snap at my boys (something pricked there, like a thorn in my awareness) if they got too rowdy with him, Shadow would lie or stand in quiet tolerance as they pretended to ride him like a pony, or tugged at his ears to make his head look like an airplane, or accidentally stepped on his toes. He'd sometimes look at me with a forlorn expression of acceptance. "It's what you do for the pups," his look seemed to say.

"Come on," I said, standing, and my knees ached a little. "Let's take the long way home. No sense hurrying back to hearth and hold." We found a field road that made a long arc around the acreage and walked it leisurely, Shadow at heel for the most part except when he saw or heard or smelled something interesting. I passed under oaks that formed an impossible canopy over my head and for a moment envisioned them uprooted and burned for development and the thought horrified me.

But I was just about to step over a small drain furrow when I saw an odd color and there, under a patch of Johnson grass, a large copperhead snake coiled. It was motionless, metabolism dulled by the cold, but at the same moment Shadow saw it and leaped.

I snatched him by the collar, dragged him back and away. "No, Shadow! No! No!" I screamed, and he wanted to obey, I just knew it, but struggled for the snake, his nostrils flaring, his body taut and coiled itself.

"No!" I screamed, frantic now, inexplicably close to tears, and I pushed him to the ground, knelt into him to pin him there. He finally acquiesced, looked at me as if I had betrayed him, but I continued to yell at him in unreasonable panic, "No! Shadow! No snakes! Leave snakes alone! *No, no, NO!*"

I let him up, led him off, away from the snake a good ways before I released his collar then took a moment to stop myself from trembling, took deep, saturating breaths. "Come on," I said, softly, trying to soothe him, apologize all at once. "Let's go home."

But he sat, staring at me. "Come on, Shadow," I said, but he only locked gaze with me. I went to him, knelt, rubbed his head. "I'm sorry, buddy, you just gotta leave snakes alone. Snakes are dangerous. Snakes can—you gotta leave 'em alone."

He swallowed, and licked my cheek and it made me laugh and the laughter pierced something, some veil I had known was there from the moment I realized I was standing at the edge of the corn field staring at the fog.

I stood. "Let's go home," I repeated, but he stood, too, and solemnly touched my hand with his nose and turned to walk away.

"No, this way," I said, a spasm of fear crawling through my gut. "Home's this way!"

He turned once and looked at me, wagged his nubby tail and continued down the headland road.

I opened my mouth to shout again, but then I realized there were tears on my face. I pushed against something holding me in place, something soft and heavy and my legs wouldn't move and I closed my eyes to push harder and when I opened them, red digital numerals told me it was three-thirty and the darkness around me and the little glow from the kitchen light we keep on all night made me gasp back a sob. I pushed away sheets and blankets, put my feet on the cold floor and trembled.

It had been so real, and I felt a tear tumble down my cheek for the sweet innocence and lost horizon of it, and for my old friend. Again, I wondered why I have been thinking of him so much these last few months, writing about him, and now he's hunting quail in my dreams, across a span of impossible years in my life, from adolescence to the present, when he was only actually here to share four of them with me in my late twenties.

He had never even hunted with me; I had long before given it up. Never retrieved a quail, never heard a gun. But the terrain of my dream-scape was that of my youth, before the casino and the highway and the houses and the expansions of municipal limits and subdivisions. He had seen none of that, but he was there. Just, I guess, as he always is.

Carefully making my way through the dark, I went and found Bogie. He's a year old now. I let him out of his kennel and he must have thought me quite the madman, because I knelt and hugged him tight. I was careful to be silent, tried to keep him quiet in his excited return of my affection. I sat on the floor, and stroked his yellow shoulder for a time, and he swallowed contentedly. Perhaps he and I were paying tribute to my old companion that I can't get out of my head these days; perhaps there is a catharsis going on, unfinished since the day a decade ago I found Shadow dead in the yard of copperhead bites.

And we sat that way for moments I didn't count, and it didn't really matter, because somehow he understood that's what I wanted, what I needed, and after a time he went back to bed and so did I and I slept, dreamless sleep, until the alarm woke me at daybreak and I showered and clothed myself, released Bogie again and we walked out into a dawning day.

What the Puppy Knows

Watching Bogie grow, from an eight-inch long ball of fur and wrinkled skin at seven weeks, to this lanky, long-legged packet of energy, has been awesome. It's been a long, long time since I had a puppy, and I've never had a large-breed one before.

He's lost his puppy fur, replaced by that more coarse, thick hair

Labs are famous for, that water-repellent mat of adulthood. I swept up hair for nearly two months, massive balls of it, every day and I couldn't believe he wasn't completely bald. The shedding has slowed considerably, at last.

It's amazing, when you think about the energies working in his little body. The cellular division, the incredible forces that grow him in leaps and bounds. The cognizance, too. Now he's learning not to bolt when he sees other people nearby, or a cat. I said learning, he's not all there yet. It's a lot to ask of a puppy, especially a Lab. He's one hundred percent on sit, ninety-five percent on stay, the five percent deficiency being a matter of duration, which we're working on. We're working on walking at heel...ninety percent good on that, on leash.

It's fun watching the world unfold for him. Every new bug is a revelation. Every scent a nirvana. He can be barreling along at ninety-to-nothing, catch a scent, stop on a dime and go back to investigate. He still tries to catch birds, with no success, of course. That's good. He's interested in them, and only has to learn to hold back and flush them when I say, mark the fall on shot, and retrieve it.

He knows that, when he gets fed, if I pour food without saying anything, he can leap into it at once. If I say simply, "Sit," even without adding "stay," he'll watch patiently until I say "Go," and then he leaps like a spring to the bowl. Every other time he responds to "come" positively, he gets one of the treats I carry around in my pockets when we're romping, and he's figured out that this hit-and-miss procedure is worth coming to find out if he won the prize, each and every time.

But he knows more than those things. The puppy is quickly turning into the dog. Not so far removed from his ancestral wolf lineage as we think. Most of the breeds we know today were developed from a handful of domesticated dogs in the last hundred and fifty years. He knows what plants are edible, and which to leave alone, somehow. Or at least the ones that aren't tasty. I see him chewing grass or other plants and notice he specifically leaves certain species completely untouched.

He knows how to swim, and is venturing farther and farther

from shore every trip. Not so far as to be worrisome, but the water dog in him is certainly apparent. That otter-like tail swishes as he goes, and his webbed feet propel him nicely. He tries to bring back to shore anything that might be floating out there, from a twig to a twelve-foot long two-by-four. He actually made it back with the two-by-four, but was pretty tuckered out after that.

The puppy will devour some things. Daisy, his matriarch predecessor, during her puppy-hood ate a length of galvanized water pipe and a boat trailer hitch. Kid you not. Bogie is not quite as ambitious; his chew repertoire includes limestone, clam shell and oak limbs. He does not, however, touch the green tomatoes the stupid squirrels steal from our bushes and carry out in the yard to half-eat. He carries them back to me, but doesn't eat them, perhaps sensing their slightly toxic nature.

He knows his daddy (that would be me) will come in the house after work, go change clothes, grab a sweet tea and a little cigar before coming to let him out of the kennel. He doesn't fuss or whine, just waits patiently. He has amazing patience for a pup. He's not sappy-dog affectionate, he's independent but not stand-offish, and lets us know when he thinks we need it that we're his best buds and his world simply revolves around us.

The puppy knows there are things on the breeze that are farther away than he can see, but that makes them no less real. As they swirl through his long snout and his eyes half-close while he studies them with instinct and perceptions we human beings lost long, long ago, he "sees" what is beyond range of his eyes.

At night, when I'm yawning and ready for some down-time, I lead him to his kennel in my piddling room. He knows to sit, because he gets one treat that way, then another is thrown in the kennel as reward for entering. He takes a little time to get comfortable but before long is snoozing peacefully, sometimes on his side, sometimes on his stomach, now and then on his back. In the middle of the night, sometimes, I hear him yipping. I went to check a couple times, because in the past the only time he ever made a sound that late was if he needed to go, bad. But there he was, sound asleep, and now and then, a *Yip!* would escape his lips and his little legs twitched. Perhaps he was, in his dreams, chasing those dang squirrels and circling the base of the tree they escaped into. Who's to know? We can't really be sure what the dog knows, but we shouldn't underestimate him. His instincts are more closely entwined with the natural world he lives in than our own. He is, after all, not that far removed from the wolf, though we might think him cuddly and cute and obedient, because that's how we've molded his lineage.

But what the puppy knows is far greater than what we can ever hope to perceive. He depends on us solely to function in our world, and to guide him in what he can do to please us. Which, in the end, the dog knows is what he most wants to do anyway.

I watch him grow, by leaps and bounds, over the scant five months he's been with me. And a haunted, mourning part of me knows that great acceleration of his growth also accounts for the brevity of his life, his fraction of an existence compared to my own. Right now that yellow bundle of joy tags along at my heel but as the years pass he'll grow older, slower, grayer, and one day, the last burst of energy will leave him, far too soon. Among my greatest wishes are to make those moments as fulfilling and joyful for him as I can before time runs out.

That's what the puppy and the dog knows. What the man knows is he is no "master" despite the arrogance of his species, and he should be honored, humbled even, to be the recipient of such loyalty and love.

If you enjoyed this book, please post a review on Amazon.

Visit our website for all our books!
www.shadowfirebooks.com

About the Author:

Roger Emile Stouff is the son of Nicholas Leonard Stouff Jr., last chief of the Chitimacha Tribe of Louisiana, and Lydia Marie Gaudet Stouff, daughter of a Cajun farmer. He has been a journalist for more than thirty years and writer of the award-winning column "From the Other Side" in the *St. Mary and Franklin Banner-Tribune*. He was featured on the television show "Fly Fishing America" in 2006, and was writer and narrator of the documentary "Native Waters: A Chitimacha Recollection" on Louisiana Public Broadcasting in 2010.

Made in the USA
Lexington, KY
31 January 2018